Arduino and MicroPython Programming Guide: ESP32 & ESP8266 for Absolute Beginners to Advanced IoT Projects

First edition
Sarful Hassan

Preface

Welcome to **"Arduino and MicroPython Programming Guide: ESP32 & ESP8266 for Absolute Beginners to Advanced IoT Projects"**. This book is designed to take you on a journey from a complete beginner in programming and IoT development to creating advanced projects using ESP32 and ESP8266 microcontrollers. Whether you're new to programming or looking to enhance your skills with these versatile devices, this book will provide you with the knowledge and tools needed to succeed.

Who This Book Is For

This book is for:

- Absolute beginners with no prior experience in Arduino or MicroPython.
- Makers, students, and professionals looking to build IoT projects using ESP32 and ESP8266.
- Developers seeking to learn both **Arduino** and **MicroPython** programming environments for versatile project development.
- Those who want to understand the fundamentals of IoT applications and microcontroller programming, moving toward advanced techniques.

How This Book Is Organized

This book is divided into several key sections to guide you through your learning journey:

1. **Getting Started**: Introduction to ESP32 and ESP8266, hardware setup, and environment configuration for both Arduino IDE and Thonny (MicroPython).

2. **Foundations of Computing and I/O**: Covering digital and analog input/output, including essential projects like LED blink, PWM control, and sensor readings.
3. **Programming Fundamentals**: Diving into arithmetic, comparison, bitwise, and boolean operators, followed by control structures, data types, variables, and more.
4. **Advanced Concepts**: Introducing communication protocols, deep sleep modes, and advanced Wi-Fi networking with ESP32 and ESP8266.
5. **Hands-on Projects**: Each chapter includes practical projects to solidify your understanding, culminating in IoT applications that connect devices to the cloud.

What Was Left Out

While this book covers a broad range of topics, we've focused on the most essential areas of Arduino and MicroPython programming for IoT with ESP32 and ESP8266. Advanced topics such as RTOS, advanced security in IoT, and enterprise-level IoT integrations have been left out to maintain a clear focus on programming fundamentals and intermediate project development.

Code Style (About the Code)

All code in this book adheres to widely-accepted coding conventions for both **Arduino** and **MicroPython**. Code snippets are designed to be simple, clean, and accessible for beginners while demonstrating the most efficient ways to implement functionality. Each code example is accompanied by explanations and troubleshooting tips, ensuring that you fully understand each concept.

Notes on the First Edition

This is the first edition of **"Arduino and MicroPython Programming Guide: ESP32 & ESP8266 for Absolute Beginners to Advanced IoT Projects"**. The book reflects the most up-to-date methods for programming these microcontrollers and focuses on current best practices. Future editions may expand on additional topics based on feedback from readers and advances in the field.

Conventions Used in This Book

- **Bold** is used for emphasis and key terms.
- Code is presented in monospace for clarity.
- Notes and warnings are presented in boxes to highlight important information.

Using Code Examples

Feel free to use the code examples in this book for your own projects and learning purposes. You are encouraged to modify and adapt the code to fit your needs. However, if you use the examples in a published project or product, proper attribution would be appreciated.

MechatronicsLAB Online Learning

To further support your learning, additional resources and tutorials are available at **mechatronicslab.net**. You can also reach out via email at **mechatronicslab@gmail.com** for any questions or to provide feedback. We are committed to providing a complete learning experience for all readers.

How to Contact Us

For questions, comments, or inquiries, please contact us at:

- **Email**: mechatronicslab@gmail.com
- **Website**: mechatronicslab.net

Acknowledgments for the First Edition

This book wouldn't have been possible without the incredible support of the ESP32 and ESP8266 development communities, the open-source contributors who continually improve the tools and libraries, and the many readers who provided feedback and suggestions. Special thanks to those who helped test the code, review drafts, and offer encouragement throughout this process.

Copyright

© 2024 MechatronicsLAB. All rights reserved. No part of this book may be reproduced, distributed, or transmitted in any form or by any means without the prior written permission of the publisher.

Disclaimer

The information contained in this book is for educational purposes only. While every effort has been made to ensure the accuracy of the information, the authors and publishers assume no responsibility for errors or omissions. The code examples provided are for learning purposes and should be tested and validated before being used in any production environment.

Table of Contents

Chapter -0 Get started with ESP 7
   1. Introduction to ESP32 and ESP8266 7
      Overview of ESP32 and ESP8266 7
      History and Evolution of ESP8266 and ESP32 10
      Timeline of Hardware Updates and Firmware Improvements 11
      ESP8266 to ESP32: The Evolution 12
      Impact on IoT Community 13
      Future of ESP32 and ESP8266 in IoT 14
   2. Pinout and Hardware Layout 15
      GPIO Pin Details and Usage for ESP32 and ESP8266 20
      Power Supply Requirements: 22
   3. Getting Started with ESP32 in Arduino IDE 24
   4. Getting Started with ESP32 in Thonny (MicroPython) 25
   5. Basic Troubleshooting for Setup (Driver Issues, Flashing Problems): 26
   6.Best Practices for Using ESP32/ESP8266: 29
Section 1: Foundations of Computing and I/O 30
Chapter 1. Digital I/O Basics: 30
      Digital Pin Modes 32
      Input/Output Declaration 35
      Digital Write 37
      Digital Read 39
      Built-in Pull-up Resistor 42
      Debouncing 44
      PWM Support 47
Chapter 2. Analog I/O Basics 50

Analog Input 52
Analog Output (PWM) 54
Analog Reference (Arduino) 56
Attenuation (MicroPython) 57
Smoothing Analog Input Readings 58
Analog-to-Digital Converter (ADC) Resolution 59
Section 2: Programming Fundamentals 63
Chapter-3 .Arithmetic Operators: 63
    Addition (+) 64
    Subtraction (-) 67
    Multiplication (*) 69
    Division (/) 71
    Modulus (%) 74
    Modulus (%) 76
    Exponentiation 78
    Integer Division 80
Chapter 4. Comparison Operators 83
    Equal to (==) 84
    Not Equal to (!=) 87
    Greater than (>) 89
    Less than (<) 91
    Greater Than or Equal To (>=) 94
    Less Than or Equal To (<=) 96
Chapter 5. Bitwise Operators 98
    AND (&) 99
    OR (|) 102
    XOR (^) 104
    NOT (~) 107
Chapter 6. Boolean Operators 109

AND (&&)	110
OR (||)	112
NOT (!)	114
Chapter-7. Trigonometry	117
Sine (sin())	118
Cosine (cos())	120
Tangent (tan())	123
Chapter 8. Variables	125
Global Variables	126
Local Variables	129
Static Variables	131
Constant Variables	134
Volatile Variables	136
Chapter 9. Data Types	139
int: 16-bit Signed Integer	141
unsigned int: 16-bit Unsigned Integer	143
long: 32-bit Signed Integer	144
unsigned long: 32-bit Unsigned Integer	146
float: 32-bit Floating-Point Number	147
double: 32-bit Floating-Point Number (Same as float)	150
char: 8-bit Signed Character	152
unsigned char / byte: 8-bit Unsigned Value	155
boolean: True/False Values	156
String: A String Object to Handle Text	159
Array: Collections of Elements of the Same Type	161
Chapter 10. Control structure	164
if: Conditional Statement	166
else if: Conditional Statement for Multiple Conditions	168
else: Conditional Statement for Default Case	171

switch-case: Conditional Statement for Multiple Options 173

for Loop: A Looping Structure for Iteration 176

while Loop: A Looping Structure for Repeated Execution 179

do-while Loop: A Looping Structure that Executes at Least Once 181

break: Exiting a Loop or Switch-Case 184

continue: Skip the Current Iteration of a Loop 187

return: Exiting a Function and Returning a Value 189

Chapter -11 . Characters and Strings 192

Characters (char): 8-bit Signed Character 193

Chapter 12. Data Conversion Techniques 196

String to Integer Conversion 197

Arduino: String to Integer Conversion 198

MicroPython: String to Integer Conversion 199

Integer to String Conversion 200

Arduino: Integer to String Conversion 200

MicroPython: Integer to String Conversion 201

Float to String Conversion 202

Arduino: Float to String Conversion 202

MicroPython: Float to String Conversion 204

Chapter 13. Communication Protocols 205

UART (Serial Communication) 207

SPI (Serial Peripheral Interface) 209

I2C (Inter-Integrated Circuit) 211

Bluetooth 214

Section Project in Programming Fundamentals section 217

Foundations of Computing and I/O 217

Project: LED Blink using ESP32/ESP8266 217

Project: Analog Temperature Sensor with LED using ESP32/ESP8266 225

Project: PWM LED Brightness Control with Potentiometer using ESP32/ESP8266 230

Programming Fundamentals (Operators and Math) 234

Project: Simple Calculator using ESP32/ESP8266 234

Project: Area and Perimeter of a Rectangle using ESP32/ESP8266 239

Project: Exponentiation Calculator using ESP32/ESP8266 242

Project: Trigonometric Calculator using ESP32/ESP8266 246

Variables, Data Types, and Control Structures 250

Project : Temperature Conversion Program using ESP32/ESP8266 250

Project: Simple ATM System using ESP32/ESP8266 254

Project : Sum and Average of Array Elements using ESP32/ESP8266 259

Project : LED Control with User Input (Digital Pin) using ESP32/ESP8266 263

Working with Data and Characters 267

Project Title: User Input Validation using ESP32/ESP8266 267

Project: String to Integer Converter using ESP32/ESP8266 271

Project: Basic Calculator with String Input using ESP32/ESP8266 274

Operators and Logical Flow 279

Project: Number Comparison Game using ESP32/ESP8266 279

Project: Simple Bitwise Calculator using ESP32/ESP8266 283

Project: Logical Flow Light Control using ESP32/ESP8266 287

Project: Grade Calculator with Compound Operators using ESP32/ESP8266 292

Chapter 14 ESP Deep Sleep 297

1. Timer Wake-up 298

Project: ESP32 Wakes Up Every 10 Seconds to Read a Sensor Value 300

2. Touchpad Wake-up 304

Project: ESP32 Wakes Up When a Touch Sensor is Activated 306

3. External GPIO Wake-up (Single GPIO) 310

Project: ESP32 Wakes Up When a Button is Pressed 312

4. Starting Sleep Modes 316

Project: Battery-powered Weather Station Using ESP32 with Deep Sleep 319

Section- Getting started with IoT in esp32 /esp8266 324

Chapter 15. WiFi Network 324

    Basic Wi-Fi Setup 326

    Connecting to WiFi 326

    Creating an Access Point 328

    Disconnecting from WiFi 330

    Project: ESP32 Wi-Fi Connection 332

2. Connection Status & IP Information 335

    Checking WiFi Connection Status 335

    Getting the Local IP Address 338

    Getting the Access Point IP Address 340

    Project: Display ESP32 IP Address 342

3. Wi-Fi Mode Selection 346

    Setting the WiFi Mode to Station 346

Setting the WiFi Mode to Access Point 348

Setting the WiFi Mode to Both Access Point and Station 350

Project: Dual Mode ESP32: Wi-Fi Client (Station) and Hotspot (AP) 352

4. Network Scanning..357

Scanning for Available WiFi Networks..............................357

Getting the SSID of a WiFi Network..................................359

Getting the Signal Strength of a WiFi Network..................361

Project: Wi-Fi Network Scanner Using ESP32...................363

5. Advanced Network Management..366

Manually Configuring Network Settings 366

Setting the Hostname for Your Device..............................369

Adjusting WiFi Transmission Power 371

Disabling WiFi Sleep Mode..373

Chapter -0 Get started with ESP

1. Introduction to ESP32 and ESP8266

Overview of ESP32 and ESP8266

The **ESP32** and **ESP8266** are microcontrollers developed by **Espressif Systems**, commonly used in **Internet of Things (IoT)** projects. These microcontrollers are known for their **built-in Wi-Fi** capabilities, which make them highly popular for connecting devices to the internet and creating smart, connected systems. Both are affordable and widely used, but they have different levels of power, features, and applications, making them suitable for different use cases.

- **ESP32**: Designed to be a high-performance microcontroller with dual-core processing, Wi-Fi, and Bluetooth capabilities, the ESP32 is ideal for more advanced IoT projects. It is suitable for applications where more computing power, additional features, and enhanced connectivity are needed.
- **ESP8266**: Known for its low cost and built-in Wi-Fi, the ESP8266 is ideal for simpler IoT projects, particularly for beginners or budget-conscious makers. It's capable of handling basic tasks and is perfect for projects that do not require the higher performance or additional connectivity options found in the ESP32.

Introduction to ESP32

The **ESP32** is a powerful and versatile microcontroller unit (MCU) created by Espressif Systems, specifically designed to enable connected, smart, and interactive devices. The key highlights of the ESP32 are:

- **Dual-Core Processor**: The ESP32 features two Xtensa LX6 processors, each capable of running up to **240 MHz**. This dual-core setup makes it powerful enough for multitasking

and managing different operations simultaneously, which is beneficial in many IoT scenarios.
- **Connectivity**: It supports **Wi-Fi** (802.11 b/g/n) and **Bluetooth**, including **Bluetooth Low Energy (BLE)**. This makes the ESP32 versatile, as it can connect to the internet or other devices via Bluetooth.
- **Power Management**: The ESP32 is known for its various **low-power modes**, which makes it ideal for battery-powered applications. It can operate in **deep sleep mode** with very low power consumption, which is an essential feature for IoT projects that need to last long on a single battery charge.
- **Peripherals and GPIO**: The ESP32 comes with a wide range of **GPIO (General Purpose Input/Output) pins**, which can be used to connect sensors, LEDs, buttons, and other devices. It also has built-in modules like **analog-to-digital converters (ADC)**, **touch sensors**, and a **temperature sensor**.
- **Applications**: It is well-suited for **smart home automation**, **wearables**, **wireless sensors**, and **other advanced IoT projects** that require a high level of connectivity and computation power.

Introduction to ESP8266

The **ESP8266** is an earlier microcontroller model from Espressif Systems, widely popular for its affordability and integrated Wi-Fi. Key characteristics of the ESP8266 are:

- **Single-Core Processor**: The ESP8266 features a **32-bit Tensilica L106 processor**, running at speeds between **80 MHz and 160 MHz**. While it's not as powerful as the ESP32, it is sufficient for less demanding IoT projects, especially those that don't require extensive data processing.
- **Built-in Wi-Fi**: The ESP8266 has a built-in **Wi-Fi module**, making it perfect for connecting small devices to the internet without needing an external Wi-Fi chip. It supports standard Wi-Fi protocols for internet access.
- **Cost-Effectiveness**: The ESP8266 is known for being **highly affordable**, which is why it became popular with

hobbyists and makers. It provides a low-cost way to add Wi-Fi capabilities to electronics.
- **GPIO and Connectivity**: It has a limited number of **GPIO pins** compared to the ESP32, which limits the number of sensors and peripherals that can be connected simultaneously. Nevertheless, it supports common communication protocols like **SPI**, **I2C**, and **UART**, making it versatile enough for many smaller projects.
- **Applications**: The ESP8266 is ideal for simple projects such as **smart light switches**, **basic wireless sensors**, and **simple automation devices** where a low-cost solution is needed.

Comparison between ESP32 and ESP8266

To help understand the differences and choose between ESP32 and ESP8266, let's compare their features:

1. **Processing Power**:
    - **ESP32**: Features a **dual-core processor**, running up to **240 MHz**, providing more processing power for demanding applications.
    - **ESP8266**: Has a **single-core processor** running at **80-160 MHz**, sufficient for simple tasks and straightforward IoT projects.
2. **Connectivity**:
    - **ESP32**: Offers both **Wi-Fi** and **Bluetooth (including BLE)** connectivity. This dual connectivity makes it ideal for projects that require a variety of communication options.
    - **ESP8266**: Offers only **Wi-Fi** connectivity, making it great for basic IoT projects that involve internet communication without the need for Bluetooth.
3. **Power Consumption**:
    - **ESP32**: Comes with advanced power-saving features, including multiple power modes (like **deep sleep mode**), which make it suitable for battery-operated projects.

- **ESP8266**: Also supports power-saving, but it is less efficient than the ESP32, which may affect long-term battery life in some projects.

4. **GPIO and Peripherals**:
   - **ESP32**: Has more **GPIO pins** and a richer set of built-in peripherals, including touch sensors, analog inputs, and a temperature sensor, giving more flexibility for complex projects.
   - **ESP8266**: Has fewer GPIO pins, limiting the number of devices that can be connected, but is still capable of handling basic hardware interfaces and common sensors.

5. **Price**:
   - **ESP8266**: **Cheaper** compared to the ESP32, making it the preferred option for budget projects and for beginners just getting into IoT.
   - **ESP32**: Slightly **more expensive** but worth the cost for projects that require more features and better performance.

6. **Suitability for Projects**:
   - **ESP32**: Best for **advanced IoT projects**, requiring high processing power, Bluetooth connectivity, and multiple sensor inputs. Examples include **smart home automation systems**, **wearable devices**, and **complex sensors**.
   - **ESP8266**: Great for **entry-level and basic IoT projects**, where cost and simplicity are the main factors. It is perfect for **home automation**, such as smart lights and switches, where only Wi-Fi is required.

History and Evolution of ESP8266 and ESP32

Release Timeline

The ESP8266 and ESP32 microcontrollers have significantly impacted the development of IoT solutions by providing affordable and powerful connectivity options. Here's a look at their release history:

- **ESP8266 Release Timeline**:
  - **2014**: The **ESP8266** was first introduced by Espressif Systems, becoming a game changer due to its integrated Wi-Fi capabilities at a very low cost. It initially gained popularity with hobbyists and DIY makers.
  - **Late 2014 - 2015**: The ESP8266 gained widespread adoption thanks to the open availability of software development tools (SDKs) that allowed developers to easily create custom firmware.
- **ESP32 Release Timeline**:
  - **2016**: Espressif Systems launched the **ESP32**, which was developed as a more powerful successor to the ESP8266. It included enhanced features like dual-core processing, Bluetooth connectivity, and improved power efficiency.
  - **Late 2016 - 2017**: The ESP32 quickly caught the attention of developers and IoT enthusiasts, largely due to its increased processing power and additional features.

Timeline of Hardware Updates and Firmware Improvements

- **ESP8266 Hardware and Firmware Evolution**:
  - **2014**: The initial version of ESP8266 had limited software support and was primarily used in basic Wi-Fi-enabled projects.
  - **2015 - 2016**: Espressif improved SDK support, adding more stable and feature-rich firmware. This enabled developers to take advantage of better Wi-Fi stability, power management, and the ability to customize applications.
  - **NodeMCU Boards**: Popular third-party development boards, like NodeMCU, made ESP8266 more

accessible by adding USB connectivity, voltage regulators, and breakout pins.
- **ESP32 Hardware and Firmware Evolution**:
    - **2016**: The first ESP32 modules, like the ESP-WROOM-32, were released. They included new features such as Bluetooth Low Energy (BLE) and multiple analog and digital peripherals.
    - **2017 - 2018**: Firmware updates focused on improving Bluetooth stack performance, reducing power consumption, and optimizing GPIO and I/O functions.
    - **New Variants**: Different versions of the ESP32 module have been introduced to cater to specific needs, such as the **ESP32-S2** (targeted towards security-sensitive applications) and **ESP32-C3** (based on the RISC-V architecture for cost-effective solutions).

ESP8266 to ESP32: The Evolution

Reasons for the Development of ESP32

The **ESP8266** was revolutionary for making Wi-Fi connectivity affordable, but it had some limitations, which led to the development of the **ESP32**. Key reasons for this evolution include:

- **Enhanced Processing Power**: The ESP8266 has a single-core processor with limited power, which restricts its multitasking capabilities. The ESP32 was developed with **dual-core processors** to provide more power for handling multiple tasks efficiently.
- **Additional Connectivity Options**: While the ESP8266 only supported Wi-Fi, the ESP32 introduced **Bluetooth** and **Bluetooth Low Energy (BLE)** capabilities, enabling a wider range of connectivity options.
- **Power Efficiency**: One key drawback of the ESP8266 was its relatively high power consumption for battery-operated applications. The ESP32 offers **low-power modes** and better power management, making it suitable for portable devices.

Enhancements Over ESP8266

The **ESP32** includes several significant improvements over the **ESP8266**:

- **More GPIO Pins**: The ESP32 features more GPIO pins, which provides greater flexibility in connecting peripherals, sensors, and other hardware.
- **Dual-Core Processor**: Unlike the single-core ESP8266, the ESP32 features a **dual-core Xtensa LX6 processor**, which enables better multitasking and overall performance.
- **Built-in Peripherals**: The ESP32 comes with a host of built-in peripherals, such as **analog-to-digital converters (ADCs), capacitive touch sensors, temperature sensors**, and even **digital-to-analog converters (DACs)**.
- **Multiple Communication Interfaces**: The ESP32 supports **SPI**, **I2C**, **UART**, and **CAN**, allowing for more versatile communication between components.

Impact on IoT Community

How ESP8266 Revolutionised Affordable Wi-Fi Modules

The **ESP8266** marked a revolutionary shift in the IoT community by significantly reducing the cost of adding Wi-Fi capabilities to electronic devices. Before the ESP8266, Wi-Fi modules were often costly, making it impractical for smaller projects or DIY enthusiasts. Key impacts of the ESP8266 include:

- **Lowered Barriers to Entry**: The low cost and ease of use of the ESP8266 democratized access to Wi-Fi-enabled microcontrollers, making them accessible for hobbyists, students, and developers on a budget.
- **Community and Ecosystem Growth**: The availability of open-source SDKs and extensive community support helped foster a large and engaged developer base. This resulted in the rapid growth of tutorials, libraries, and projects that further popularized the module.

- **Rise of DIY IoT Projects**: ESP8266 enabled the development of countless **DIY projects**, such as smart lights, Wi-Fi weather stations, and connected sensors, inspiring more people to engage in IoT development.

The Adoption of ESP32 in Advanced IoT Applications

The **ESP32** took the success of the ESP8266 a step further by introducing features that made it suitable for more advanced IoT applications:

- **Complex Applications**: With its **dual-core processing**, **Bluetooth**, and more GPIO options, the ESP32 is commonly used in complex projects such as **robotics**, **real-time monitoring systems**, and **wearables**.
- **Industrial IoT**: The increased power and versatility of the ESP32 have also made it a popular choice in industrial IoT (IIoT) applications, such as remote monitoring, data logging, and automation systems.
- **Expanded Use Cases**: Bluetooth and Bluetooth Low Energy (BLE) support have allowed the ESP32 to be used in projects that require device-to-device communication, such as **smart health** devices, **home automation**, and **mesh networks**.

Future of ESP32 and ESP8266 in IoT

Future of ESP8266

- **Continued Use in Basic IoT Projects**: Given its affordability, the **ESP8266** is likely to remain a popular choice for basic IoT projects that do not require high processing power or Bluetooth. It will continue to be used by beginners and makers looking to create simple, internet-connected devices.
- **Educational Use**: The ESP8266 will remain an educational tool for learning about IoT and microcontrollers. Its simplicity makes it an ideal choice for introducing students and new developers to Wi-Fi-based projects.

Future of ESP32

- **Expanded Industrial Applications**: With its robust processing capabilities and connectivity options, the **ESP32** will continue to be adopted in more advanced industrial applications and environments where more reliable and flexible connectivity is needed.
- **Growing Integration with AI and Machine Learning**: As AI and edge computing become more prevalent, the ESP32, with its processing power, is well-positioned to support **machine learning models** at the edge, making it suitable for applications like **smart cameras**, **voice recognition**, and **predictive maintenance**.
- **New Variants and Features**: Espressif has continued to expand the ESP32 family with variants like **ESP32-S3** and **ESP32-C3**, each with unique features that cater to specific use cases (e.g., enhanced AI capabilities, reduced cost). This diversification ensures that the ESP32 line remains adaptable and versatile for various IoT needs.

2. Pinout and Hardware Layout

Understanding the pinout and hardware layout of microcontrollers like **ESP32** and **ESP8266** is essential for connecting sensors, peripherals, and other electronic components effectively. Both ESP32 and ESP8266 have different sets of pins with specific functions that define their use cases in projects.

ESP32 Pinout Diagram

The **ESP32** microcontroller comes with numerous **GPIO pins** and a variety of other specialized pins that can be used for different purposes. Here's a high-level description of the **ESP32 pinout**:

- **GPIO Pins**: The ESP32 typically has **36 GPIO pins** (depending on the variant). These pins can be used as digital

inputs or outputs. Many of these pins also have additional functions, such as PWM, ADC, or touch sensors.
- **Power Pins**:
    - **3.3V Pin**: Supplies 3.3 volts of power to the board.
    - **Vin Pin**: This pin is used to power the ESP32 from an external 5V power source.
    - **Ground (GND) Pins**: Connect to the ground of the circuit.
- **Analog Input Pins (ADC)**: The ESP32 has multiple ADC pins that can be used to read analog sensors. There are **18 channels** available, with a resolution of up to **12 bits**.
- **Touch Sensors**: The ESP32 has **capacitive touch pins** (T0 to T9), allowing for touch-based input detection.

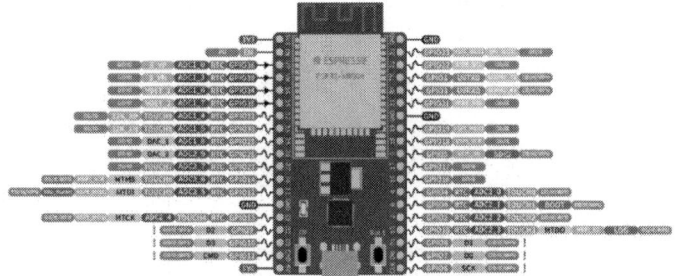

- **UART, SPI, I2C, and PWM Pins**: These pins provide communication interfaces to connect peripherals.
    - **UART**: Supports up to 3 UART interfaces for serial communication.
    - **SPI/I2C**: Multiple SPI and I2C pins allow for interfacing with sensors and other devices.
    - **PWM**: Most GPIOs can be used for **PWM** (Pulse Width Modulation), useful for controlling LEDs and motors.
- **Other Special Pins**:
    - **EN Pin**: The **Enable** pin (EN) is used to reset the microcontroller.
    - **Boot Pin (IO0)**: Used to put the ESP32 into **bootloader mode** for uploading firmware.

ESP8266 Pinout Diagram

The **ESP8266** has fewer pins compared to the ESP32, and understanding its pinout is crucial for using it effectively in simpler projects.

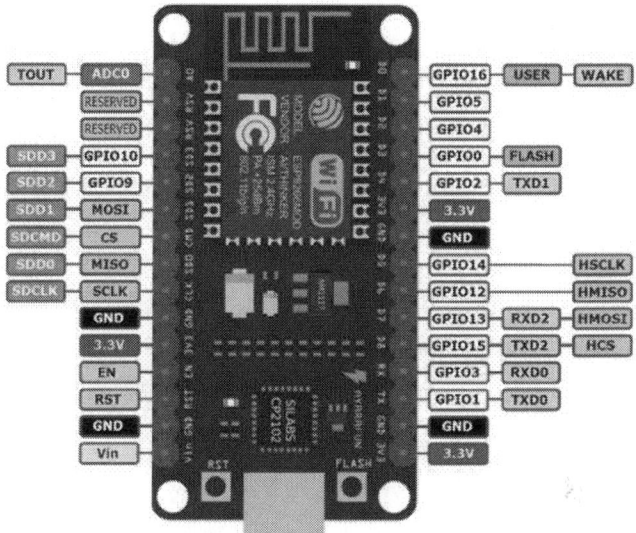

- **GPIO Pins**: The ESP8266 generally has **17 GPIO pins** available (depending on the development board). These pins serve multiple functions and can be configured as digital input or output.
- **Power Pins**:
    - **3.3V Pin**: Supplies power to the ESP8266 (typically operates at 3.3V).
    - **Vin Pin**: Powers the module with an input voltage range of 4.5V to 12V, depending on the board.
    - **Ground (GND) Pins**: Connects to the ground of the circuit.
- **Analog Input Pin (ADC0)**: The ESP8266 has **one analog input pin** (ADC0), which can measure voltages from 0 to 1V.
- **UART, SPI, I2C, and PWM Pins**:
    - **UART**: Supports serial communication for programming and debugging.

- **SPI/I2C**: Fewer communication options compared to ESP32, but SPI and I2C are still supported for external components.
- **PWM**: Limited GPIO pins can be configured for PWM, mainly for controlling simple components like LEDs.
- **CH_PD Pin**: The **Chip Power-Down** pin is used to enable or disable the chip.

Pin Functions and Description

Power Pins

- **ESP32 and ESP8266 both have 3.3V and GND pins** for power supply. It's crucial to ensure that the **input voltage** is regulated to prevent damaging the microcontrollers.
- The **Vin pin** can be used to provide external power; however, the voltage requirements for ESP32 and ESP8266 may vary slightly depending on the board.

Input/Output Pins

- Both **ESP32** and **ESP8266** GPIO pins can be configured as **inputs or outputs**, making them versatile for controlling components like LEDs, motors, or reading sensor values.
- **ESP32**: Offers **more GPIO pins** (typically 36), which allows more components to be connected simultaneously.
- **ESP8266**: Offers fewer GPIO pins (usually **17**), which can be a limitation when attempting to connect multiple peripherals.

GPIO Limitations and Considerations

- **ESP32**:
  - Not all GPIO pins are available for general use. Some pins have specific functions (e.g., flash, boot mode) and should be avoided in general-purpose use unless configured correctly.
  - Pins like **GPIO6 to GPIO11** are used for the internal flash and should **not** be used for other purposes.

- **ESP8266**:

- **GPIO0, GPIO2, and GPIO15**: These pins have special functions during boot mode and should be used carefully to avoid conflicts during power-up.
- **Limited Number of GPIOs**: With fewer GPIOs, you may need to use **multiplexing** techniques or **GPIO expanders** to connect additional components.

Interrupt Capabilities

- **ESP32**: Supports **interrupts** on almost all GPIO pins. This feature is crucial when you need the microcontroller to respond immediately to an event, like a button press.
- **ESP8266**: Interrupts are also supported but are more limited. Care should be taken to avoid using certain pins that may not properly support interrupts.

Analog Input Limitations

- **ESP32**:
  - The ESP32 has **multiple ADC channels** (up to 18), with a 12-bit resolution, which provides more precise analog readings.
  - However, the **ADC** is known to be **non-linear**, and calibration may be required to get accurate results.
- **ESP8266**:
  - The **ESP8266** has only **one ADC pin** (ADC0), and its range is limited to 0-1V, which can be restrictive when trying to read analog signals with higher voltages.
  - A voltage divider may be needed to bring the input voltage within the acceptable range of the ADC.

GPIO Pin Details and Usage for ESP32 and ESP8266

GPIO Pin Numbe	Pin Type	ESP32	ESP8266	Use

r				
GPIO 0	Digital I/O	Yes	Yes	Boot mode selection, LED control
GPIO 1 (TX)	UART TX	Yes	Yes	Serial communication (data transmission)
GPIO 2	Digital I/O	Yes	Yes	LED control, status indication
GPIO 3 (RX)	UART RX	Yes	Yes	Serial communication (data reception)
GPIO 4	Digital I/O	Yes	Yes	General-purpose tasks, sensors, LEDs
GPIO 5	Digital I/O	Yes	Yes	Motor control, PWM
GPIO 6-11	Flash Memory	No	No	Reserved (do not use)
GPIO 12	Digital I/O	Yes	Yes	General-purpose tasks, output devices
GPIO 13	Digital I/O, PWM	Yes	Yes	LED dimming, motor control
GPIO 14	Digital I/O, PWM	Yes	Yes	PWM for motor or LED, sensor input
GPIO 15	Digital I/O, PWM	Yes	Yes	PWM, sensor or device control

GPIO 16	Digital I/O, Wake	Yes	Yes	Wake from deep sleep, low-power projects
GPIO 17	Digital I/O	Yes	No	General-purpose tasks
GPIO 18	SPI SCK	Yes	No	SPI communication (clock line)
GPIO 19	SPI MISO	Yes	No	SPI communication (data reception)
GPIO 21	I2C SDA	Yes	No	I2C communication (data line)
GPIO 22	I2C SCL	Yes	No	I2C communication (clock line)
GPIO 23	SPI MOSI	Yes	No	SPI communication (data transmission)
GPIO 25-27	Digital I/O, ADC	Yes	No	Reading analog values from sensors
GPIO 32-39	ADC	Yes	No	Analog input (e.g., sensors like LDRs)

Power Supply Requirements:

Voltage Range and Power Consumption:

- **ESP32**: The ESP32 operates within a voltage range of **3.0V to 3.6V**, with an ideal input voltage of **3.3V**. It is capable of drawing a substantial amount of current, especially during Wi-Fi transmission. During peak usage (like Wi-Fi transmission), the ESP32 can consume around **160-240 mA**, while in idle mode, it typically consumes around **20-30 mA**.
- **ESP8266**: The ESP8266 also operates in a voltage range of **3.0V to 3.6V**, typically running at **3.3V**. Its power consumption is slightly lower than that of the ESP32, with peak currents reaching **170 mA** during Wi-Fi transmission. In idle mode, the current draw is roughly **10-20 mA**.

Power Management Hardware: Both ESP32 and ESP8266 have built-in capabilities to manage power consumption effectively:

- **Voltage Regulators**: Most development boards for the ESP32 and ESP8266 (such as NodeMCU or ESP32 DevKit) come with onboard **voltage regulators** that convert higher input voltages (like 5V from USB) to the required **3.3V** for the microcontroller. These voltage regulators ensure that the input power is within the safe operating range.
- **Decoupling Capacitors**: To ensure stable voltage supply and avoid fluctuations during peak power usage, decoupling capacitors are often included on development boards.

Battery Power and USB Power Options:

- **Battery Power**: Both ESP32 and ESP8266 can be powered using batteries, making them ideal for portable projects. Typical battery options include **Li-ion/Li-Po** batteries (3.7V nominal voltage). For battery-powered setups, a voltage regulator is necessary to step down the voltage to **3.3V**. The ESP32 is designed with several power-saving modes, making it suitable for long-term battery-powered applications.

- **USB Power**: Development boards for both ESP32 and ESP8266 generally have a **micro USB port** for powering and programming the microcontroller. The USB power supplies **5V**, which is then regulated down to **3.3V** on the board.

Current Draw During Different States:

Active Mode:

- **ESP32**: In active mode, when all components are running, including Wi-Fi, the ESP32 can consume between **160-240 mA**. This high power draw occurs primarily during transmission and data processing. The dual-core processor adds to the power requirements when both cores are in operation.
- **ESP8266**: In active mode with Wi-Fi enabled, the ESP8266 draws about **150-170 mA**. This is slightly lower compared to the ESP32 due to its simpler architecture and lower processing power.

Sleep Mode:

- **ESP32**: The ESP32 is highly optimized for low-power operation, offering several sleep modes, including **light sleep** and **deep sleep**. In **deep sleep mode**, the ESP32 can reduce its power consumption to around **10 µA**, making it suitable for battery-powered devices where long operational life is required. **Light sleep** typically uses a bit more power, around **1-5 mA**.
- **ESP8266**: The ESP8266 also offers sleep modes, although they are less sophisticated compared to the ESP32. In **deep sleep mode**, the ESP8266 can reduce power consumption to about **20 µA**, which is higher than the ESP32. The wake-up process from deep sleep is relatively slower, which may affect its use in some applications requiring quick responses.

3. Getting Started with ESP32 in Arduino IDE

Step 1: Install Arduino IDE

- **Download Arduino IDE** from here.
- Install it just like any other software (follow the prompts).

Step 2: Add ESP32 Support to Arduino IDE

1. Open Arduino IDE.
2. Go to **File > Preferences**.

In the **Additional Boards Manager URLs** box, paste this link:

```
https://dl.espressif.com/dl/package_esp32_index.json
```

3. Click **OK**.

Step 3: Install ESP32 Board

1. Go to **Tools > Board > Boards Manager**.
2. Search for "ESP32" in the Boards Manager.
3. Click **Install** next to **ESP32 by Espressif Systems**.

Step 4: Connect Your ESP32

1. Plug your ESP32 into your computer using a USB cable.
2. Go to **Tools > Board** and select your ESP32 board (for example, "ESP32 Dev Module").
3. Under **Tools > Port**, select the correct port (e.g., COM3 on Windows).

Step 5: Upload Your First Program

1. Open the **Blink** example: **File > Examples > Basics > Blink**.
2. Click the **Upload** button (right arrow icon).
3. Your ESP32's built-in LED should start blinking once the program is uploaded.

4. Getting Started with ESP32 in Thonny (MicroPython)

Step 1: Install Thonny IDE

- **Download Thonny IDE** from here.
- Install it by following the installation steps, like any regular program.

Step 2: Install MicroPython on Your ESP32

1. **Download the MicroPython firmware** for your ESP32 from here.

Install **esptool** by opening the command prompt (Windows) or terminal (macOS/Linux) and running:

```
pip install esptool
```

Erase the ESP32 memory by running this command:
`esptool.py --chip esp32 erase_flash`

Flash the MicroPython firmware with this command (replace `firmware.bin` with the actual filename of the firmware you downloaded):
`esptool.py --chip esp32 --port COM3 --baud 460800 write_flash -z 0x1000 firmware.bin`

2. *(Replace COM3 with your actual port name if needed.)*

Step 3: Set Up Thonny for MicroPython

1. Open Thonny IDE.
2. Go to **Tools > Options > Interpreter**.
3. Select **MicroPython (ESP32)** as the interpreter.
4. Choose the port where your ESP32 is connected.

Step 4: Write Your First MicroPython Script

1. In Thonny, write a simple script to control the ESP32 (such as blinking the LED).
2. Click the **Run** button (green arrow) to upload the code and execute it on the ESP32.

Which to Choose?

- **Arduino IDE**: Best for those who are new to programming and want a simple, beginner-friendly platform with plenty of resources and examples.
- **Thonny with MicroPython**: Ideal if you are comfortable with Python or want to learn it. It's great for quick, simple projects and easy-to-read code.

5. Basic Troubleshooting for Setup (Driver Issues, Flashing Problems):

Driver Issues:

- If your computer does not recognize the ESP32 or ESP8266, you may need to install drivers for **USB-to-Serial chips** like **CP2102**, **CH340**, or **FTDI**.
- Ensure that the correct COM port is selected in the **Arduino IDE** under **Tools > Port**.

Flashing Problems:

- **Common Errors**: "Failed to connect to ESP32" is a common error when the microcontroller is not in bootloader mode. Press and hold the **BOOT** button while uploading code to put the ESP32 in flashing mode.
- Ensure the **baud rate** is set correctly (usually *115200*).

Flashing Firmware:

Using ESP-Tool to Flash:

- **ESP-Tool** is a command-line utility provided by Espressif for flashing firmware onto ESP32 and ESP8266 devices.
- **Installation**: Install `esptool` using Python's package manager: *pip install esptool*
- **Usage**: Connect your ESP board and run the following command to erase the flash memory: *esptool.py erase_flash* To flash new firmware: *esptool.py --port COM3 write_flash -z 0x0000 firmware.bin* Replace *COM3* with the appropriate port (e.g., */dev/ttyUSB0* on Linux) and *firmware.bin* with the path to your firmware file.

Troubleshooting Common Issues:

USB Connectivity Problems (Beyond Initial Setup): Even after setting up the initial development environment, you might encounter USB connectivity issues:

- **USB Port Not Recognized**:
    - *Check USB Cable*: Some USB cables are power-only and do not support data transfer. Make sure you are using a **data-capable USB cable**.
    - *Port Selection*: Ensure the correct **COM port** is selected in the **Arduino IDE** under **Tools > Port**.
    - *Reinstall Drivers*: Sometimes, drivers may become corrupted. Reinstalling drivers for **CP2102**, **CH340**, or **FTDI** can help resolve recognition issues.
- **Board Keeps Disconnecting**:
    - *Power Supply Issue*: Ensure that the board is receiving stable power. A poor-quality USB cable or insufficient power from the USB port can cause disconnections. Using a powered USB hub can provide a more stable power supply.
    - *USB Port Overload*: Avoid plugging multiple power-consuming devices into the same USB hub as your

ESP board, as this may cause voltage drops, resulting in random disconnections.

Wi-Fi Connectivity Issues:
- **Unable to Connect to Wi-Fi**:
    - *Wrong Credentials*: Double-check the **SSID** and **password**. Simple typos can lead to connection failures.
    - *Wi-Fi Signal Strength*: Place the ESP module closer to the router or access point, and ensure there aren't many obstacles. Use the **WiFi.RSSI()** function in **Arduino IDE** or similar methods to check signal strength.
    - *Channel Overcrowding*: Many Wi-Fi networks on the same channel can cause interference. If possible, change the router's channel to a less crowded one.
- **Intermittent Wi-Fi Disconnection**:
    - *Power Supply Stability*: Ensure a stable power supply, as Wi-Fi transmission draws significant current. Voltage fluctuations can cause the microcontroller to reset or disconnect from Wi-Fi.
    - *Firmware Update*: Older firmware may have issues maintaining a stable Wi-Fi connection. Updating to the latest **ESP32** or **ESP8266 firmware** can resolve such issues.

Debugging Tools and Techniques:
- **Serial Monitor**:
    - The **Serial Monitor** in **Arduino IDE** is a fundamental tool for debugging. Use *Serial.print()* statements to understand the flow of your code and identify where errors occur.
- **Logic Analyzers**:
    - For communication issues (such as **I2C** or **SPI**), a **logic analyzer** can help you understand what data is being transmitted and identify where errors might be occurring.
-
-

- **ESP-IDF Monitor**:
    - If using **ESP-IDF**, the integrated **ESP-IDF Monitor** provides useful logs and real-time debugging information. It is especially useful for understanding deeper issues like crashes or stack traces.

6.Best Practices for Using ESP32/ESP8266:

Power Supply Stability:

- Ensure a **reliable 3.3V power supply**. Both ESP32 and ESP8266 can draw spikes of current during Wi-Fi transmissions. If you are using a linear regulator, make sure it can handle at least **500 mA** of current.
- When using battery power, consider a **Li-Po battery** with a **DC-DC buck converter** to ensure stable voltage, as voltage drops can cause unexpected reboots.

Proper GPIO Usage:

- **ESP32**: Not all GPIO pins are available for general use, as some are used internally by the microcontroller (e.g., for flash or boot). Avoid using **GPIO6 to GPIO11** for other purposes, as these are connected to the integrated flash memory.
- **ESP8266**: Special GPIO pins like **GPIO0**, **GPIO2**, and **GPIO15** are involved in the boot process. Ensure proper connections if these pins are used, as incorrect connections can cause the board to not boot correctly.
- Use **current-limiting resistors** (typically **220 ohms to 1k ohms**) when connecting LEDs or other components to GPIO pins to protect both the pins and external components.

Antenna Placement for Wi-Fi:

- **Avoid Obstacles**: The onboard antenna should not be obstructed by metal components, power supplies, or other electronics that could interfere with signal transmission.

- **Distance from Power Sources**: Place the ESP module away from power supplies, as electromagnetic interference can degrade Wi-Fi performance.
- **Proper Orientation**: The onboard PCB antenna is directional. Make sure the module is oriented so that the antenna faces outward for optimal coverage.

Section 1: Foundations of Computing and I/O

Chapter 1. Digital I/O Basics:

Chapter Overview

In this chapter, you will learn how to control and interact with external devices using the **Digital Input/Output (I/O)** functionality of microcontrollers like the Arduino and ESP32 using MicroPython. You'll understand how to set pins as inputs or outputs, control devices like LEDs and motors, and read signals from sensors and buttons. This chapter covers fundamental operations that allow microcontrollers to interact with the physical world through GPIO (General Purpose Input/Output) pins.

Chapter Purpose

By the end of this chapter, you will be able to:

- **Set pins** on a microcontroller as inputs or outputs to interact with external devices.
- **Control devices** like LEDs and motors using digital signals.
- **Read inputs** from buttons, sensors, and other devices to detect their state.
- **Implement pull-up resistors** to ensure stable readings from input pins.
- **Use debouncing** to handle noisy button presses.
- **Use PWM** (Pulse Width Modulation) to simulate analog output for controlling brightness, motor speed, etc.

Chapter Syntax Table

Topics	Arduino Syntax	MicroPython Syntax
Digital Pin Modes	`pinMode(pin, mode);`	`pin = machine.Pin(pin_number, mode)`
Digital Write	`digitalWrite(pin, value);`	`pin.value(1)` (HIGH) or `pin.value(0)` (LOW)
Digital Read	`digitalRead(pin);`	`pin.value()`
Built-in Pull-up Resistor	`pinMode(pin, INPUT_PULLUP);`	`pin = machine.Pin(pin_number, machine.Pin.IN, machine.Pin.PULL_UP)`
Debouncing	`delay(milliseconds);`	`time.sleep_ms(milliseconds)`
PWM (Pulse Width Modulation)	`analogWrite(pin, value);`	`pwm = machine.PWM(machine.Pin(pin))` and `pwm.duty_u16(value)`

Digital Pin Modes

Digital pin modes define how a pin on a microcontroller (such as an Arduino or MicroPython board) will behave—either as an *input* (to read signals) or as an *output* (to send signals). This setting tells the microcontroller how to interact with devices like sensors, buttons, or LEDs.

Use Purpose

The main purpose of setting digital pin modes is to communicate with external devices. You can either receive signals from components like sensors (input mode) or control components like LEDs or motors (output mode).

Arduino Syntax Use

```
pinMode(pin, mode);
```

Arduino Syntax Explanation

In Arduino, the *pinMode()* function is used to define how a specific pin will behave:

- *pin*: The number of the pin you're configuring (e.g., pin 7).
- *mode*: You can set the pin to be either *INPUT*, *OUTPUT*, or *INPUT_PULLUP*.

Arduino Simple Code Example

```
pinMode(7, OUTPUT);
pinMode(2, INPUT);
```

- Pin 7 is set as an output (e.g., to control an LED).
- Pin 2 is set as an input (e.g., to read a button press).

Notes

- By default, Arduino pins are set to *INPUT*.
- *INPUT_PULLUP* is useful when you need an internal pull-up resistor to avoid noisy readings from input devices like buttons.

Warnings

- Setting a pin incorrectly can damage components or cause them to function improperly. Always verify the pin mode when working with external devices.

MicroPython Syntax Use

```
pin = machine.Pin(pin_number, machine.Pin.OUT)
pin = machine.Pin(pin_number, machine.Pin.IN)
```

MicroPython Syntax Explanation

In MicroPython, the *machine.Pin()* function is used to set a pin's behavior:

- *pin_number*: The specific pin you're configuring (e.g., pin 15).
- *OUT* or *IN*: Defines whether the pin will act as an output or input.

MicroPython Simple Code Example

```
pin = machine.Pin(15, machine.Pin.OUT)
pin = machine.Pin(4, machine.Pin.IN)
```

- Pin 15 is set as an output (e.g., to control an LED).
- Pin 4 is set as an input (e.g., to read a sensor).

Notes

- Like Arduino, MicroPython pins default to *IN* mode.
- Pull-up resistors can be activated for input pins to improve signal quality.

Warnings

- Misconfiguring the pin mode could lead to unexpected behavior or even damage to connected devices. Double-check the pin mode before using external components.

Input/Output Declaration

Input/Output (I/O) declaration refers to the process of defining which pins on a microcontroller will be used for input (to receive data or signals) and which pins will be used for output (to send data or signals). This is crucial in controlling external devices such as sensors, motors, and LEDs.

Use Purpose
The purpose of declaring pins as either input or output is to properly set up communication between the microcontroller and the external components. Inputs allow the microcontroller to read data (like from a button), while outputs allow it to send data (like turning on an LED).

Arduino Syntax Use

```
pinMode(pin, mode);
```

Arduino Syntax Explanation
In Arduino, the *pinMode()* function is used to set the mode of a pin:

- *pin*: The specific pin number to configure.
- *mode*: The mode can be *INPUT* (for receiving data), *OUTPUT* (for sending data), or *INPUT_PULLUP* (for internal pull-up resistor use).

Arduino Simple Code Example

```
pinMode(13, OUTPUT);
pinMode(2, INPUT);
```

- Pin 13 is set as an output (to control an LED, for example).
- Pin 2 is set as an input (to read the state of a button).

Notes

- Input pins can be used to detect external signals, such as pressing a button or receiving sensor data.
- Output pins can drive components like LEDs, motors, or send signals to other devices.
- Use *INPUT_PULLUP* when you need a weak internal pull-up resistor to avoid adding an external one.

Warnings

- Incorrectly setting a pin's mode (e.g., configuring an output pin as input) may lead to errors or hardware damage. Always verify the correct mode for the pins in use.

MicroPython Syntax Use

```
pin = machine.Pin(pin_number, machine.Pin.OUT)
pin = machine.Pin(pin_number, machine.Pin.IN)
```

MicroPython Syntax Explanation

In MicroPython, the *machine.Pin()* function configures a pin:

- *pin_number*: Specifies the pin to configure.
- *OUT* or *IN*: Defines whether the pin will be an output or an input.

MicroPython Simple Code Example

```
pin = machine.Pin(12, machine.Pin.OUT)
pin = machine.Pin(16, machine.Pin.IN)
```

- Pin 12 is configured as an output (to control an LED or other devices).
- Pin 16 is configured as an input (to read a button or sensor data).

Notes

- Just like Arduino, pins default to *IN* mode unless otherwise specified.
- You can use internal pull-up or pull-down resistors when configuring input pins in MicroPython for more stable readings.

Warnings

- If you configure an output pin as an input by mistake, or vice versa, it may cause malfunction or even damage the connected components. Always check your pin configuration carefully.

Digital Write

Digital write is a function that allows a microcontroller, such as an Arduino or a MicroPython-based board, to send a digital signal (either HIGH or LOW) to an output pin. This is commonly used to control components like LEDs, motors, or relays.

Use Purpose
The purpose of using digital write is to control external devices by sending either a HIGH (on) or LOW (off) signal from the microcontroller's digital output pins. For example, turning an LED on or off based on the pin state.

Arduino Syntax Use

```
digitalWrite(pin, value);
```

Arduino Syntax Explanation
In Arduino, the *digitalWrite()* function is used to set a digital pin to either HIGH or LOW:

- *pin*: The number of the pin where the signal is being sent.
- *value*: Either *HIGH* (to send a 5V signal, turn the component on) or *LOW* (to send a 0V signal, turn the component off).

Arduino Simple Code Example

```
digitalWrite(13, HIGH);
digitalWrite(13, LOW);
```

- Pin 13 is set to HIGH, turning on the connected device (like an LED).
- Pin 13 is then set to LOW, turning off the device.

Notes

- Ensure the pin has been set as an *OUTPUT* using the *pinMode()* function before calling *digitalWrite()*.
- Digital pins only have two states: *HIGH* (on) and *LOW* (off).

Warnings

- Be cautious when using digital write on pins connected to sensitive devices, as sending incorrect signals may damage components.
- Make sure the pin mode is correctly set to output; otherwise, the digital write won't work.

MicroPython Syntax Use

```
pin.value(1)
pin.value(0)
```

MicroPython Syntax Explanation

In MicroPython, the *pin.value()* method is used to set a pin's output state:

- *pin*: The pin object you created.
- *1*: Sets the pin to HIGH (on).
- *0*: Sets the pin to LOW (off).

MicroPython Simple Code Example

```
pin.value(1)
pin.value(0)
```

- The pin is set to HIGH, turning on the connected device.
- The pin is set to LOW, turning off the device.

Notes

- Always configure the pin as an output before attempting to write a value to it.
- MicroPython simplifies the process by using *1* for HIGH and *0* for LOW.

Warnings

- Writing incorrect values or using the wrong pin mode may lead to hardware issues or unexpected behavior.
- Double-check pin configurations and ensure connected devices can handle the signals being sent.

Digital Read

Digital read is a function used to check the state of a digital input pin on a microcontroller, such as an Arduino or MicroPython-based board. It tells whether the pin is receiving a HIGH (on) or LOW (off) signal from an external device, like a sensor or button.

Use Purpose
The purpose of using digital read is to allow the microcontroller to detect the state of an external device. This is commonly used to read input from buttons, switches, or sensors and take action based on whether the signal is HIGH or LOW.

Arduino Syntax Use

```
digitalRead(pin);
```

Arduino Syntax Explanation
In Arduino, the *digitalRead()* function is used to read the state of a digital pin:

- *pin*: The number of the pin from which you want to read the input signal.
- The function returns either *HIGH* (if the input signal is 5V) or *LOW* (if the input signal is 0V).

Arduino Simple Code Example

```
int buttonState = digitalRead(2);
```

This reads the state of pin 2 (where a button may be connected) and stores the result (either *HIGH* or *LOW*) in the *buttonState* variable.

Notes

- Ensure that the pin is configured as an *INPUT* using the *pinMode()* function before using *digitalRead()*.
- *HIGH* means the pin is receiving a 5V signal, while *LOW* means it is receiving a 0V signal.

Warnings

- Improper wiring of the input devices (such as buttons or sensors) may cause inaccurate readings.
- If no external components are connected, the input pin can "float," resulting in unreliable readings. Use a pull-up or pull-down resistor to avoid this.

MicroPython Syntax Use

```
pin.value()
```

MicroPython Syntax Explanation

In MicroPython, the *pin.value()* method reads the current state of the pin:

- *pin*: The pin object that you have created for the input.
- The method returns *1* for HIGH or *0* for LOW.

MicroPython Simple Code Example

```
button_state = pin.value()
```

This reads the value of the input pin and stores it in the variable *button_state*, either as *1* (HIGH) or *0* (LOW).

Notes

- Similar to Arduino, ensure that the pin is set as an input when using *pin.value()* to read the pin state.
- MicroPython defaults to using internal pull-up or pull-down resistors to stabilize the input signal if needed.

Warnings

- Floating pins (unconnected input pins) can result in unpredictable behavior. Use appropriate resistors to stabilize the signal.
- Ensure that external components like sensors or buttons are properly connected to avoid incorrect readings.

Built-in Pull-up Resistor

A built-in pull-up resistor is a feature available in many microcontrollers, such as Arduino and MicroPython-based boards, that helps stabilize the input pin when it is not connected to any external component. Without it, an input pin can "float," causing unpredictable behavior or false readings.

Use Purpose
The main purpose of a pull-up resistor is to ensure a consistent, default HIGH state for an input pin, avoiding unreliable or fluctuating input values when the pin is not actively connected to a signal (e.g., when a button is not pressed).

Arduino Syntax Use

```
pinMode(pin, INPUT_PULLUP);
```

Arduino Syntax Explanation
In Arduino, you can enable the internal pull-up resistor for a digital input pin by using the *INPUT_PULLUP* mode in the *pinMode()* function:

- *pin*: The pin number you want to configure.
- *INPUT_PULLUP*: Activates the built-in pull-up resistor, setting the pin to a default HIGH state when no input is detected.

Arduino Simple Code Example

```
pinMode(2, INPUT_PULLUP);
int buttonState = digitalRead(2);
```

- This sets pin 2 as an input with a built-in pull-up resistor, ensuring that the pin reads HIGH when the button is not pressed.
- *digitalRead()* is then used to detect if the button has been pressed.

Notes

- When using *INPUT_PULLUP*, the logic is inverted: pressing the button will result in a LOW signal, and releasing it will give a HIGH signal.
- This method saves you from needing to add an external pull-up resistor to your circuit.

Warnings

- Be aware of the inverted logic when using pull-up resistors. A pressed button will return LOW, while an unpressed button will return HIGH.

MicroPython Syntax Use

```
pin = machine.Pin(pin_number, machine.Pin.IN, machine.Pin.PULL_UP)
```

MicroPython Syntax Explanation

In MicroPython, the built-in pull-up resistor can be enabled by adding the *PULL_UP* argument when configuring a pin:

- *pin_number*: The pin you are setting as input.
- *IN*: Configures the pin as input.
- *PULL_UP*: Enables the internal pull-up resistor.

MicroPython Simple Code Example

```
pin = machine.Pin(4, machine.Pin.IN, machine.Pin.PULL_UP)
button_state = pin.value()
```

- This configures pin 4 as an input with an internal pull-up resistor, so it will read HIGH by default and LOW when the button is pressed.

Notes

- Like Arduino, the logic is inverted when using the pull-up resistor in MicroPython. Expect a LOW signal when the button is pressed and HIGH when it is released.
- MicroPython also allows you to use pull-down resistors if needed, depending on your circuit design.

Warnings

- Be careful when interpreting input values, as the use of pull-up resistors inverts the expected logic (pressed = LOW, not pressed = HIGH).
- Ensure that your wiring and logic account for the inverted signals when using internal pull-up resistors to avoid confusion in your program.

Debouncing

Debouncing is the process of eliminating multiple false signals caused by mechanical switches, such as buttons, when they are pressed or released. Due to the nature of mechanical components, a button press may cause several rapid, unintended on/off signals before settling. Debouncing ensures that only one clear signal is detected.

Use Purpose
The purpose of debouncing is to avoid reading multiple unintended signals when a button is pressed or released. This helps improve the accuracy and reliability of input readings, especially when working with buttons or switches.

Arduino Syntax Use

```
delay(milliseconds);
```

Arduino Syntax Explanation
In Arduino, debouncing is typically handled using a small delay after

detecting a button press. The *delay()* function pauses the program for a specific amount of time to allow the bouncing to settle:

- *milliseconds*: The amount of time (in milliseconds) to wait before re-checking the button state.

Arduino Simple Code Example

```
int buttonState = digitalRead(2);
if (buttonState == LOW) {
delay(50);
if (digitalRead(2) == LOW) {
// Perform action
}
}
```

- The button is connected to pin 2.
- When the button is pressed (LOW), the program waits 50 milliseconds to ensure the input is stable before checking again. If the state is still LOW after the delay, the button press is confirmed.

Notes

- A delay of around 20-50 milliseconds is typically enough to debounce a button. Adjust based on the specific behavior of your switch or button.
- Debouncing can be done either in software (with code) or in hardware (with capacitors or specialized components).

Warnings

- Using too long of a delay may make your system feel unresponsive to button presses.
- Be cautious when using delays in time-sensitive programs, as the entire system pauses during the delay.

MicroPython Syntax Use

```
time.sleep_ms(milliseconds)
```

MicroPython Syntax Explanation
In MicroPython, debouncing is commonly handled by using the *time.sleep_ms()* function to pause for a short period after detecting a button press:

- *milliseconds*: The duration (in milliseconds) for the pause to allow for debouncing.

MicroPython Simple Code Example

```
if pin.value() == 0:
time.sleep_ms(50)
if pin.value() == 0:
# Perform action
```

- The button is connected to the input pin.
- When the button is pressed (*pin.value() == 0*), the program pauses for 50 milliseconds to let the signal stabilize, then checks again to confirm the button press.

Notes

- Similar to Arduino, 20-50 milliseconds is a typical debouncing delay in MicroPython. Adjust as needed for your button or switch.
- Debouncing in MicroPython can also be handled with event-driven programming or interrupt-based methods for more advanced setups.

Warnings

- Like Arduino, using too long of a debounce delay can make the system feel slow or unresponsive.

- Consider alternative methods for debouncing in more complex programs where timing is critical, such as using interrupts or timers.

PWM Support

PWM (Pulse Width Modulation) is a technique used to simulate an analog signal by rapidly switching a digital pin between HIGH and LOW states. By adjusting the ratio of time the signal stays HIGH to the time it stays LOW (called duty cycle), you can control devices like LEDs, motors, and servos with variable intensity or speed.

Use Purpose
PWM is commonly used to control the brightness of LEDs, the speed of DC motors, or the position of servos. It allows for fine control over devices that require more than just on/off functionality by simulating varying power levels through rapid switching.

Arduino Syntax Use

```
analogWrite(pin, value);
```

Arduino Syntax Explanation
In Arduino, the *analogWrite()* function is used to generate a PWM signal on pins that support it:

- *pin*: The number of the pin where you want to output the PWM signal.
- *value*: A value between 0 and 255 that sets the duty cycle of the PWM. A value of 0 means always LOW, and 255 means always HIGH. Any value in between controls the pulse width, thus adjusting brightness or speed.

Arduino Simple Code Example

```
analogWrite(9, 128);
```

- Pin 9 is set to output a PWM signal with a 50% duty cycle (128 out of 255), which could, for example, dim an LED to half brightness.

Notes

- Not all Arduino pins support PWM. Check the documentation to see which pins on your board are capable of generating a PWM signal.
- The *analogWrite()* function outputs a 490 Hz PWM signal on most pins.

Warnings

- PWM outputs only simulate an analog signal; they do not produce true analog voltages.
- Ensure that the components you're controlling (e.g., LEDs, motors) are compatible with PWM signals to avoid damage.

MicroPython Syntax Use

```
pwm = machine.PWM(machine.Pin(pin_number))
pwm.duty_u16(value)
```

MicroPython Syntax Explanation
In MicroPython, PWM is handled by the *machine.PWM()* class. You can create a PWM object for the pin you want to control:

- *pin_number*: The pin number where you want to output the PWM signal.
- *duty_u16(value)*: Sets the duty cycle with a value between 0 (always LOW) and 65535 (always HIGH). Intermediate values control the pulse width.

MicroPython Simple Code Example

```
pwm = machine.PWM(machine.Pin(15))
pwm.duty_u16(32768)
```

- Pin 15 is set to output a PWM signal with a 50% duty cycle (32768 out of 65535), which could control the brightness of an LED or the speed of a motor.

Notes

- Different microcontrollers may have different numbers of PWM-capable pins, so check the documentation of your specific board.
- MicroPython allows for more fine-grained control of the duty cycle using 16-bit values (0-65535).

Warnings

- As in Arduino, PWM in MicroPython simulates an analog signal but does not output true analog voltages.
- Ensure the devices connected to PWM pins can handle the signals properly to avoid malfunction or damage.

Chapter 2. Analog I/O Basics

Chapter Overview

This chapter explains how microcontrollers (like Arduino and MicroPython boards) can handle signals from the outside world. These signals can be something like the brightness of a light, the temperature, or how fast a motor should spin. To work with these signals, we need to understand two important things: **analog input** (reading signals that can change continuously) and **analog output** (sending out signals that can smoothly control things like motors or lights). We'll also learn how these signals are converted into numbers that the microcontroller can understand and work with.

Chapter Purpose

The purpose of this chapter is to:

1. Help you understand the difference between analog input and output.
2. Show you how to use these functions in both Arduino and MicroPython with easy-to-follow examples.
3. Explain why the number of steps (called "resolution") is important for accurate readings.
4. Provide simple techniques to make your sensor readings more stable and accurate.
5. Compare how Arduino and MicroPython handle these signals.

Chapter Syntax Table

Topics	Arduino Syntax	MicroPython Syntax
Analog Input	`analogRead(pin)`	`adc = machine.ADC(pin_number)` `value = adc.read_u16()`
Analog Output (PWM)	`analogWrite(pin, value)`	`pwm = machine.PWM(machine.Pin(pin_number))` `pwm.duty_u16(value)`
Analog Reference	`analogReference(type)`	Not applicable
Attenuation	Not applicable	`adc.atten(adc.ATTN_11DB)`

Smoothing Analog Input Readings	`for (int i = 0; i < num_readings; i++)`
	`{ total += analogRead(pin); }`
	`average = total / num_readings;`
		`def smooth_adc(num_samples)`
		`{ total += adc.read_u16() }`
		`return total // num_samples`

ADC Resolution	10-bit (0-1023) `analogRead(pin)`	12-bit to 16-bit `adc.read_u16()`

Analog Input

An **analog input** allows a microcontroller to read a continuous (varying) signal, like from a temperature sensor, light sensor, or potentiometer (a dial). These sensors provide signals that can have any value between 0 and a certain maximum, not just ON or OFF.

Why Use It?

You use analog inputs when you need more detailed information than just ON/OFF. For example, to measure how bright a light is, or how warm it is, the microcontroller needs to know more than just "light on" or "light off." Analog input provides a range of values that help with this.

Arduino Syntax:

```
analogRead(pin);
```

Explanation:

- **pin**: This is the analog pin number where you've connected the sensor (for example, A0, A1).
- When you call `analogRead(pin)`, it converts the voltage from the sensor (0V to 5V) into a number between 0 and 1023. For instance, 0V = 0 and 5V = 1023.

Example:

```
int sensorValue = analogRead(A0);
```

This reads the value from pin A0 and stores it in the variable `sensorValue`. If the voltage is around 2.5V, the value of `sensorValue` will be close to 512.

Notes:

- The range 0 to 1023 comes from the 10-bit Analog-to-Digital Converter (ADC) used in most Arduino boards.
- Most Arduino boards can read signals up to 5V (on 5V boards) or up to 3.3V (on 3.3V boards).

Warnings:

- Don't connect a signal higher than the board's maximum voltage (5V or 3.3V) to an analog pin, as this could damage the board.

MicroPython Syntax:

```
adc = machine.ADC(pin_number)
value = adc.read_u16()
```

Explanation:

- `pin_number`: This is the pin number you're using for the analog input.
- The `adc.read_u16()` function reads the analog value as a 16-bit number, meaning the value will range from 0 to 65535 (more precision than Arduino's 1023).

Example:

```
adc = machine.ADC(0)
sensor_value = adc.read_u16()
```

This reads the analog value from pin 0 (typically connected to an ADC pin) and stores it in `sensor_value`. If the signal is halfway, `sensor_value` will be about 32768.

Notes:

- MicroPython offers higher precision with 16-bit resolution (0 to 65535).
- Some MicroPython boards use 3.3V as the maximum input voltage for analog pins.

Warnings:

- Just like Arduino, connecting a higher-than-allowed voltage can damage your board.

Analog Output (PWM)

PWM (Pulse Width Modulation) simulates an analog output by turning a digital pin on and off very quickly. This creates an effect that looks like a varying output, like controlling the brightness of an LED or the speed of a motor.

Why Use It?

You use PWM to simulate analog output because most microcontrollers don't have true analog outputs. For example, you can dim an LED or control the speed of a motor by using different PWM values instead of just turning them fully ON or OFF.

Arduino Syntax:

```
analogWrite(pin, value);
```

Explanation:

- **pin**: The pin number you're using for the output (only certain pins support PWM).
- **value**: A number between 0 and 255, where 0 means "fully off" and 255 means "fully on". Any number in between changes the intensity.

Example:

```
analogWrite(9, 128);
```

This sets pin 9 to output a PWM signal with a duty cycle of 50%, meaning the LED connected to pin 9 will be half as bright as it can be (since 128 is half of 255).

Notes:

- PWM is not true analog output. It rapidly switches between HIGH and LOW, but because it switches so fast, it appears to act like a smooth signal (like dimming a light).
- Arduino uses an 8-bit value (0-255) for PWM.

Warnings:

- Not all pins support PWM. Check your board's documentation to know which pins can do PWM.

MicroPython Syntax:

```
pwm = machine.PWM(machine.Pin(pin_number))
pwm.duty_u16(value)
```

Explanation:

- **`pin_number`**: The pin number you want to use for the PWM output.
- **`duty_u16(value)`**: A value between 0 and 65535 that controls the duty cycle, where 0 is fully off and 65535 is fully on. This gives finer control than Arduino's 0-255 range.

Example:

```
pwm = machine.PWM(machine.Pin(15))
pwm.duty_u16(32768)
```

This sets pin 15 to a PWM signal with a 50% duty cycle (since 32768 is half of 65535), making an LED glow at half brightness or controlling the speed of a motor at half speed.

Notes:

- MicroPython uses 16-bit PWM (0-65535), so it offers more control than Arduino's 8-bit PWM (0-255).

Warnings:

- Make sure your components (like motors or LEDs) can handle PWM signals to avoid damage.

Analog Reference (Arduino)

The **analog reference** defines the highest voltage the Arduino uses to read analog signals. By default, this is 5V (or 3.3V on some boards), but you can change this to get more accurate readings from low-voltage sensors.

Why Use It?

When dealing with sensors that provide a low voltage (like 0V to 1V), using the default 5V reference makes the readings less accurate. Setting the analog reference to match the maximum expected voltage improves precision.

Arduino Syntax:

```
analogReference(type);
```

Explanation:

- **type**: Sets the analog reference type. Options are:
    - DEFAULT: Uses the board's default voltage (5V or 3.3V).
    - INTERNAL: Uses the internal reference voltage (1.1V or 2.56V, depending on the board).
    - EXTERNAL: You provide your own reference voltage through the AREF pin.

Example:

```
analogReference(INTERNAL);
int sensorValue = analogRead(A0);
```

This changes the reference voltage to 1.1V, so the Arduino will now map 0V to 1023 across 0 to 1.1V instead of 0 to 5V.

Notes:

- If your sensor only outputs a small voltage, lowering the reference voltage will give you more accurate readings.
- INTERNAL uses a built-in reference of 1.1V, which is useful for low-voltage sensors.

Warnings:

- Be careful when using EXTERNAL mode. Don't exceed the board's allowed reference voltage (typically 5V or 3.3V), or you could damage the Arduino.

Attenuation (MicroPython)

Attenuation reduces the voltage input on analog pins so that higher voltages can be measured safely. For example, attenuation allows you to measure up to 3.6V instead of being limited to 1.2V.

Why Use It?

On boards like the ESP32, the ADC can only measure up to a certain voltage (typically 1.2V). Attenuation expands this range, so you can safely measure voltages up to 3.6V without damaging the ADC.

MicroPython Syntax:

```
adc.atten(adc.ATTN_11DB)
```

Explanation:

- **atten(attenuation)**: Sets how much the input signal is reduced before the ADC reads it:
    - ADC.ATTN_0DB: 0 to 1.2V range (no attenuation).
    - ADC.ATTN_11DB: 0 to 3.6V range (maximum attenuation).

Example:
```
adc = machine.ADC(machine.Pin(32))
adc.atten(adc.ATTN_11DB)
value = adc.read_u16()
```

This allows the ADC on pin 32 to safely read voltages up to 3.6V.

Notes:

- Use attenuation if your input voltage is higher than 1.2V to avoid damaging the ADC.

Warnings:

- Make sure the input voltage doesn't exceed the attenuated range (for example, 3.6V with 11dB attenuation), or you might still damage the ADC.

Smoothing Analog Input Readings

Smoothing is the process of taking multiple analog readings and averaging them to reduce noise. This results in more stable sensor values, especially useful for sensors that fluctuate rapidly.

Why Use It?

Analog sensors often have small fluctuations or noise in their output. Smoothing helps clean up these readings so that you can get a more stable value, which is especially important for temperature or light sensors.

Arduino Example:
```
int sensorValue = analogRead(A0);
int total = 0;
for (int i = 0; i < 10; i++) {
  total += analogRead(A0);  // Take multiple readings
}
sensorValue = total / 10;  // Average the readings
```

This averages 10 readings from the sensor to smooth out fluctuations.

Notes:

- Smoothing helps reduce noise from sensors, giving you more reliable data.
- You can adjust the number of readings based on how much smoothing you need.

Warnings:

- Too much smoothing might make your system slow to react to quick changes.

MicroPython Example:

```
adc = machine.ADC(machine.Pin(32))
def smooth_adc(num_samples=10):
    total = 0
    for _ in range(num_samples):
        total += adc.read_u16()   # Take multiple readings
        time.sleep_ms(10)   # Add a small delay between readings
    return total // num_samples
smoothed_value = smooth_adc()
```

This averages 10 readings from the ADC to reduce noise in the sensor data.

Analog-to-Digital Converter (ADC) Resolution

An **Analog-to-Digital Converter (ADC)** converts analog signals (continuous voltage levels) into digital numbers that a microcontroller can process. **ADC resolution** refers to how many distinct digital values the ADC can represent from an analog input. The higher the resolution, the more accurately the analog signal can be represented.

For example:

- A **10-bit ADC** provides 1024 possible values (from 0 to 1023).
- A **12-bit ADC** provides 4096 possible values (from 0 to 4095).
- A **16-bit ADC** provides 65536 possible values (from 0 to 65535).

The **resolution** directly affects how detailed the conversion of the input voltage is. Higher resolution gives more "steps" between the lowest and highest voltage the ADC can read, allowing for finer detail in the readings.

Why is ADC Resolution Important?

Higher ADC resolution means more precise readings from sensors, which is especially useful when dealing with analog sensors like temperature, light, or pressure sensors. For example, with a 10-bit ADC, the range between 0V and 5V is divided into 1024 steps, giving each step a size of approximately 4.88 millivolts (5V ÷ 1024). If you increase the resolution to 12 bits, each step becomes 1.22 millivolts (5V ÷ 4096), allowing for more accurate measurements.

If the sensor you are using outputs a small signal, or if you need precise control, a higher resolution will allow for finer adjustments or more detailed readings.

How ADC Resolution Works

Let's say you have a 5V Arduino or microcontroller:

- With **8-bit resolution**, the ADC divides the 0-5V range into 256 steps (0 to 255).
    - Each step represents 19.53 mV (5V ÷ 256).
- With **10-bit resolution**, the ADC divides the same 0-5V range into 1024 steps (0 to 1023).
    - Each step represents 4.88 mV (5V ÷ 1024).
- With **12-bit resolution**, the ADC divides the same range into 4096 steps (0 to 4095).
    - Each step represents 1.22 mV (5V ÷ 4096).
- With **16-bit resolution**, the ADC divides the 0-5V range into 65536 steps (0 to 65535).
    - Each step represents 0.076 mV (5V ÷ 65536).

This shows how increasing the resolution allows for smaller differences in voltage to be detected, making the reading more precise.

Arduino ADC Resolution

Most Arduino boards, like the **Uno**, use a 10-bit ADC, which means analog inputs are measured as values from **0** to **1023**.

- **Default range**: 0V to 5V (if you're using a 5V board).
- **Steps**: 1024 steps (from 0 to 1023).

If the input is 0V, `analogRead()` will return **0**. If the input is 5V, `analogRead()` will return **1023**. If the input is 2.5V (halfway), it will return around **512**.

Arduino Syntax:

```
analogRead(pin);
```

Explanation:

- `pin`: This is the analog pin you're reading from (e.g., A0, A1).
- The `analogRead()` function converts the input voltage (0-5V for most Arduino boards) into a number between 0 and 1023.

Arduino Simple Code Example:

```
int sensorValue = analogRead(A0);
```

This reads the analog value from pin A0 and stores it in `sensorValue`. The value will be between 0 and 1023, depending on the input voltage.

Notes:

- The range for `analogRead()` is **0 to 1023** for most Arduino boards, meaning the 10-bit ADC converts 0-5V into 1024 possible values.
- You can change the upper voltage limit (reference voltage) using `analogReference()`.

Warnings:

- If you input a voltage higher than the board's reference voltage (typically 5V or 3.3V), you risk damaging the ADC or getting incorrect readings.

MicroPython ADC Resolution

In MicroPython, the resolution is typically higher. For example, on the **ESP32**, the ADC has a **12-bit resolution**, providing a more detailed reading range from **0 to 4095**. This allows for more precise sensor readings compared to Arduino's 10-bit ADC.

Some boards in MicroPython, such as the **Pyboard**, use a **16-bit ADC**, which gives even more precise readings, converting analog values into numbers between **0 and 65535**.

MicroPython Syntax:

```
adc = machine.ADC(pin_number)
value = adc.read_u16()
```

Explanation:

- `pin_number`: The analog input pin connected to the sensor.
- `read_u16()`: Reads the value from the ADC with 16-bit resolution (from 0 to 65535).

MicroPython Simple Code Example:

```
adc = machine.ADC(machine.Pin(32))   # Use pin 32 for the ADC input
sensor_value = adc.read_u16()   # Read the analog value
```

This reads the analog value from pin 32 and stores it in `sensor_value`. The value will be between 0 and 65535, depending on the input voltage.

Notes:

- The **ESP32** typically has **12-bit resolution**, meaning values from 0 to 4095.
- The **Pyboard** or other high-precision boards may have a **16-bit ADC**, meaning values range from 0 to 65535.

Warnings:

- Ensure the input voltage is within the allowable range for your board (typically 3.3V or 5V), as exceeding this can cause damage to the ADC.

Section 2: Programming Fundamentals

Chapter-3 .Arithmetic Operators:

Chapter Overview: Arithmetic Operators

In this chapter, we'll explore basic arithmetic operations such as addition, subtraction, multiplication, division, modulus, exponentiation, and integer division. These operations are fundamental to performing mathematical calculations in programming. We will cover how these arithmetic operators work in both Arduino and MicroPython, along with their syntax, examples, and warnings to help you avoid common pitfalls.

Chapter Purpose
The purpose of this chapter is to:

1. Introduce basic arithmetic operators used in programming.
2. Show how to use these operators in both Arduino and MicroPython.
3. Provide examples and highlight potential issues such as overflow, precision loss, and data type compatibility.

4. Explain key concepts like integer division and modulus to beginners.

Chapter Syntax Table

Topics	Arduino Syntax	MicroPython Syntax
Addition (+)	result = number1 + number2;	result = number1 + number2
Subtraction (-)	result = number1 - number2;	result = number1 - number2
Multiplication (*)	result = number1 * number2;	result = number1 * number2
Division (/)	result = number1 / number2;	result = number1 / number2
Modulus (%)	result = number1 % number2;	result = number1 % number2
Exponentiation () / pow()**	result = pow(base, exponent);	result = base ** exponent or pow(base, exponent)
Integer Division (//)	Not available	result = number1 // number2

Addition (+)

Addition is a basic mathematical operation that combines two numbers to get their sum. In programming, the addition operator + is used to add two values or variables together.

Use Purpose
The addition operator is used when you need to calculate the total of two or more numbers. It can be applied to simple numbers or variables holding numerical values in programming, like adding sensor values, counters, or creating mathematical expressions.

Arduino Syntax Use

```
result = number1 + number2;
```

Arduino Syntax Explanation
In Arduino, the + operator is used to add two numbers or variables:

- *number1*: The first number or variable.
- *number2*: The second number or variable.
- The result of the addition is stored in a variable (*result*).

Arduino Simple Code Example

```
int sum = 5 + 3;
int total = sensorValue + offset;
```

- The first line adds 5 and 3, and stores the result (8) in the variable *sum*.
- The second line adds the value of the variable *sensorValue* to *offset* and stores the result in *total*.

Notes

- You can use the + operator to add both constants (fixed values) and variables.
- Arduino supports addition with integer, float, and other numerical data types.

Warnings

- Be mindful of data type limitations. For example, adding two large integers can cause overflow if the result exceeds the data type's limit.

- Adding floating-point numbers can lead to precision issues depending on the value range.

MicroPython Syntax Use

```
result = number1 + number2
```

MicroPython Syntax Explanation

In MicroPython, the + operator works similarly to Arduino, adding two numbers or variables:

- *number1*: The first value or variable.
- *number2*: The second value or variable.
- The result is stored in a variable (*result*).

MicroPython Simple Code Example

```
sum = 10 + 7
total = temperature + correction
```

- The first line adds 10 and 7, and stores the result (17) in the variable *sum*.
- The second line adds the variable *temperature* to *correction* and stores the result in *total*.

Notes

- The + operator can be used with integers, floats, and other numerical data types in MicroPython.
- MicroPython allows you to perform addition on both fixed values (like 10 and 7) and variables.

Warnings

- Just like Arduino, watch for overflow issues when adding large numbers, especially with small data types like integers.

- Ensure that both values being added are of compatible data types to avoid errors or unexpected behavior.

Subtraction (-)

Subtraction is a basic arithmetic operation that removes one number from another. In programming, the subtraction operator - is used to find the difference between two numbers or variables.

Use Purpose
The subtraction operator is used when you need to calculate the difference between two values. This can be useful in various applications, such as adjusting sensor readings, counting down, or tracking changes in values over time.

Arduino Syntax Use

```
result = number1 - number2;
```

Arduino Syntax Explanation
In Arduino, the - operator is used to subtract one number from another:

- *number1*: The value or variable from which you are subtracting.
- *number2*: The value or variable you are subtracting from *number1*.
- The result of the subtraction is stored in the variable (*result*).

Arduino Simple Code Example

```
int difference = 10 - 3;
int adjustment = sensorReading - calibrationValue;
```

- The first line subtracts 3 from 10, storing the result (7) in the variable *difference*.

- The second line subtracts *calibrationValue* from *sensorReading* and stores the result in *adjustment*.

Notes

- Subtraction can be used with integer and floating-point variables.
- You can subtract both constants (fixed numbers) and variables.

Warnings

- Be mindful of data type limitations. Subtracting a larger number from a smaller number may result in negative values.
- Integer subtraction can cause underflow if the result is lower than the minimum allowed value for the data type.

MicroPython Syntax Use

```
result = number1 - number2
```

MicroPython Syntax Explanation

In MicroPython, the - operator works similarly to Arduino, subtracting one value from another:

- *number1*: The value from which you are subtracting.
- *number2*: The value to subtract from *number1*.
- The result is stored in the variable (*result*).

MicroPython Simple Code Example

```
difference = 15 - 8
adjustment = measuredValue - baselineValue
```

- The first line subtracts 8 from 15, and the result (7) is stored in the variable *difference*.
- The second line subtracts *baselineValue* from *measuredValue* and stores the result in *adjustment*.

Notes

- Subtraction in MicroPython works for both integers and floating-point numbers.
- Just like in Arduino, you can subtract constants or variables.

Warnings

- Be careful when subtracting large numbers from smaller ones to avoid negative values if they are not intended.
- Pay attention to the data types of the numbers you are subtracting to prevent underflow or other calculation issues.

Multiplication (*)

Multiplication is a basic arithmetic operation that calculates the product of two numbers. In programming, the multiplication operator * is used to multiply two values or variables together.

Use Purpose
The multiplication operator is used to calculate the total when one number is multiplied by another. This can be used in various scenarios, such as calculating areas, scaling values, or applying coefficients in formulas.

Arduino Syntax Use

```
result = number1 * number2;
```

Arduino Syntax Explanation
In Arduino, the * operator is used to multiply two numbers or variables:

- *number1*: The first number or variable to be multiplied.
- *number2*: The second number or variable.
- The product of the multiplication is stored in the variable (*result*).

Arduino Simple Code Example

```
int product = 5 * 4;
int total = distance * factor;
```

- The first line multiplies 5 and 4, storing the result (20) in the variable *product*.
- The second line multiplies the variable *distance* by *factor* and stores the result in *total*.

Notes

- Multiplication can be performed on both integers and floating-point numbers.
- You can use multiplication to scale values, apply coefficients, or perform other numerical calculations.

Warnings

- Be careful of data type overflow when multiplying large numbers. The result of the multiplication may exceed the storage capacity of the data type (e.g., integers).
- Ensure that both numbers being multiplied are compatible in terms of data types to avoid errors.

MicroPython Syntax Use

```
result = number1 * number2
```

MicroPython Syntax Explanation

In MicroPython, the * operator works similarly to Arduino, multiplying two values or variables:

- *number1*: The first value or variable.
- *number2*: The second value or variable.
- The product is stored in the variable (*result*).

MicroPython Simple Code Example

```
product = 7 * 3
total = speed * time
```

- The first line multiplies 7 and 3, and the result (21) is stored in *product*.
- The second line multiplies *speed* by *time* and stores the result in *total*.

Notes

- Multiplication can be used for integer and floating-point numbers in MicroPython.
- Just like in Arduino, multiplication is useful for scaling values or applying mathematical formulas.

Warnings

- Multiplying large values may result in overflow or loss of precision with certain data types.
- Check the data types of the variables to ensure compatibility during multiplication to prevent errors or unexpected behavior.

Division (/)

Division is an arithmetic operation that divides one number by another to calculate how many times the second number fits into the first. In programming, the division operator / is used to divide two numbers or variables.

Use Purpose
The division operator is used to calculate the quotient when one number is divided by another. It is commonly used in programming

for operations like calculating averages, determining ratios, or converting units.

Arduino Syntax Use

```
result = number1 / number2;
```

Arduino Syntax Explanation

In Arduino, the / operator divides one number or variable by another:

- *number1*: The dividend or number you are dividing.
- *number2*: The divisor or number you are dividing by.
- The result of the division is stored in the variable (*result*).

Arduino Simple Code Example

```
int quotient = 10 / 2;
float average = totalSum / numberOfItems;
```

- The first line divides 10 by 2, storing the result (5) in the variable *quotient*.
- The second line divides *totalSum* by *numberOfItems* to calculate an average, stored in the variable *average*.

Notes

- If both numbers are integers, the result will be an integer, and any remainder will be discarded (integer division).
- If one or both numbers are floating-point, the result will include the decimal portion (floating-point division).

Warnings

- Be careful when dividing by zero, as this will result in an error or undefined behavior.
- Integer division can lead to rounding down the result if both numbers are integers.

MicroPython Syntax Use

```
result = number1 / number2
```

MicroPython Syntax Explanation

In MicroPython, the / operator divides one value or variable by another:

- *number1*: The value being divided.
- *number2*: The value to divide by.
- The result is stored in the variable (*result*).

MicroPython Simple Code Example

```
quotient = 15 / 3
average = totalDistance / timeElapsed
```

- The first line divides 15 by 3, and the result (5) is stored in the variable *quotient*.
- The second line divides *totalDistance* by *timeElapsed* to calculate the average speed and stores it in *average*.

Notes

- Division in MicroPython behaves similarly to Arduino: integer division truncates the decimal part, while floating-point division provides more accurate results.
- MicroPython automatically supports floating-point division when either of the operands is a floating-point number.

Warnings

- Ensure you are not dividing by zero, as it will cause an error.
- Be aware of the data types being used, as integer division may lead to loss of precision.

Modulus (%)

The modulus operator % returns the remainder of a division between two integers. It only works with whole numbers and is useful when you need to determine how much is left over after performing a division.

Use Purpose
The modulus operator is commonly used to determine whether one number is divisible by another, to check for even or odd numbers, or to cycle through a range of values (e.g., for creating loops or patterns in programs).

Arduino Syntax Use

```
result = number1 % number2;
```

Arduino Syntax Explanation
In Arduino, the % operator divides two integers and returns the remainder:

- *number1*: The dividend or the number you want to divide.
- *number2*: The divisor or the number you're dividing by.
- The result of the modulus operation (the remainder) is stored in the variable (*result*).

Arduino Simple Code Example

```
int remainder = 10 % 3;
if (counter % 2 == 0) { // Do something }
```

- The first line divides 10 by 3 and stores the remainder (1) in the variable *remainder*.
- The second line checks if the variable *counter* is even by using the modulus operator (% 2 == 0 checks if the remainder is 0).

Notes

- The modulus operator is useful for determining divisibility. If the result is 0, the first number is evenly divisible by the second.
- It can also be used to alternate behavior in programs, such as toggling between two states.

Warnings

- The modulus operator only works with integers. Using it with floating-point numbers will result in an error.
- Ensure that the divisor (number2) is not zero, as dividing by zero will result in an error.

MicroPython Syntax Use

```
result = number1 % number2
```

MicroPython Syntax Explanation

In MicroPython, the % operator works the same way as in Arduino, returning the remainder when dividing two integers:

- *number1*: The dividend or the number to be divided.
- *number2*: The divisor or the number you're dividing by.
- The remainder is stored in the variable (*result*).

MicroPython Simple Code Example

```
remainder = 17 % 4
if index % 3 == 0:
```

Do something

- The first line divides 17 by 4 and stores the remainder (1) in *remainder*.

- The second line checks if *index* is divisible by 3 by using % 3 == 0.

Notes

- As in Arduino, the modulus operator is primarily used to determine divisibility or to cycle through values.
- The result of the modulus operation is always an integer.

Warnings

- The modulus operator works only with integers. Trying to use it with floats or dividing by zero will cause an error.
- Ensure the divisor is not zero to avoid runtime errors.

Modulus (%)

The modulus operator % returns the remainder of a division between two integers. It tells you what's left over after one number is divided by another, but it only works with integers. For example, in the division 10 ÷ 3, the quotient is 3 and the remainder is 1, so 10 % 3 returns 1.

Use Purpose
The modulus operator is used when you need to know the remainder of a division rather than the result itself. This can be helpful in tasks like checking if a number is even or odd, looping at regular intervals, or detecting overflow conditions in counters.

Arduino Syntax Use

```
result = number1 % number2;
```

Arduino Syntax Explanation
In Arduino, the % operator calculates the remainder of dividing one integer by another:

- *number1*: The dividend, or the number you want to divide.
- *number2*: The divisor, or the number you're dividing by.

- The result of the operation is the remainder of the division, stored in the variable (*result*).

Arduino Simple Code Example

```
int remainder = 10 % 3;
int evenOrOdd = number % 2;
```

- The first line divides 10 by 3, storing the remainder (1) in the variable *remainder*.
- The second line checks if *number* is even or odd by calculating the remainder when dividing by 2. If the remainder is 0, the number is even.

Notes

- The modulus operator only works with integers. Using it with floating-point numbers will result in an error.
- Modulus is useful for determining factors or checking if one number is a multiple of another.

Warnings

- Ensure that the divisor (*number2*) is not zero, as dividing by zero will cause an error.
- Modulus only returns the remainder for integers; it does not work with non-integer values.

MicroPython Syntax Use

```
result = number1 % number2
```

MicroPython Syntax Explanation

In MicroPython, the % operator works the same way as in Arduino, returning the remainder of dividing two integers:

- *number1*: The integer being divided.
- *number2*: The integer you are dividing by.
- The result is the remainder, stored in the variable (*result*).

MicroPython Simple Code Example

```
remainder = 15 % 4
evenOrOdd = counter % 2
```

- The first line divides 15 by 4, with a remainder of 3, which is stored in *remainder*.
- The second line checks if *counter* is even or odd by calculating *counter % 2*.

Notes

- Just like Arduino, the modulus operator only works with integers in MicroPython.
- It's a useful tool for checking for factors, detecting patterns, or working with cyclic operations (such as looping every few steps).

Warnings

- Do not use a divisor of zero, as this will result in an error.
- Since the modulus operator only works with integers, using it with floats will cause errors.

Exponentiation

Exponentiation is a mathematical operation where a number (called the base) is raised to the power of another number (called the exponent). For example, 3 raised to the power of 2 is written as 3^2, which equals 9.

Use Purpose
Exponentiation is used when you need to calculate powers, such as squaring a number, cubing, or any higher powers. It is common in scientific, engineering, and mathematical calculations.

Arduino Syntax Use

```
result = pow(base, exponent);
```

Arduino Syntax Explanation
In Arduino, exponentiation is done using the *pow()* function:

- *base*: The number you want to raise to a power.
- *exponent*: The power to which the base is raised.
- The result is stored in the variable *result*.

Arduino Simple Code Example

```
float result = pow(3, 2);
float square = pow(number, 2);
```

- The first line calculates 3 raised to the power of 2, resulting in 9, stored in *result*.
- The second line calculates the square of *number* and stores it in *square*.

Notes

- The *pow()* function returns a floating-point result, even if both the base and exponent are integers.
- This function works with positive and negative exponents.

Warnings

- Large exponents may cause overflow or loss of precision due to data type limitations.
- Using a negative base with a fractional exponent may result in complex numbers, which Arduino does not support.

MicroPython Syntax Use

```
result = pow(base, exponent)
result = base ** exponent
```

MicroPython Syntax Explanation

In MicroPython, exponentiation can be done using either the *pow()* function or the ** operator:

- *base*: The number you want to raise to a power.
- *exponent*: The power to which the base is raised.
- The result is stored in *result*.

MicroPython Simple Code Example

```
result = pow(4, 3)
result = 5 ** 2
```

- The first line calculates 4 raised to the power of 3 (64) and stores it in *result*.
- The second line calculates 5 raised to the power of 2 (25) and stores the result in *result*.

Notes

- MicroPython allows exponentiation with both integers and floating-point numbers using either *pow()* or **.
- The ** operator is a simpler way to perform exponentiation in MicroPython.

Warnings

- Large exponents can cause overflow or loss of precision, especially with integers.
- Be cautious when using negative bases with fractional exponents, as they may yield unexpected results.

Integer Division

Integer division is a division operation where both operands (numbers) are integers, and the result is also an integer. The fractional part is discarded, meaning you only get the whole number result of the division. For example, 5 divided by 2 in integer division results in 2, with the remainder ignored.

Use Purpose
Integer division is useful when you need to divide whole numbers and you only care about the integer part of the result, such as when counting items or calculating steps in loops.

Arduino Syntax Use

```
result = number1 / number2;
```

Arduino Syntax Explanation
In Arduino, when both *number1* and *number2* are integers, the division automatically performs integer division:

- *number1*: The integer to be divided (the dividend).
- *number2*: The integer that divides *number1* (the divisor).
- The result is stored in *result*, and any fractional part is discarded.

Arduino Simple Code Example

```
int result = 5 / 2;
int totalSteps = totalDistance / stepSize;
```

- The first line divides 5 by 2, resulting in 2 (the fractional part is ignored), and stores it in *result*.
- The second line calculates the number of steps by dividing *totalDistance* by *stepSize* and stores the result in *totalSteps*.

Notes

- Integer division in Arduino will discard any decimal portion. To preserve the fractional part, you need to use floating-point numbers (e.g., *float*).

- If either of the numbers is a floating-point type, regular division (with decimal results) will occur.

Warnings

- Be cautious when using integer division, as it may lead to inaccurate results if you are expecting a decimal value.
- Dividing by zero will cause an error or undefined behavior, so always ensure the divisor is not zero.

MicroPython Syntax Use

```
result = number1 // number2
```

MicroPython Syntax Explanation

In MicroPython, integer division is explicitly performed using the // operator.

- *number1*: The integer to be divided (the dividend).
- *number2*: The integer that divides *number1* (the divisor).
- The result is stored in *result*, with the fractional part discarded.

MicroPython Simple Code Example

```
result = 9 // 4
steps = distance // stepLength
```

- The first line divides 9 by 4, resulting in 2 (fraction discarded), stored in *result*.
- The second line divides *distance* by *stepLength* to calculate the number of steps and stores it in *steps*.

Notes

- The *// operator* in MicroPython is specifically used for integer division, ensuring that only whole numbers are returned.
- If you want to keep the decimal portion, use regular division with a single slash (/).

Warnings

- Like in Arduino, be careful when performing integer division where fractional precision is required, as this method discards decimals.
- Avoid dividing by zero, as it will result in a runtime error.

Chapter 4. Comparison Operators

Chapter Overview

In this chapter, we explore comparison operators that are essential in controlling the flow of programs by making decisions based on the comparison of two values. These operators return either **true** or **false**, helping to decide whether a block of code should run. This chapter covers common comparison operators like **Equal to (==)**, **Not equal to (!=)**, **Greater than (>)**, **Less than (<)**, **Greater than or equal to (>=)**, and **Less than or equal to (<=)**. We'll learn how these operators are used in Arduino and MicroPython with examples, explanations, and warnings to avoid common mistakes.

Chapter Purpose

The purpose of this chapter is to:

1. Introduce basic comparison operators used for decision-making in programming.
2. Provide syntax examples and explanations for how these operators work in both Arduino and MicroPython.
3. Explain typical use cases for each operator.

4. Highlight common mistakes and issues such as precision problems with floating-point comparisons.
5. Equip beginners with the knowledge to write condition-based programs.

Chapter Syntax Table

Operator	Arduino Syntax	MicroPython Syntax
Equal to (==)	`if (variable1 == variable2)`	`if variable1 == variable2:`
Not equal to (!=)	`if (variable1 != variable2)`	`if variable1 != variable2:`
Greater than (>)	`if (variable1 > variable2)`	`if variable1 > variable2:`
Less than (<)	`if (variable1 < variable2)`	`if variable1 < variable2:`
Greater than or equal to (>=)	`if (variable1 >= variable2)`	`if variable1 >= variable2:`
Less than or equal to (<=)	`if (variable1 <= variable2)`	`if variable1 <= variable2:`

Equal to (==)

The *equal to* operator == is a comparison operator used to check whether two values are equal. It evaluates the two values on either side of the operator and returns *true* if they are equal and *false* if they are not. This operator is typically used in conditional statements, such as *if* statements, to control the flow of the program based on value comparisons.

Use Purpose

The == operator is used when you need to compare two values to check if they are the same. It is commonly used in decision-making processes, such as checking if a button is pressed, verifying sensor data, or comparing input values.

Arduino Syntax Use

```
if (variable1 == variable2) {
// Code to execute if the values are equal
}
```

Arduino Syntax Explanation

In Arduino, the == operator checks whether *variable1* and *variable2* are equal. If they are, the condition evaluates to *true*, and the code inside the *if* block is executed. Otherwise, the condition is *false*.

Arduino Simple Code Example

```
int sensorValue = analogRead(A0);
if (sensorValue == 500) {
Serial.println("Sensor value is exactly 500!");
}
```

- In this example, the *if* statement checks whether the sensor value is exactly equal to 500. If true, the message "Sensor value is exactly 500!" is printed to the serial monitor.

Notes

- The == operator is used to compare values, not to assign them. If you need to assign a value, use the = operator.
- The comparison can be between numbers, characters, or even other data types, as long as they are comparable.

Warnings

- Be careful not to confuse == (comparison) with = (assignment). Using = instead of == will assign the value rather than compare it, leading to incorrect behavior.
- Floating-point comparisons may not always work as expected due to precision issues. For floats, consider comparing within a small range of tolerance.

MicroPython Syntax Use

```
if variable1 == variable2:
# Code to execute if the values are equal
```

MicroPython Syntax Explanation
In MicroPython, the == operator works the same way as in Arduino. It checks if *variable1* is equal to *variable2*. If true, the code inside the *if* block runs.

MicroPython Simple Code Example

```
sensor_value = 500 if
sensor_value == 500:
print("Sensor value is exactly 500!")
```

- This example checks if *sensor_value* is equal to 500. If the condition is true, the message "Sensor value is exactly 500!" is printed.

Notes

- As in Arduino, == is used to compare values, not assign them.
- The == operator can compare integers, floats, strings, or other objects, as long as they can be meaningfully compared.

Warnings

- Ensure that you use == for comparisons and not for assignments.
- Be cautious when comparing floating-point values in MicroPython due to possible precision issues. Consider using a small tolerance range when comparing floats.

Not Equal to (!=)

The *not equal to* operator != is a comparison operator used to check whether two values are not equal. It evaluates the two values on either side of the operator and returns *true* if they are not equal and *false* if they are equal. This operator is often used in conditional statements to execute code when values are different.

Use Purpose
The *!=* operator is used when you want to verify that two values are different. It is commonly applied in decision-making scenarios, such as checking if a sensor reading has changed, verifying user input, or skipping certain operations when a condition is not met.

Arduino Syntax Use

```
if (variable1 != variable2) {
// Code to execute if the values are not equal
}
```

Arduino Syntax Explanation
In Arduino, the *!=* operator checks whether *variable1* and *variable2* are not equal. If they are not equal, the condition evaluates to *true*,

and the code inside the *if* block is executed. Otherwise, the condition is *false*.

Arduino Simple Code Example

```
int sensorValue = analogRead(A0);
if (sensorValue != 500) {
Serial.println("Sensor value is not 500!");
}
```

- In this example, the *if* statement checks whether the sensor value is not equal to 500. If true, the message "Sensor value is not 500!" is printed to the serial monitor.

Notes

- The != operator is the opposite of ==. It is used when you want to check for inequality between two values.
- This operator can be used with numbers, characters, or other comparable data types.

Warnings

- Make sure you do not confuse != (not equal) with == (equal). Both serve opposite purposes and may lead to unintended behavior if used incorrectly.
- As with ==, avoid direct comparisons with floating-point numbers due to possible precision issues. For floats, consider checking if the difference between two numbers is within a small tolerance.

MicroPython Syntax Use

```
if variable1 != variable2:
# Code to execute if the values are not equal
```

MicroPython Syntax Explanation

In MicroPython, the *!=* operator works in the same way as in Arduino. It checks if *variable1* is not equal to *variable2*. If true, the code inside the *if* block runs.

MicroPython Simple Code Example

```
sensor_value = 500
if sensor_value != 300:
print("Sensor value is not 300!")
```

- This example checks if *sensor_value* is not equal to 300. If true, it prints the message "Sensor value is not 300!".

Notes

- As with Arduino, *!=* is used for comparing values that should be different.
- This operator can be applied to integers, floats, strings, and other comparable objects.

Warnings

- Ensure that you are using *!=* to check for inequality and not *==* to check for equality, as they serve opposite purposes.
- Be cautious when comparing floating-point values due to precision issues. Consider using a tolerance range when comparing floats in MicroPython.

Greater than (>)

The *greater than* operator > is a comparison operator used to check if the value on the left side is larger than the value on the right side. If the left value is greater, it returns *true*; otherwise, it returns *false*. This operator is often used to compare numerical values, such as sensor readings, counters, or input data.

Use Purpose
The *greater than* operator is used when you need to compare two values and verify whether the first value is larger than the second. It is helpful in scenarios such as checking if a reading exceeds a threshold or determining if a counter has reached a certain level.

Arduino Syntax Use

```
if (variable1 > variable2) {
// Code to execute if variable1 is greater than variable2
}
```

Arduino Syntax Explanation
In Arduino, the *greater than* operator checks whether *variable1* is larger than *variable2*. If this condition is true, the code inside the *if* block runs. If the condition is false, the code inside the block is skipped.

Arduino Simple Code Example

```
int temperature = analogRead(A0);
if (temperature > 30) {
Serial.println("Temperature is above 30 degrees!");
}
```

- In this example, the *if* statement checks if the *temperature* value is greater than 30. If true, the message "Temperature is above 30 degrees!" is printed to the serial monitor.

Notes

- The *greater than* operator can be used to compare numbers, including integers and floating-point values.
- This operator is particularly useful in control flow structures where an action needs to be taken if one value exceeds another.

Warnings

- Be mindful of floating-point comparisons. Due to precision issues, direct comparisons might not work as expected, especially for very small differences.
- Ensure that the variables being compared are of compatible types (e.g., comparing an integer with a float).

MicroPython Syntax Use

```
if variable1 > variable2:
# Code to execute if variable1 is greater than variable2
```

MicroPython Syntax Explanation

In MicroPython, the *greater than* operator works the same way as in Arduino. It checks if *variable1* is larger than *variable2*. If true, the code inside the *if* block runs.

MicroPython Simple Code Example

```
temperature = 35
if temperature > 30:
print("Temperature is above 30 degrees!")
```

- This example checks if the *temperature* is greater than 30. If true, it prints "Temperature is above 30 degrees!".

Notes

- The *greater than* operator works for comparing integers, floats, and other numerical values in MicroPython.
- Python automatically handles integer and float comparisons, making it easy to use *greater than* without worrying about type casting.

Warnings

- Be cautious with floating-point values due to potential precision errors. If the values are very close, the comparison might not behave as expected.
- Ensure you are comparing compatible data types (e.g., comparing a string to a number may result in an error).

Less than (<)

The *less than* operator < is a comparison operator used to check if the value on the left side is smaller than the value on the right side. If the left value is smaller, it returns *true*; otherwise, it returns *false*. This operator is often used in conditions that involve thresholds or limits, such as checking sensor values or counters.

Use Purpose
The *less than* operator is used to compare two values and verify whether the first value is smaller than the second. It is useful in decision-making structures where an action needs to be performed if a value is below a certain limit, such as turning off a device if a temperature drops below a certain point.

Arduino Syntax Use

```
if (variable1 < variable2) {
// Code to execute if variable1 is less than variable2
}
```

Arduino Syntax Explanation
In Arduino, the *less than* operator compares whether *variable1* is smaller than *variable2*. If the condition is true, the code inside the *if* block is executed. If the condition is false, the code inside the block is skipped.

Arduino Simple Code Example

```
int temperature = analogRead(A0);
if (temperature < 20) {
Serial.println("Temperature is below 20 degrees!");
}
```

- In this example, the *if* statement checks if the *temperature* value is less than 20. If true, the message "Temperature is below 20 degrees!" is printed to the serial monitor.

Notes

- The *less than* operator can be used with numbers, including integers and floating-point values.
- It is useful for range checking, such as verifying whether a value is below a certain threshold before taking action.

Warnings

- Be careful with floating-point comparisons. Due to precision issues, very close values may not behave as expected when compared directly.
- Ensure that the variables being compared are of compatible types (e.g., comparing an integer with a float).

MicroPython Syntax Use

```
if variable1 < variable2:
# Code to execute if variable1 is less than variable2
```

MicroPython Syntax Explanation

In MicroPython, the *less than* operator works the same way as in Arduino. It checks if *variable1* is smaller than *variable2*. If true, the code inside the *if* block runs.

MicroPython Simple Code Example

```
temperature = 15
if temperature < 20:
    print("Temperature is below 20 degrees!")
```

- This example checks if the *temperature* is less than 20. If true, it prints "Temperature is below 20 degrees!".

Notes

- The *less than* operator works with integers, floats, and other numerical values in MicroPython.
- Python automatically handles integer and float comparisons, making it easy to use the *less than* operator without worrying about data types.

Warnings

- Be cautious with floating-point comparisons due to potential precision issues. Comparing very close floating-point values might not work as expected.
- Ensure that the variables being compared are compatible (e.g., avoid comparing a number with a string).

Greater Than or Equal To (>=)

The "Greater Than or Equal To" (>=) operator is used in programming to compare two values. It checks if the value on the left is greater than or equal to the value on the right. If the condition is true, it returns a "true" value; otherwise, it returns "false."

Use Purpose
This operator is often used in conditions where you want to check if one value meets or exceeds another value. For example, it can be used to check if a sensor value is greater than or equal to a threshold.

Arduino Syntax Use

```
if (value1 >= value2)
```

Arduino Syntax Explanation

In Arduino, the >= operator is used in conditions (like an *if* statement) to compare two values:

- *value1*: The first value to compare (e.g., a sensor reading).
- *value2*: The second value or threshold to compare against.

If *value1* is greater than or equal to *value2*, the condition is true.

Arduino Simple Code Example

```
if (sensorValue >= 100) {
digitalWrite(LEDpin, HIGH);
}
```

This checks if the sensor value is greater than or equal to 100. If true, it turns the LED on by writing a HIGH signal to the LED pin.

Notes

- The >= operator can be used with any numerical values, including integers and floats.
- Common use cases include comparing sensor readings, counting loops, or checking input values.

Warnings

- Be careful with comparing floating-point numbers, as rounding errors might affect the result in certain cases.
- Ensure that the variables being compared are of compatible types to avoid unexpected behavior.

MicroPython Syntax Use

```
if value1 >= value2
```

MicroPython Syntax Explanation

In MicroPython, the >= operator works similarly, used in conditional statements to compare values:

- *value1*: The first value to compare (e.g., a sensor reading).
- *value2*: The second value to compare against.

If *value1* is greater than or equal to *value2*, the condition is true.

MicroPython Simple Code Example

```
if temperature >= 30:
led.value(1)
```

This checks if the temperature is greater than or equal to 30. If true, it turns on the LED by setting the pin value to 1.

Notes

- The >= operator in MicroPython is used in the same way as in Arduino for comparing values.
- It's often used to compare sensor data or other input values.

Warnings

- When comparing values from sensors, ensure that the values are properly scaled or converted to avoid errors.
- Double-check for type compatibility between values to prevent unexpected outcomes.

Less Than or Equal To (<=)

The "Less Than or Equal To" (<=) operator is used in programming to compare two values. It checks if the value on the left is less than or equal to the value on the right. If the condition is true, the result is "true"; otherwise, it returns "false."

Use Purpose
This operator is often used to ensure a value does not exceed a certain limit or to check if a value has fallen below a threshold. It is useful in conditions like stopping an action when a value reaches or goes below a set point.

Arduino Syntax Use

```
if (value1 <= value2)
```

Arduino Syntax Explanation
In Arduino, the <= operator is used within conditional statements like *if* to compare two values:
- *value1*: The value you are checking (e.g., a sensor reading).
- *value2*: The comparison value (e.g., a threshold or limit).

If *value1* is less than or equal to *value2*, the condition is considered true.

Arduino Simple Code Example

```
if (sensorValue <= 50) {
digitalWrite(LEDpin, LOW);
}
```

This code checks if the sensor value is less than or equal to 50. If the condition is true, it turns off the LED by writing a LOW signal to the LED pin.

Notes

- The <= operator can be applied to any numerical data types, such as integers and floats.

- It is commonly used for checking conditions where a value should not exceed or should drop below a specific limit.

Warnings

- Be mindful of rounding errors when comparing floating-point numbers, as small variations may affect the result.
- Ensure the data types of the values being compared are compatible to avoid unexpected behavior.

MicroPython Syntax Use

```
if value1 <= value2
```

MicroPython Syntax Explanation

In MicroPython, the <= operator is used in a similar way as in Arduino, within conditional statements to compare values:

- *value1*: The value being checked.
- *value2*: The reference value.

If *value1* is less than or equal to *value2*, the condition evaluates as true.

MicroPython Simple Code Example

```
if temperature <= 20:
fan.value(0)
```

This checks if the temperature is less than or equal to 20. If true, it turns off the fan by setting the pin value to 0.

Notes

- In MicroPython, the <= operator functions the same way as in Arduino for comparison operations.

- It is often used in control systems or to manage sensor-based operations where limits are critical.

Warnings

- Floating-point comparison may be unreliable due to small rounding errors, so care should be taken with precision.
- Make sure the variables being compared are of compatible types to prevent errors or unexpected results.

Chapter 5. Bitwise Operators

Chapter Overview

Bitwise operators allow manipulation of data at the bit level, enabling programmers to work with individual bits of integers. These operators are essential for low-level programming, such as hardware control, flags, or binary data manipulation. This chapter will cover key bitwise operators like **AND (&)**, **OR (|)**, **XOR (^)**, and **NOT (~)**, demonstrating how they work in both Arduino and MicroPython with code examples, use cases, and warnings.

Chapter Purpose

The purpose of this chapter is to:

1. Introduce the functionality of bitwise operators and their applications.
2. Provide explanations and examples of how these operators work in both Arduino and MicroPython.
3. Highlight scenarios where bitwise operations are crucial, such as setting specific bits or performing low-level tasks.
4. Warn about common pitfalls, especially when dealing with signed numbers and integer data types.

Chapter Syntax Table

Operator	Arduino Syntax	MicroPython Syntax
AND (&)	result = value1 & value2;	result = value1 & value2
**OR (	)**	`result = value1
XOR (^)	result = value1 ^ value2;	result = value1 ^ value2
NOT (~)	result = ~value;	result = ~value

AND (&)

The "AND" operator (&) is a bitwise operator used in programming to compare each bit of two numbers. It performs a logical AND operation between corresponding bits of two values, returning a new value where each bit is 1 only if both compared bits are 1. Otherwise, the resulting bit is 0.

Use Purpose
The bitwise AND operator is often used to manipulate or evaluate specific bits within a number, such as setting or checking flags, masks, or controlling certain bits of data. It is commonly used in low-level programming where direct manipulation of hardware bits is required.

Arduino Syntax Use

```
result = value1 & value2;
```

Arduino Syntax Explanation
In Arduino, the bitwise AND operator (&) compares each bit of *value1* and *value2*.

- *value1*: The first number to compare.
- *value2*: The second number to compare.

For each pair of corresponding bits, the resulting bit is 1 if both bits are 1, and 0 if one or both are 0.

Arduino Simple Code Example

```
int result = 6 & 3;
```

Here's how the bitwise AND works:

- 6 in binary: 0110
- 3 in binary: 0011
    Result: 0010 (which is 2 in decimal)

This code would assign the value 2 to the variable *result*.

Notes

- Bitwise operations work at the level of individual bits, making them useful for low-level tasks like controlling hardware.
- The AND (&) operator is different from the logical AND (&&) operator, which is used to compare conditions rather than bits.

Warnings

- Make sure you understand the difference between bitwise AND (&) and logical AND (&&) to avoid logical errors in your code.
- Bitwise operators only work with integer data types like int, char, etc.

MicroPython Syntax Use

```
result = value1 & value2
```

MicroPython Syntax Explanation

In MicroPython, the bitwise AND operator works the same way as in Arduino. It performs a bitwise comparison between *value1* and *value2*, returning a value where only the bits that are 1 in both numbers will be set to 1.

MicroPython Simple Code Example

```
result = 5 & 2
```

Here's how the bitwise AND works:

- 5 in binary: 0101
- 2 in binary: 0010
    Result: 0000 (which is 0 in decimal)

This assigns the result of the AND operation (0) to the variable *result*.

Notes

- As with Arduino, the bitwise AND operator can be used to check or manipulate individual bits in a number.
- It's often used in situations where you need to isolate or manipulate certain bits.

Warnings

- Be careful to use the correct operator for the task (bitwise AND vs logical AND) to avoid confusion in your code.
- Ensure the data types you are working with are integers, as bitwise operations do not apply to floating-point values.

OR (|)

The "OR" operator (|) is a bitwise operator used to compare two numbers at the bit level. It performs a logical OR operation between corresponding bits of two values. For each bit, the result is 1 if at least one of the compared bits is 1. If both bits are 0, the result is 0.

Use Purpose
The bitwise OR operator is useful for setting specific bits in a number or combining flags and binary values. It's often used when you want to ensure that one or more specific bits in a value are set to 1.

Arduino Syntax Use

```
result = value1 | value2;
```

Arduino Syntax Explanation
In Arduino, the bitwise OR operator (|) compares each bit of *value1* and *value2*.

- *value1*: The first number to compare.
- *value2*: The second number to compare.

For each pair of corresponding bits, the resulting bit is 1 if either or both of the bits are 1; if both are 0, the result is 0.

Arduino Simple Code Example

```
int result = 6 | 3;
```

Here's how the bitwise OR works:

- 6 in binary: 0110
- 3 in binary: 0011
    Result: 0111 (which is 7 in decimal)

This code would assign the value 7 to the variable *result*.

Notes

- The OR (|) operator is useful when you need to combine multiple binary values or ensure certain bits are set to 1.
- Unlike the logical OR (||) operator, which is used to compare boolean conditions, the bitwise OR operator works at the bit level.

Warnings

- Be careful not to confuse the bitwise OR (|) with the logical OR (||). Both serve different purposes.
- Bitwise operators only work on integer types like int, char, etc.

MicroPython Syntax Use

```
result = value1 | value2
```

MicroPython Syntax Explanation

In MicroPython, the bitwise OR operator works similarly to Arduino. It compares the bits of *value1* and *value2*, returning a value where the bits are set to 1 if either of the compared bits is 1.

MicroPython Simple Code Example

```
result = 5 | 2
```

Here's how the bitwise OR works:

- 5 in binary: 0101
- 2 in binary: 0010
  Result: 0111 (which is 7 in decimal)

This assigns the result of the OR operation (7) to the variable *result*.

Notes

- The bitwise OR operator can be used in various scenarios where you need to manipulate or combine individual bits.
- It's often used in control systems and low-level programming to combine or modify bit flags.

Warnings

- Ensure that the bitwise OR (|) is used correctly and not confused with the logical OR (||), which is for comparing boolean expressions.
- Be aware that bitwise operations only work with integers and may cause errors if used with floating-point values.

XOR (^)

XOR (Exclusive OR) is a bitwise operator that compares two binary numbers and performs a logical exclusive OR operation on each corresponding bit. It returns 1 if the bits are different (one is 1 and the other is 0) and 0 if they are the same (both 0 or both 1).

Use Purpose
The XOR operator is often used in programming for toggling specific bits, error detection algorithms, and encryption techniques. It's useful for comparing values and performing certain operations where you need to know if bits are different.

Arduino Syntax Use

```
result = value1 ^ value2;
```

Arduino Syntax Explanation
In Arduino, the XOR operator (^) compares the bits of *value1* and *value2*.

- *value1*: The first value for the XOR operation.
- *value2*: The second value for the XOR operation.

For each bit, the result is 1 if the corresponding bits are different, and 0 if they are the same.

Arduino Simple Code Example

```
int result = 6 ^ 3;
```

Here's how the XOR works:

- 6 in binary: 0110
- 3 in binary: 0011
  Result: 0101 (which is 5 in decimal)

This code assigns the result of the XOR operation, 5, to the variable *result*.

Notes

- XOR is useful for toggling bits in a binary number.
- If you XOR a number with itself, the result is 0, as all bits will be the same (0 ^ 0 = 0, 1 ^ 1 = 0).

Warnings

- Be cautious when using XOR, as it can behave unexpectedly if you're unfamiliar with bitwise operations.
- XOR only works with integers, so avoid using it with floating-point numbers.

MicroPython Syntax Use

```
result = value1 ^ value2
```

MicroPython Syntax Explanation

In MicroPython, the XOR operator works the same way as in Arduino. It compares the bits of *value1* and *value2*, returning a value where the bits are 1 if the corresponding bits are different.

MicroPython Simple Code Example

```
result = 5 ^ 2
```

Here's how the XOR works:

- 5 in binary: 0101
- 2 in binary: 0010
  Result: 0111 (which is 7 in decimal)

This assigns the result of the XOR operation (7) to the variable *result*.

Notes

- XOR is a commonly used operation in algorithms that require bit manipulation, such as encryption and checksum calculations.
- It's useful for toggling or flipping specific bits.

Warnings

- Make sure you understand how XOR operates on binary values to avoid unexpected results.
- Remember that XOR only works with integers and cannot be applied to floating-point numbers.

NOT (~)

The NOT (~) operator is a bitwise operator that inverts all the bits of a number. For each bit in the number, it changes a 1 to a 0 and a 0 to a 1. It essentially "flips" the bits in the binary representation of the number.

Use Purpose
The bitwise NOT operator is useful for inverting values, toggling bits, or performing operations where you need to change the binary representation of a number. It's commonly used in low-level programming tasks involving hardware control.

Arduino Syntax Use

```
result = ~value;
```

Arduino Syntax Explanation
In Arduino, the ~ operator flips all the bits in *value*:

- *value*: The integer number you want to invert.

The result is the bitwise complement of *value*, where each bit is the opposite of what it was before.

Arduino Simple Code Example

```
int result = ~5;
```

Here's how the bitwise NOT works:

- 5 in binary: 00000000 00000000 00000000 00000101
- Applying NOT: 11111111 11111111 11111111 11111010 (which is -6 in decimal, due to two's complement representation in most systems).

This code assigns the value -6 to *result*.

Notes

- In most systems, the bitwise NOT operation on positive numbers results in negative numbers due to the two's complement representation of integers.
- Use bitwise NOT carefully when working with signed numbers, as it may yield unexpected negative results.

Warnings

- Be cautious when using the NOT operator with signed integers. The result may be confusing due to the way negative numbers are represented.

- Bitwise NOT only works on integers, so avoid using it with floating-point numbers.

MicroPython Syntax Use

```
result = ~value
```

MicroPython Syntax Explanation

In MicroPython, the bitwise NOT operator works the same way as in Arduino. It inverts all the bits in the binary representation of *value*, flipping 1s to 0s and 0s to 1s.

MicroPython Simple Code Example

```
result = ~5
```

Here's how the NOT operator works:

- 5 in binary: 00000000 00000000 00000000 00000101
- Applying NOT: 11111111 11111111 11111111 11111010 (which is -6 in decimal).

The result of this operation is -6.

Notes

- Just like in Arduino, the NOT operation inverts all the bits in the value, resulting in a two's complement representation for signed integers.
- This is useful when you need to toggle or invert the bits of a number for certain operations.

Warnings

- As with Arduino, the NOT operator may produce unexpected results when used with signed numbers due to the way negative numbers are represented in binary.

- Ensure that the number you're using the NOT operator on is an integer, as this operation doesn't work with floating-point values.

Chapter 6. Boolean Operators

Chapter Overview

Boolean operators allow for logical comparisons between conditions, enabling decision-making in programs. These operators evaluate expressions as either true or false and help control the flow of a program. In this chapter, we will cover the basic Boolean operators: **AND (&&)**, **OR (||)**, and **NOT (!)**. These operators are used in both Arduino and MicroPython to evaluate multiple conditions and reverse logic. You'll learn how to use them, with examples and explanations for each operator.

Chapter Purpose

The purpose of this chapter is to:

1. Explain how Boolean operators are used to make logical decisions in programming.
2. Provide syntax examples and usage for **AND**, **OR**, and **NOT** operators in both Arduino and MicroPython.
3. Demonstrate common use cases, such as controlling devices based on multiple sensor readings.
4. Highlight potential issues with complex conditions and provide guidance on writing clean, readable code.

Chapter Syntax Table

Operator	Arduino Syntax	MicroPython Syntax
AND (&&)	`if (condition1 && condition2)`	`if condition1 and condition2:`

| NOT (!) | if (!condition) | if not condition: |

AND (&&)

The AND (&&) operator is a logical operator used in programming to evaluate two conditions. It checks if both conditions are true. If both conditions are true, the result is true. If one or both conditions are false, the result is false.

Use Purpose
The AND (&&) operator is commonly used in conditional statements, such as *if* statements, where you want to check if multiple conditions must be true for a block of code to execute. It is used to combine conditions that must both be true for the overall condition to pass.

Arduino Syntax Use

```
if (condition1 && condition2)
```

Arduino Syntax Explanation
In Arduino, the && operator is used within conditional statements to check if both conditions are true:

- *condition1*: The first condition that needs to be true.
- *condition2*: The second condition that also needs to be true.

If both *condition1* and *condition2* are true, the overall condition is true, and the code inside the *if* block will execute.

Arduino Simple Code Example

```
if (temperature > 20 && humidity < 50)
{
digitalWrite(fanPin, HIGH);
}
```

This checks if the temperature is greater than 20 **and** the humidity is less than 50. If both conditions are true, it turns the fan on by setting the fan pin to HIGH.

Notes

- The AND (&&) operator is useful for combining multiple conditions into one, making your code more concise and readable.
- If either condition is false, the block of code inside the *if* statement will not execute.

Warnings

- Be cautious with using complex conditions inside the AND (&&) operator, as it can make debugging more difficult.
- Ensure that both conditions are properly evaluated to avoid logic errors.

MicroPython Syntax Use

```
if condition1 and condition2:
```

MicroPython Syntax Explanation

In MicroPython, the logical AND operator is represented by the word *and*. It works similarly to Arduino's && operator:

- *condition1*: The first condition that must be true.
- *condition2*: The second condition that also needs to be true.

If both conditions are true, the block of code following the *if* statement will execute.

MicroPython Simple Code Example

```
if temperature > 20 and humidity < 50:
    fan.value(1)
```

This checks if the temperature is greater than 20 **and** the humidity is less than 50. If both are true, the fan is turned on by setting the pin value to 1.

Notes

- Just like in Arduino, the *and* operator allows you to check multiple conditions at once.
- It is commonly used in control systems or to monitor sensors when multiple inputs must be true.

Warnings

- Using too many conditions in an *and* statement can make the code harder to read and debug.
- Make sure all conditions are valid and properly checked to avoid logical errors in the code.

OR (||)

The OR (||) operator is a logical operator used in programming to evaluate two conditions. It checks if at least one of the conditions is true. If one or both conditions are true, the result is true. If both conditions are false, the result is false.

Use Purpose
The OR (||) operator is commonly used in situations where you want to execute code if at least one of several conditions is met. It helps combine multiple conditions where only one of them needs to be true for the action to occur.

Arduino Syntax Use

```
if (condition1 || condition2)
```

Arduino Syntax Explanation
In Arduino, the || operator is used in conditional statements to check if at least one of the conditions is true:

- *condition1*: The first condition to evaluate.
- *condition2*: The second condition to evaluate.

If either *condition1* or *condition2* is true (or both), the block of code inside the *if* statement will execute.

Arduino Simple Code Example

```
if (temperature > 30 || humidity > 70)
{
digitalWrite(fanPin, HIGH);
}
```

This checks if the temperature is greater than 30 **or** the humidity is greater than 70. If either condition is true, it turns on the fan by writing a HIGH signal to the fan pin.

Notes

- The OR (||) operator allows you to simplify your code by combining multiple conditions that might trigger the same action.
- If both conditions are false, the code block inside the *if* statement will not execute.

Warnings

- Be mindful when using the OR (||) operator with multiple conditions, as it can make debugging more difficult if the conditions are complex.
- Ensure that the conditions are properly evaluated to avoid unexpected behavior.

MicroPython Syntax Use

```
if condition1 or condition2:
```

MicroPython Syntax Explanation

In MicroPython, the logical OR operator is represented by the word *or*. It works similarly to Arduino's || operator:

- *condition1*: The first condition to evaluate.
- *condition2*: The second condition to evaluate.

If either condition is true, the block of code following the *if* statement will execute.

MicroPython Simple Code Example

```
if temperature > 30 or humidity > 70:
    fan.value(1)
```

This checks if the temperature is greater than 30 **or** the humidity is greater than 70. If either condition is true, the fan is turned on by setting the pin value to 1.

Notes

- The *or* operator allows you to check multiple conditions in a single statement, making the code more concise.
- It is useful for control systems or sensor monitoring where multiple inputs can trigger the same action.

NOT (!)

The NOT (!) operator is a logical operator that inverts the value of a condition or expression. If the condition is true, applying the NOT operator makes it false, and if the condition is false, applying the NOT operator makes it true. It is used to reverse logical conditions.

Use Purpose
The NOT operator is used when you want to check if a condition is false, or when you want to execute code only if a condition is not met. It helps in simplifying logical checks by inverting conditions in *if* or *while* statements.

Arduino Syntax Use

```
if (!condition)
```

Arduino Syntax Explanation

In Arduino, the *!* operator is used to invert the value of *condition*:

- *condition*: The condition you want to invert.

If *condition* is true, *!condition* will evaluate to false, and vice versa. This is useful when you want to check if a condition is not true.

Arduino Simple Code Example

```
if (!buttonPressed) {
digitalWrite(LEDpin, HIGH);
}
```

In this example, if *buttonPressed* is false (the button is not pressed), the code turns on the LED by setting the LED pin to HIGH.

Notes

- The NOT operator is useful for simplifying code when you need to check if a condition is false.
- It is often used in situations where the logic needs to be inverted, such as turning an LED off when a button is pressed.

Warnings

- Be careful not to overuse the NOT operator, as it can sometimes make the code harder to read, especially in complex logical statements.
- Make sure the condition you are negating behaves as expected when inverted.

MicroPython Syntax Use

```
if not condition:
```

MicroPython Syntax Explanation

In MicroPython, the NOT operator is represented by the word *not*. It works similarly to the Arduino *!* operator:

- *condition*: The condition to invert.

If *condition* is true, *not condition* will evaluate to false, and if *condition* is false, *not condition* will evaluate to true.

MicroPython Simple Code Example

```
if not buttonPressed:
    led.value(1)
```

In this example, if *buttonPressed* is false (the button is not pressed), the code turns on the LED by setting the pin value to 1.

Notes

- Just like in Arduino, the NOT operator is useful for inverting logical conditions in MicroPython.
- It helps simplify code by directly checking the opposite of a condition.

Warnings

- Be cautious when using the NOT operator in more complex expressions, as it can make logic harder to follow.
- Ensure that the condition being inverted works properly and results in the intended behavior when negated.

Chapter-7. Trigonometry

Chapter Overview

Trigonometry functions like **sine (sin)**, **cosine (cos)**, and **tangent (tan)** are essential mathematical tools often used in programming for calculating angles, waveforms, and circular motion. These functions are useful in a variety of fields, including geometry, physics, and engineering. In this chapter, we will explore how to use trigonometric functions in both Arduino and MicroPython to perform calculations involving angles, oscillations, and wave patterns. All angles in these functions must be expressed in radians, not degrees.

Chapter Purpose
The purpose of this chapter is to:

1. Introduce the key trigonometric functions used in programming: **sin()**, **cos()**, and **tan()**.
2. Explain the syntax and usage of these functions in both Arduino and MicroPython.
3. Demonstrate real-world applications, such as generating waveforms or calculating angles in motion.
4. Provide notes and warnings on how to handle radians, precision, and hardware limitations when using trigonometric functions.

Chapter Syntax Table

Function	Arduino Syntax	MicroPython Syntax
Sine	result = sin(angle);	result = math.sin(angle)
Cosine	result = cos(angle);	result = math.cos(angle)
Tangent	result = tan(angle);	result = math.tan(angle)

Sine (sin())

The sine function, represented by *sin()*, is a mathematical function that calculates the sine of an angle. In programming, the angle is measured in radians, not degrees. The sine of an angle in a right triangle is the ratio of the length of the opposite side to the hypotenuse.

Use Purpose
The sine function is commonly used in applications involving waveforms, oscillations, or circular motion. It's also used in geometry and physics for calculating angles, trajectories, or generating smooth movements.

Arduino Syntax Use

```
result = sin(angle);
```

Arduino Syntax Explanation
In Arduino, the *sin()* function calculates the sine of an angle (in radians):

- *angle*: The angle in radians for which you want to calculate the sine.
- The result is stored in the variable *result*, which will be a floating-point number between -1 and 1.

Arduino Simple Code Example

```
float result = sin(1.5708);
float waveValue = sin(time);
```

- The first line calculates the sine of 1.5708 radians (which is approximately π/2), and stores the result (1) in *result*.

- The second line calculates the sine of the variable *time*, which could be used in wave generation or smooth animations.

Notes

- The *sin()* function expects the angle to be in radians. To convert degrees to radians, multiply degrees by π/180.
- The output of the sine function is a value between -1 and 1.

Warnings

- Be careful when working with angles in degrees; Arduino's *sin()* function works only with radians.
- The precision of the result may vary depending on the hardware used, especially when dealing with very small or large values.

MicroPython Syntax Use

```
result = math.sin(angle)
```

MicroPython Syntax Explanation

In MicroPython, the *math.sin()* function from the math library is used to calculate the sine of an angle (in radians):

- *angle*: The angle in radians for which to calculate the sine.
- The result is stored in *result*, which is a floating-point number between -1 and 1.

MicroPython Simple Code Example

```
import math
result = math.sin(3.1416 / 2)
waveValue = math.sin(time)
```

- The first line imports the math module, and the second line calculates the sine of π/2 radians (approximately 1).

- The third line calculates the sine of the variable *time*.

Notes

- As in Arduino, MicroPython's *sin()* function works with radians. Use the conversion formula degrees × π/180 to convert degrees to radians.
- The result is a floating-point value between -1 and 1, representing the sine of the angle.

Warnings

- Ensure you import the *math* module before using the *sin()* function in MicroPython.
- MicroPython's hardware precision may affect the result's accuracy, especially with extreme values or limited floating-point precision.

Cosine (cos())

The cosine function, represented by *cos()*, is a mathematical function that calculates the cosine of an angle. In programming, the angle is measured in radians, not degrees. The cosine of an angle in a right triangle is the ratio of the adjacent side to the hypotenuse.

Use Purpose
The cosine function is commonly used in applications involving waveforms, oscillations, or circular motion. It's also used in geometry, physics, and engineering for calculating angles, distances, or generating smooth movements.

Arduino Syntax Use

```
result = cos(angle);
```

Arduino Syntax Explanation
In Arduino, the *cos()* function calculates the cosine of an angle (in radians):

- *angle*: The angle in radians for which you want to calculate the cosine.
- The result is stored in the variable *result*, which will be a floating-point number between -1 and 1.

Arduino Simple Code Example

```
float result = cos(0);
float waveValue = cos(time);
```

- The first line calculates the cosine of 0 radians (which is 1), and stores the result in *result*.
- The second line calculates the cosine of the variable *time*, which could be used in wave generation or animations.

Notes

- The *cos()* function expects the angle in radians. To convert degrees to radians, multiply degrees by π/180.
- The output of the cosine function is a value between -1 and 1.

Warnings

- Ensure the angle is in radians when using *cos()*; Arduino does not support degrees directly.
- Like with sine, the precision of the cosine result can be affected by hardware limitations.

MicroPython Syntax Use

```
result = math.cos(angle)
```

MicroPython Syntax Explanation

In MicroPython, the *math.cos()* function from the math library calculates the cosine of an angle (in radians):

- *angle*: The angle in radians for which you want to calculate the cosine.
- The result is stored in *result*, which is a floating-point number between -1 and 1.

MicroPython Simple Code Example

```
import math
result = math.cos(3.1416 / 3)
waveValue = math.cos(time)
```

- The first line imports the math module, and the second line calculates the cosine of π/3 radians (approximately 0.5).
- The third line calculates the cosine of the variable *time*.

Notes

- Like in Arduino, MicroPython's *cos()* function requires the angle in radians. Use degrees × π/180 to convert degrees to radians.
- The output of *cos()* ranges between -1 and 1, representing the cosine of the given angle.

Warnings

- In MicroPython, you must import the *math* module before using *cos()*.
- Be cautious when working with extremely large or small angles, as precision may vary based on the hardware and floating-point limitations.

Tangent (tan())

The tangent function, represented by *tan()*, is a mathematical function that calculates the tangent of an angle. In programming, the angle is measured in radians, not degrees. The tangent of an angle in a right triangle is the ratio of the opposite side to the adjacent side.

Use Purpose
The tangent function is useful in applications that involve trigonometry, waveforms, and angles in geometry or physics. It helps in calculating slopes, angles, and projections in circular or oscillating systems.

Arduino Syntax Use

```
result = tan(angle);
```

Arduino Syntax Explanation
In Arduino, the *tan()* function calculates the tangent of an angle (in radians):

- *angle*: The angle in radians for which you want to calculate the tangent.
- The result is stored in the variable *result*, which will be a floating-point number.

Arduino Simple Code Example

```
float result = tan(0.7854);
float angleValue = tan(time);
```

- The first line calculates the tangent of 0.7854 radians (which is π/4 or 45 degrees) and stores the result in *result*.
- The second line calculates the tangent of the variable *time*, which could be used in animations or motion calculations.

Notes

- The *tan()* function requires the angle to be in radians. To convert degrees to radians, multiply degrees by π/180.
- The result of the tangent function can range from negative infinity to positive infinity, depending on the angle.

Warnings

- Be cautious when calculating the tangent of angles close to π/2 (90 degrees) or multiples thereof, as the tangent function becomes undefined (division by zero) at these points.
- Ensure the angle is in radians, as using degrees directly will give incorrect results.

MicroPython Syntax Use

```
result = math.tan(angle)
```

MicroPython Syntax Explanation

In MicroPython, the *math.tan()* function from the math library calculates the tangent of an angle (in radians):

- *angle*: The angle in radians for which you want to calculate the tangent.
- The result is stored in *result*, which will be a floating-point number.

MicroPython Simple Code Example

```
import math
result = math.tan(3.1416 / 4)
angleValue = math.tan(time)
```

- The first line imports the math module, and the second line calculates the tangent of π/4 radians (approximately 1).
- The third line calculates the tangent of the variable *time*.

Notes

- Like Arduino, MicroPython requires the angle in radians for the *tan()* function. To convert degrees to radians, use degrees × π/180.

- The tangent of an angle can grow very large or small, depending on how close the angle is to π/2 or 90 degrees.

Warnings

- In MicroPython, you must import the *math* module before using the *tan()* function.
- The tangent function becomes undefined at angles near π/2 or 90 degrees, so avoid calculating the tangent at these points.

Chapter 8. Variables

Chapter Overview

Variables are essential elements in programming, used to store and manipulate data. They can be categorized into global, local, static, constant, and volatile, each serving a specific purpose in how and where the variable's value is used and retained in the program. Understanding the differences between these types of variables allows you to write more efficient, readable, and organized code. This chapter will explore each type of variable in both Arduino and MicroPython, providing explanations, use cases, and code examples.

Chapter Purpose
The purpose of this chapter is to:

1. Explain the various types of variables used in programming, such as global, local, static, constant, and volatile.
2. Provide syntax examples for how to declare and use these variables in both Arduino and MicroPython.
3. Offer guidance on when to use each type of variable based on the scope and behavior needed.
4. Highlight common issues and best practices when working with variables to avoid memory or logical errors.

Chapter Syntax Table

Variable Type	Arduino Syntax	MicroPython Syntax
Global	`type variableName;`	`global variableName`
Local	`type variableName;`	`variableName = value`
Static	`static type variableName = value;`	Use class or global for persistence
Constant	`const type variableName = value;`	`LED_PIN = const(13)` or use uppercase
Volatile	`volatile type variableName;`	Handle with care in interrupt context

Global Variables

What are Global Variables?

Global variables are variables that are declared outside of all functions and are accessible from any part of the program. Unlike local variables (which are only accessible within the function they are declared in), global variables can be used by any function in the program, making them useful for sharing data across multiple functions.

Use Purpose

Global variables are used when you need a variable to be accessible throughout the entire program, across multiple functions. This is useful when different parts of the code need to share or update the same data, such as sensor values, counters, or configuration settings.

Arduino Syntax Use

```
type variableName;
```

Arduino Syntax Explanation
In Arduino, global variables are declared outside of any function, typically at the top of the program:

- *type*: The data type of the variable (e.g., *int*, *float*, *boolean*).
- *variableName*: The name of the variable.

Arduino Simple Code Example

```
int counter = 0; // Global variable
void setup() {
Serial.begin(9600);
}
void loop() {
counter++; // Modify global variable
Serial.println(counter); // Access global variable
delay(1000);
}
```

- The variable *counter* is declared globally and can be accessed and modified inside both the *setup()* and *loop()* functions.

Notes

- Global variables are initialized at the start of the program and retain their value throughout the program's execution.
- Declaring too many global variables may lead to memory issues, especially on devices with limited RAM, like Arduino.

Warnings

- Be cautious when using global variables in large programs, as they can make debugging more difficult if many functions modify the same variable.
- Global variables should be used sparingly to avoid unintended side effects and to keep the code organized.

MicroPython Syntax Use

```
global variableName
```

MicroPython Syntax Explanation

In MicroPython, global variables are declared similarly to Arduino. If you want to modify a global variable inside a function, you must use the *global* keyword within the function:

- *global variableName*: Tells the function to use the global version of the variable, not a local one.

MicroPython Simple Code Example

```
counter = 0 # Global variable
def increment_counter():
global counter # Access global variable
counter += 1
print(counter)
increment_counter()
increment_counter()
```

- The variable *counter* is declared globally, and the *increment_counter()* function modifies it using the *global* keyword.

Notes

- In MicroPython, global variables can be accessed from any function, but you need the *global* keyword if you want to modify their value inside a function.
- Just like in Arduino, global variables are initialized at the start of the program and retain their values throughout execution.

Warnings

- Overusing global variables can lead to confusion and potential errors if many parts of the program are modifying the same variables.
- Be careful when modifying global variables from within functions to avoid unintended side effects, especially in complex programs.

Local Variables

What are Local Variables?
Local variables are variables that are declared within a function or a block of code and are only accessible inside that specific function or block. Once the function finishes executing, the local variables are destroyed, and their values are no longer accessible.

Use Purpose
Local variables are used when you only need a variable to store data temporarily within a specific function or block of code. They help avoid conflicts with global variables and ensure that the variable is only used in the context where it's needed.

Arduino Syntax Use

```
type variableName;
```

Arduino Syntax Explanation
In Arduino, local variables are declared inside a function:

- *type*: The data type of the variable (e.g., *int, float, boolean*).
- *variableName*: The name of the variable.

Arduino Simple Code Example

```
void loop() {
int counter = 0; // Local variable
counter++;
Serial.println(counter);
delay(1000);
}
```

- In this example, *counter* is a local variable declared inside the *loop()* function. It is reinitialized to 0 every time the function runs and only exists within the scope of the *loop()* function.

Notes

- Local variables are only available within the function or block where they are declared. They cannot be accessed by other functions.
- Each time the function is called, the local variable is created and destroyed, meaning its value is reset unless otherwise handled.

Warnings

- Be careful not to rely on the value of a local variable across different function calls because it gets reinitialized each time the function runs.
- Using too many local variables in a function can lead to increased memory usage, especially in resource-limited environments like Arduino.

MicroPython Syntax Use

```
variableName = value
```

MicroPython Syntax Explanation

In MicroPython, local variables are declared within a function or block of code. They are used in the same way as in Arduino, but no explicit data type declaration is required:

- *variableName*: The name of the local variable.
- *value*: The initial value assigned to the variable.

MicroPython Simple Code Example

```
def my_function():
    counter = 0 # Local variable
    counter += 1
    print(counter)
my_function()
my_function()
```

- Here, *counter* is a local variable inside the function *my_function()*. Every time the function is called, *counter* is reinitialized to 0 and incremented by 1.

Notes

- In MicroPython, local variables are automatically destroyed once the function execution is complete, similar to how they work in Arduino.
- Local variables make the code more modular and prevent variable conflicts across different parts of the program.

Warnings

- Like in Arduino, local variables in MicroPython are not preserved between function calls. If you need a variable to retain its value, consider using a global variable or passing it as a parameter.
- Avoid excessive use of local variables in deeply nested functions, as this can lead to memory issues on devices with limited resources.

Static Variables

What are Static Variables?
Static variables are variables that retain their value between function calls. Unlike local variables, which are reinitialized every time the function is called, static variables keep their previous value even after the function finishes executing. Static variables are typically used within functions but are preserved throughout the program's execution.

Use Purpose
The purpose of static variables is to maintain state across multiple function calls without having to use global variables. This is useful in situations where you need a variable to "remember" its value from previous calls, such as in counting operations or managing states in embedded systems.

Arduino Syntax Use

```
static type variableName = initialValue;
```

Arduino Syntax Explanation
In Arduino, the `static` keyword is used to declare a static variable inside a function:

- *type*: The data type of the variable (e.g., *int*, *float*).
- *variableName*: The name of the variable.
- *initialValue*: The initial value assigned to the variable (optional, but recommended).

Arduino Simple Code Example

```
void loop() {
static int counter = 0; // Static variable
counter++;
Serial.println(counter);
delay(1000);
}
```

- In this example, *counter* is a static variable declared inside the *loop()* function. Even though the function completes after every loop iteration, the value of *counter* will be retained and incremented on the next call, resulting in an increasing count.

Notes
- Static variables are initialized only once, and their value is preserved across multiple calls to the function.
- You don't need to reinitialize the static variable on every function call, unlike regular local variables.

Warnings
- Be mindful of memory usage when declaring many static variables, especially on devices with limited RAM, like the Arduino.
- Static variables are local to the function in which they are declared, meaning they cannot be accessed outside that function.

MicroPython Syntax Use
In MicroPython, there is no direct `static` keyword. However, you can achieve the same behavior using global variables or by storing the variable in an external data structure (like a class or module) that retains its state between function calls.

MicroPython Syntax Explanation
In MicroPython, using global variables or data structures like classes can help retain a variable's value across function calls, mimicking the behavior of static variables.

MicroPython Simple Code Example Using a Class

```
class Counter:
value = 0 # Static-like behavior across function calls
def increment_counter():
Counter.value += 1 print(Counter.value)
increment_counter()
increment_counter()
```

- In this example, *Counter.value* behaves similarly to a static variable. The value is retained across calls to *increment_counter()*.

Notes

- MicroPython does not have a `static` keyword, but you can achieve static-like behavior by using class attributes or module-level variables.
- Global variables can also be used, but managing state in a class is often a cleaner and more modular approach.

Warnings

- Overusing global variables for static-like behavior can lead to cluttered and confusing code. Consider using a class to encapsulate the static data.
- Be cautious about memory management when using large static-like variables in resource-constrained environments.

Constant Variables

What are Constant Variables?
Constant variables are variables whose value is set once and cannot be changed throughout the program's execution. They are typically used to define values that should remain unchanged, such as configuration settings, physical constants, or pin assignments.

Use Purpose
The purpose of constant variables is to ensure that certain values remain fixed during the execution of the program. This prevents accidental modifications of important values that should stay constant, improving code reliability and readability.

Arduino Syntax Use

```
const type variableName = value;
```

Arduino Syntax Explanation
In Arduino, the `const` keyword is used to declare a constant variable:

- *type*: The data type of the variable (e.g., *int*, *float*).
- *variableName*: The name of the variable.
- *value*: The fixed value assigned to the constant.

Arduino Simple Code Example

```
const int ledPin = 13; // Constant variable
void setup() {
pinMode(ledPin, OUTPUT);
}
void loop() {
digitalWrite(ledPin, HIGH);
delay(1000);
digitalWrite(ledPin, LOW);
delay(1000);
}
```

- In this example, *ledPin* is declared as a constant variable, meaning its value (13) cannot be changed throughout the program. This makes the code more readable and ensures the pin assignment remains fixed.

Notes

- Constant variables are useful for defining fixed values, like pin numbers, that should not be altered during the program.
- The `const` keyword ensures that the variable's value is protected from accidental modification.

Warnings

- Constant variables are read-only, meaning attempting to change their value in the program will result in a compilation error.
- Ensure that constant values are defined at the start of the program to avoid reusing or modifying them later.

MicroPython Syntax Use

In MicroPython, there is no specific `const` keyword, but you can achieve the same behavior by conventionally defining variables that you treat as constants (using uppercase naming) or using the *const()* function from the *machine* module.

MicroPython Simple Code Example Using Naming Convention

```
LED_PIN = 13 # Treat as constant variable
def setup():
pin = machine.Pin(LED_PIN, machine.Pin.OUT)
def toggle_led():
pin.toggle()
```

- In this example, *LED_PIN* is treated as a constant by using uppercase naming, indicating that its value should not be changed.

MicroPython Syntax Use with `const()` Function

```
from machine import
const LED_PIN = const(13)
```

- The *const()* function can be used to define constant variables that behave similarly to constants in Arduino.

Notes

- In MicroPython, using all uppercase letters for constant variable names is a common convention to indicate they should not be changed.
- The *const()* function can be used for optimization by telling the interpreter that the value will not change.

Warnings

- Although the *const()* function helps indicate a constant, it does not prevent the value from being modified later in the code. Stick to best practices and avoid changing the value of a constant.

Volatile Variables

What are Volatile Variables?
Volatile variables are special types of variables that can be changed unexpectedly by external factors, such as hardware interrupts or processes outside the main program flow. Declaring a variable as *volatile* tells the compiler that the value of this variable may change at any time, preventing the compiler from optimizing it in ways that assume its value will stay constant.

Use Purpose
Volatile variables are used to ensure that the program always fetches the most up-to-date value of the variable. They are often used when variables are modified within interrupt service routines (ISRs) or by hardware peripherals in embedded systems.

Arduino Syntax Use

```
volatile type variableName;
```

Arduino Syntax Explanation
In Arduino, the *volatile* keyword declares a variable as volatile:

- *type*: The data type of the variable (e.g., *int*, *float*).
- *variableName*: The name of the variable.

Arduino Simple Code Example

```
volatile int flag = 0; // Volatile variable
void setup() {
attachInterrupt(digitalPinToInterrupt(2), ISR, CHANGE);
}
void loop() {
if (flag == 1) {
// Do something
flag = 0;
}
}
void ISR() {
flag = 1; // Modify volatile variable in ISR
}
```

- In this example, *flag* is a volatile variable that is modified in an interrupt service routine (ISR). The main program continuously checks the value of *flag*, which may change unexpectedly due to the ISR.

Notes

- Volatile variables are mainly used in ISRs or hardware peripherals that may modify variables asynchronously to the main program.
- Declaring a variable as *volatile* ensures that the compiler fetches the variable's value directly from memory each time it's accessed, avoiding optimizations that could lead to incorrect behavior.

Warnings

- Declaring a variable as *volatile* does not make it thread-safe or atomic. If the variable is shared between the main code and an ISR and is larger than 1 byte, you may need to

disable interrupts when accessing the variable to ensure safe operations.
- Overusing volatile variables can reduce program efficiency because it limits compiler optimizations.

MicroPython Syntax Use

MicroPython does not have a specific *volatile* keyword like Arduino. However, for variables that might be modified by hardware or within interrupt contexts, you should handle the synchronization carefully.

MicroPython Simple Code Example Using Interrupt Handling

```
flag = False // Treat as volatile-like
def handler(pin):
global flag flag = True // Variable modified in ISR-like function
pin.irq(trigger=machine.Pin.IRQ_RISING, handler=handler)
while True:
if flag:
print("Interrupt triggered")
flag = False
```

- In this example, *flag* is treated like a volatile variable, updated by an interrupt handler when a rising edge is detected on a pin.

Notes

- Although MicroPython does not have the *volatile* keyword, variables that are modified inside interrupt handlers should be handled as if they were volatile.
- Synchronization may be needed if the variable is accessed in both the main program and the interrupt handler.

Warnings

- Like in Arduino, shared variables between the main program and an interrupt handler should be treated carefully. If the variable is larger than 1 byte, you may need to ensure atomicity by temporarily disabling interrupts while accessing the variable.

Chapter 9. Data Types

Chapter Overview

In programming, data types are essential for managing and storing different kinds of values. In Arduino and MicroPython, understanding how to use various data types like integers, floats, characters, and arrays is critical for working with hardware, sensors, and calculations efficiently. This chapter will explain common data types, their purpose, and the differences between Arduino and MicroPython syntax for handling them.

Chapter Purpose

The goal of this chapter is to:

1. Introduce the most common data types used in Arduino and MicroPython.
2. Explain how to declare and use these data types in different contexts.
3. Provide code examples for each data type to demonstrate real-world usage.
4. Highlight key differences between Arduino and MicroPython data type handling, including limitations and warnings for each system.

Chapter Syntax Table

Data Type	Arduino Syntax	MicroPython Syntax
int	`int variableName = value;`	`variableName = value`
unsigned int	`unsigned int variableName = value;`	Not applicable (handled by int)
long	`long variableName = value;`	`variableName = value`
unsigned long	`unsigned long variableName = value;`	Not applicable (handled by int)
float	`float variableName = value;`	`variableName = value`
double	`double variableName = value;` (same as float)	`variableName = value`
char	`char variableName = 'A';`	`variableName = 'A'`
byte/unsigned char	`byte variableName = value;`	Not applicable (handled by int)
boolean	`boolean variableName = true;`	`variableName = True or False`
String	`String variableName = "text";`	`variableName = "text"`
Array	`type arrayName[arraySize];`	`arrayName = [value1, value2]`

int: 16-bit Signed Integer

In Arduino, *int* is a 16-bit signed integer data type that can store whole numbers ranging from -32,768 to 32,767. This means it can handle both positive and negative integers. It is useful for basic arithmetic operations, sensor readings, and variables that need to store small numerical values.

Use Purpose
The *int* data type is commonly used when you need to store whole numbers and the values fall within the range of -32,768 to 32,767. It's suitable for counting, controlling loops, reading sensors, or storing small numerical values.

Arduino Syntax Use

```
int variableName = value;
```

Arduino Syntax Explanation
In Arduino, the *int* keyword is used to declare a 16-bit signed integer:

- *variableName*: The name of the variable.
- *value*: The initial value assigned to the variable (optional).

Arduino Simple Code Example

```
int counter = 0;
int sensorValue = analogRead(A0);
```

- The first line declares an *int* variable called *counter* and initializes it to 0.
- The second line reads a value from analog pin A0 and stores it in *sensorValue*.

Notes

- The range of values an *int* can store is from -32,768 to 32,767.
- If you need to store numbers outside of this range, consider using a larger data type, such as *long*.

Warnings

- Be cautious when performing calculations that might exceed the maximum value of 32,767 or fall below -32,768, as this can cause overflow and lead to incorrect results.
- For larger numbers, using *int* might not be suitable. Use *long* or *unsigned int* for higher ranges.

MicroPython Syntax Use

```
variableName = value
```

MicroPython Syntax Explanation

In MicroPython, there is no fixed 16-bit limit for integers. Python automatically handles large integers, so there is no need to specify *int* explicitly.

MicroPython Simple Code Example

```
counter = 0
sensor_value = analog_read(pin)
```

- The first line declares a variable *counter* and initializes it to 0.
- The second line simulates reading a sensor value and storing it in *sensor_value*.

Notes

- In MicroPython, integers automatically grow as needed, and there is no specific 16-bit integer limit as in Arduino.
- You don't need to declare the data type for variables in MicroPython, as Python handles them dynamically.

Warnings

- Although MicroPython handles large integers automatically, using large numbers on memory-constrained devices may affect performance or memory usage.
- Be aware of hardware limitations when working with large numbers in embedded systems.

unsigned int: 16-bit Unsigned Integer

In Arduino, *unsigned int* is a 16-bit data type that can store whole numbers without a sign, meaning it only represents non-negative values. The range of an *unsigned int* is from 0 to 65,535, allowing it to store larger positive values compared to a regular *int*, which can store both negative and positive values.

Use Purpose
The *unsigned int* data type is used when you need to store only positive whole numbers and require a larger range than a signed integer (which includes negative numbers). It's commonly used for counting, time tracking, or working with hardware values that cannot be negative, such as pin states or sensor data.

Arduino Syntax Use

```
unsigned int variableName = value;
```

Arduino Syntax Explanation
In Arduino, the *unsigned int* keyword is used to declare a 16-bit unsigned integer:

- *variableName*: The name of the variable.
- *value*: The initial value assigned to the variable (optional).

Arduino Simple Code Example

```
unsigned int counter = 0;
unsigned int sensorValue = analogRead(A0);
```

- The first line declares an *unsigned int* variable called *counter* and initializes it to 0.
- The second line reads a value from analog pin A0 and stores it in *sensorValue*, which is guaranteed to be non-negative.

Notes

- The range of values an *unsigned int* can store is from 0 to 65,535, which is double the positive range of a regular *int*.
- It is useful in situations where negative numbers are not expected or allowed, such as with hardware counters or sensor readings.

Warnings

- Be cautious when performing operations that might produce negative results, as *unsigned int* cannot store negative values. If a negative value is produced, it will wrap around to a large positive number, causing unexpected behavior.
- For very large values exceeding 65,535, consider using *unsigned long* for an even larger range.

MicroPython Syntax Use

In MicroPython, there is no specific *unsigned int* type. Integers in MicroPython are automatically handled, and Python does not distinguish between signed and unsigned integers.

long: 32-bit Signed Integer

In Arduino, *long* is a 32-bit signed integer data type. It can store whole numbers ranging from -2,147,483,648 to 2,147,483,647. This allows it to handle larger positive and negative values than the 16-bit *int* type. It is useful when you need to work with large integers that exceed the range of an *int*.

Use Purpose
The *long* data type is used when you need to store larger whole numbers than what *int* can handle. It is especially useful for large calculations, counters, or tracking time with millisecond precision, such as when using the *millis()* function.

Arduino Syntax Use

```
long variableName = value;
```

Arduino Syntax Explanation
In Arduino, the *long* keyword is used to declare a 32-bit signed integer:

- *variableName*: The name of the variable.
- *value*: The initial value assigned to the variable (optional).

Arduino Simple Code Example

```
long counter = 0;
long time = millis();
```

- The first line declares a *long* variable called *counter* and initializes it to 0.
- The second line stores the value returned by *millis()*, which can be a large number, in the *time* variable.

Notes

- The range of values a *long* can store is from -2,147,483,648 to 2,147,483,647.
- If you only need to work with non-negative numbers, you can use *unsigned long* for an even larger range of up to 4,294,967,295.

Warnings

- Be cautious when performing calculations that could exceed the maximum or minimum value of a *long* to avoid overflow.
- If you do not need such a large range of values, consider using *int* to save memory.

MicroPython Syntax Use
In MicroPython, there is no specific *long* data type. Python automatically handles large integers, so there's no need to distinguish between *int* and *long*.

unsigned long: 32-bit Unsigned Integer

In Arduino, *unsigned long* is a 32-bit unsigned integer data type. It can store whole numbers from 0 to 4,294,967,295. Since it is unsigned, it only represents non-negative values, which gives it a larger positive range compared to a signed *long*, which includes both positive and negative numbers.

Use Purpose
The *unsigned long* data type is used when you need to store large positive whole numbers, typically for timers, counters, or working with hardware values like time intervals, where negative values are not needed. It is especially useful when using the *millis()* or *micros()* functions for tracking time.

Arduino Syntax Use

```
unsigned long variableName = value;
```

Arduino Syntax Explanation
In Arduino, the *unsigned long* keyword is used to declare a 32-bit unsigned integer:

- *variableName*: The name of the variable.
- *value*: The initial value assigned to the variable (optional).

Arduino Simple Code Example
```
unsigned long startTime = millis();
unsigned long counter = 0;
```

- The first line declares an *unsigned long* variable called *startTime* and stores the current value of *millis()*, which can be a large number.
- The second line declares an *unsigned long* variable *counter* and initializes it to 0.

Notes

- The range of values an *unsigned long* can store is from 0 to 4,294,967,295, making it ideal for tracking time or counting large values.
- Since it's unsigned, *unsigned long* is best suited for situations where negative values are not expected, such as timekeeping or distance measurement.

Warnings

- Be cautious when performing arithmetic that could result in a negative value, as *unsigned long* cannot represent negative numbers. If a calculation produces a negative value, it will wrap around to a large positive value, which can cause unexpected behavior.
- For very large numbers exceeding the range of 32-bit values, consider using 64-bit data types like *unsigned long long* in more complex systems.

MicroPython Syntax Use
In MicroPython, there is no specific *unsigned long* type. Python automatically handles integers dynamically, and there is no need to specify whether an integer is signed or unsigned.

float: 32-bit Floating-Point Number

In Arduino, *float* is a 32-bit floating-point data type used to represent real numbers with decimal points. It can store both positive and negative values, and is commonly used in applications that require fractional or very precise numerical values, such as sensor readings or mathematical calculations.

Use Purpose
The *float* data type is used when you need to store numbers with decimal points or require more precision than integers can provide. It's ideal for representing real-world quantities, such as temperature, pressure, distance, or any value that needs decimal precision.

Arduino Syntax Use

```
float variableName = value;
```

Arduino Syntax Explanation
In Arduino, the *float* keyword is used to declare a floating-point number:

- *variableName*: The name of the variable.
- *value*: The initial value assigned to the variable (optional, but typically includes a decimal point).

Arduino Simple Code Example

```
float temperature = 23.75;
float result = sin(1.57);
```

- The first line declares a *float* variable called *temperature* and assigns it a decimal value of 23.75.
- The second line calculates the sine of 1.57 radians and stores the result in *result*, which requires decimal precision.

Notes

- The precision of a *float* in Arduino is limited to 6-7 decimal digits, which is sufficient for many applications but not as precise as a 64-bit double precision.
- Operations on *float* values can be slower than operations on integers due to the additional complexity of floating-point arithmetic.

Warnings

- Arduino's *float* is only 32-bit, so it may not provide enough precision for applications requiring highly accurate calculations (e.g., scientific simulations).
- If higher precision is needed, Arduino does not natively support the *double* data type at 64 bits, as it is typically implemented as a 32-bit float.

MicroPython Syntax Use

```
variableName = value
```

MicroPython Syntax Explanation
In MicroPython, floating-point numbers are handled automatically. There is no need to declare a specific *float* data type, as numbers with decimals are automatically treated as floating-point values.

MicroPython Simple Code Example

```
temperature = 23.75
result = math.sin(1.57)
```

- The first line declares a variable *temperature* and assigns it the decimal value of 23.75.
- The second line calculates the sine of 1.57 radians and stores the result in *result*.

Notes

- MicroPython supports floating-point numbers automatically and dynamically, with precision that may vary depending on the hardware.
- There's no need to specify a *float* type as Python dynamically adjusts to floating-point or integer values based on the data.

Warnings

- While MicroPython handles floating-point numbers, performance can be slower on devices with limited resources. Be mindful of memory usage when performing many floating-point calculations.
- Ensure that your hardware supports floating-point operations efficiently if you're working on a constrained system like an embedded device.

double: 32-bit Floating-Point Number (Same as float)

In Arduino, *double* is a 32-bit floating-point data type, just like *float*. This means it stores real numbers with decimal points, and the precision and range are the same as *float*. Although *double* typically refers to a 64-bit floating-point number in other programming languages, in Arduino it is simply an alias for *float* and offers no extra precision.

Use Purpose
The *double* data type is used when you need to work with numbers that require decimal points, such as measurements or calculations involving fractions. Since *double* is the same as *float* in Arduino, it is used for the same purposes—storing values like sensor readings, temperature, and other real-world data that require precision beyond integers.

Arduino Syntax Use

```
double variableName = value;
```

Arduino Syntax Explanation
In Arduino, the *double* keyword is used to declare a 32-bit floating-point number, which is the same as *float*:

- *variableName*: The name of the variable.
- *value*: The initial value assigned to the variable (typically including a decimal point).

Arduino Simple Code Example

```
double distance = 123.456;
double pi = 3.14159;
```

- The first line declares a *double* variable called *distance* and assigns it a value of 123.456.
- The second line declares a *double* variable *pi* with the value of 3.14159 for use in calculations.

Notes

- On Arduino boards, *double* is exactly the same as *float* and provides no additional precision. Both are limited to 6-7 decimal digits of precision.
- If higher precision is needed for more complex calculations, Arduino does not offer native support for 64-bit floating-point numbers on most boards.

Warnings

- Be aware that using *double* in Arduino does not provide 64-bit precision, as you might expect from other programming environments.
- Floating-point operations can be slower than integer operations and consume more memory, so use *double* or *float* only when necessary.

MicroPython Syntax Use

```
variableName = value
```

MicroPython Syntax Explanation
In MicroPython, floating-point numbers are handled dynamically, and there is no specific *double* type. All numbers with decimal points are automatically treated as floating-point values, and the precision depends on the hardware.

MicroPython Simple Code Example

```
pi = 3.14159
distance = 123.456
```

- The first line declares a variable *pi* with the value of 3.14159, representing a floating-point number.
- The second line declares a variable *distance* with a value of 123.456.

Notes

- In MicroPython, you don't need to distinguish between *float* and *double*. Python handles floating-point numbers automatically with precision determined by the system.
- The precision of floating-point values in MicroPython may vary depending on the hardware used.

Warnings

- Be mindful of the memory limitations when performing many floating-point calculations on resource-constrained devices.
- Ensure that the hardware you are using supports floating-point operations efficiently, especially if you are performing many calculations.

char: 8-bit Signed Character

In Arduino, *char* is an 8-bit data type used to store a single character or small integer value. Since it's signed, it can represent values from -128 to 127. In addition to storing characters, it can also be used to hold small numerical values. A *char* variable stores a single ASCII character, such as a letter, digit, or punctuation mark.

Use Purpose
The *char* data type is commonly used to store single characters, such as letters or punctuation, or small integer values. It's also useful for handling text data when working with strings or sending/receiving characters through serial communication.

Arduino Syntax Use

```
char variableName = 'character';
```

Arduino Syntax Explanation
In Arduino, the *char* keyword is used to declare a variable that holds a single character:

- *variableName*: The name of the variable.
- *character*: The single character to be stored, enclosed in single quotes (e.g., 'A').

Arduino Simple Code Example

```
char letter = 'A';
char numberChar = '5';
```

- The first line declares a *char* variable named *letter* and assigns it the value 'A'.
- The second line declares a *char* variable *numberChar* and assigns it the character '5'.

Notes

- Each *char* variable occupies 1 byte of memory.
- A *char* can hold not only characters but also small integers, where the value represents the ASCII code for the character. For example, the ASCII code for 'A' is 65.

Warnings

- Be careful not to confuse characters (like '5') with their numeric values (5). The character '5' is not the same as the number 5.
- Make sure to use single quotes around characters in *char* variables. If you use double quotes, it will be treated as a string (an array of characters).

MicroPython Syntax Use

```
variableName = 'character'
```

MicroPython Syntax Explanation
In MicroPython, single characters are also stored as strings, since there is no distinct *char* type. A single character is treated as a string of length 1.

MicroPython Simple Code Example

```
letter = 'A'
number_char = '5'
```

- The first line declares a variable *letter* and assigns it the character 'A'.
- The second line declares a variable *number_char* and assigns it the character '5'.

Notes

- In MicroPython, single characters are simply strings of length 1, so there is no separate *char* type.
- String operations can be performed on these variables, as MicroPython handles strings and characters in the same way.

Warnings

- Since Python treats characters as strings, you cannot perform arithmetic operations directly on characters as you might in C-based languages like Arduino.
- Be cautious when manipulating characters, as they are stored and treated as strings, not as individual ASCII values.

unsigned char / byte: 8-bit Unsigned Value

In Arduino, *unsigned char* and *byte* are both 8-bit unsigned data types. They can store values ranging from 0 to 255. Unlike *char*, which is signed and can store negative numbers, *unsigned char* and *byte* can only store positive values. The *byte* type is just an alias for *unsigned char*, and they can be used interchangeably.

Use Purpose

The *unsigned char* or *byte* data types are commonly used when working with binary data, such as reading or writing bytes from/to a buffer, storing sensor values, or handling raw data from hardware. Since the range is from 0 to 255, it's ideal for data that doesn't require negative values.

Arduino Syntax Use

```
unsigned char variableName = value;
byte variableName = value;
```

Arduino Syntax Explanation

In Arduino, both *unsigned char* and *byte* are used to declare 8-bit unsigned integers:

- *variableName*: The name of the variable.
- *value*: The initial value assigned to the variable (optional), between 0 and 255.

Arduino Simple Code Example

```
byte sensorData = 100;
unsigned char status = 255;
```

- The first line declares a *byte* variable called *sensorData* and assigns it the value 100.
- The second line declares an *unsigned char* variable *status* and assigns it the value 255.

Notes

- *byte* and *unsigned char* are interchangeable, but *byte* is more commonly used for readability when dealing with raw data or communication protocols.
- Both types are unsigned, meaning they can only represent positive numbers, making them ideal for binary operations, bit manipulation, and storing data that doesn't require negative values.

Warnings

- Be careful not to assign values outside the range of 0 to 255, as this will cause overflow and result in unexpected behavior.
- If you need to store negative numbers, use a *char* or *int* instead of *unsigned char* or *byte*.

MicroPython Syntax Use

```
variableName = value
```

MicroPython Syntax Explanation
In MicroPython, there is no specific *unsigned char* or *byte* type. Instead, you can use regular integers to store values in the range of 0 to 255. MicroPython automatically handles values based on their size.

boolean: True/False Values

In Arduino, *boolean* is a data type that can store one of two possible values: *true* or *false*. These values represent logical states and are commonly used in control structures, such as conditional statements and loops. The *boolean* data type occupies 1 byte of memory.

Use Purpose
The *boolean* data type is used for logical operations where you only need to know if something is either true or false. It is commonly used for conditions like checking whether a sensor is activated, a button is pressed, or if a certain threshold has been reached.

Arduino Syntax Use

```
boolean variableName = true;
boolean variableName = false;
```

Arduino Syntax Explanation

In Arduino, the *boolean* keyword is used to declare a variable that holds a *true* or *false* value:

- *variableName*: The name of the variable.
- *true* or *false*: The initial value assigned to the variable, representing a logical state.

Arduino Simple Code Example

```
boolean isButtonPressed = false;
void loop() {
if (digitalRead(2) == HIGH) {
isButtonPressed = true;
} else {
isButtonPressed = false;
}
}
```

- The first line declares a *boolean* variable called *isButtonPressed* and initializes it to *false*.
- The code inside the loop checks if pin 2 is HIGH (button pressed) and updates *isButtonPressed* accordingly.

Notes

- *boolean* variables store either *true* (1) or *false* (0).
- This data type is useful when you need to check or set conditions, such as reading sensor states or toggling hardware on/off.

Warnings

- While *boolean* values are represented as 1 (true) and 0 (false), assigning values other than 1 or 0 may still result in unexpected behavior. Stick to using *true* or *false* for clarity.

- Be mindful of the fact that a *boolean* in Arduino uses 1 byte of memory, which may be a consideration when working with memory-constrained devices.

MicroPython Syntax Use

```
variableName = True
variableName = False
```

MicroPython Syntax Explanation
In MicroPython, *boolean* values are represented by the built-in *True* and *False* keywords. There is no specific *boolean* data type, but *True* and *False* are treated as logical values.

MicroPython Simple Code Example

```
is_button_pressed = False
if pin.value() == 1:
    is_button_pressed = True
```

- The first line declares a variable *is_button_pressed* and initializes it to *False*.
- The code checks if the pin value is 1 (indicating a button press) and updates *is_button_pressed* to *True*.

Notes

- In MicroPython, booleans are handled using the built-in *True* and *False* values.
- Boolean values can be used in control structures like *if* statements to check conditions.

Warnings

- Boolean values in Python are case-sensitive, so always use *True* and *False* (with capital T and F). Using lowercase will cause an error.
- Booleans in Python do not take up as much memory as in Arduino, as Python automatically manages data types.

String: A String Object to Handle Text

In Arduino, *String* is a data type that allows you to store and manipulate sequences of characters (text). It is an object, which provides more flexibility and functions for working with text compared to traditional character arrays. A *String* object can be used to concatenate, compare, and extract parts of text.

Use Purpose
The *String* object is used when you need to handle and manipulate text in your Arduino programs. It simplifies working with text, making it easier to join, split, and format strings. This is commonly used in scenarios like displaying text on screens, sending or receiving text via serial communication, or handling user input.

Arduino Syntax Use

```
String variableName = "text";
```

Arduino Syntax Explanation
In Arduino, the *String* keyword is used to declare a string object:

- *variableName*: The name of the String variable.
- *"text"*: The initial text (string) assigned to the variable.

Arduino Simple Code Example

```
String message = "Hello, World!";
void setup() {
Serial.begin(9600);
Serial.println(message);
}
```

- The first line declares a *String* object named *message* and initializes it with the text "Hello, World!".
- Inside the *setup()* function, the message is printed to the serial monitor.

Notes

- The *String* object in Arduino provides many useful functions like *length()*, *substring()*, *concat()*, and *indexOf()*, allowing you to easily manipulate text.
- *String* objects offer flexibility but can use more memory compared to simple character arrays.

Warnings

- Be cautious when using *String* objects in memory-constrained environments (like smaller Arduino boards), as dynamic memory allocation with strings can cause memory fragmentation and lead to crashes or unexpected behavior.
- For memory efficiency, consider using character arrays if you only need simple text handling.

MicroPython Syntax Use

```
variableName = "text"
```

MicroPython Syntax Explanation

In MicroPython, strings are handled as immutable sequences of characters. There is no special *String* object as in Arduino; instead, Python's built-in *str* type is used to handle text.

MicroPython Simple Code Example

```
message = "Hello, World!"
print(message)
```

- The first line declares a variable *message* and initializes it with the text "Hello, World!".
- The second line prints the message to the console.

Notes

- In MicroPython, strings are automatically handled as *str* objects, which means you can use string methods like *len()*, *upper()*, and *split()* without needing to import any additional libraries.
- Strings in Python are immutable, meaning once a string is created, it cannot be changed. If you modify a string, a new string object is created.

Warnings

- In MicroPython, string operations can be slower on resource-limited devices. Be mindful of using large or complex string manipulations in performance-critical sections of your program.
- Python strings are case-sensitive, so ensure you handle text with the correct casing when working with string comparisons or operations.

Array: Collections of Elements of the Same Type

In Arduino, an *array* is a collection of elements of the same data type, stored in contiguous memory locations. Each element in the array can be accessed using an index, starting from 0. Arrays allow you to store and manage multiple values of the same type (e.g., integers, floats, characters) using a single variable.

Use Purpose

Arrays are used when you need to store and manage multiple values of the same type. They are especially useful when dealing with repetitive data, like sensor readings, or when you need to iterate over multiple elements for tasks like calculations, storing a series of inputs, or performing batch operations.

Arduino Syntax Use

```
type arrayName[arraySize];
type arrayName[arraySize] = {value1, value2, value3};
```

Arduino Syntax Explanation

In Arduino, arrays are declared by specifying the data type, array name, and the number of elements (*arraySize*):

- *type*: The data type of the array elements (e.g., *int*, *float*, *char*).
- *arrayName*: The name of the array variable.
- *arraySize*: The number of elements in the array.
- Values can be assigned directly using curly braces.

Arduino Simple Code Example

```
int numbers[5] = {10, 20, 30, 40, 50};
void setup() {
Serial.begin(9600);
for (int i = 0; i < 5; i++) {
Serial.println(numbers[i]);
}
}
```

- The first line declares an *int* array named *numbers* with 5 elements initialized to {10, 20, 30, 40, 50}.
- The loop prints each element of the array to the serial monitor.

Notes

- The size of the array must be specified when it is declared, and arrays are zero-indexed, meaning the first element is accessed using index 0.
- You can update or access specific elements in the array using the index, e.g., *numbers[2]* refers to the third element in the array.

Warnings

- Accessing an element outside the declared array size (out of bounds) will result in undefined behavior, potentially leading to memory corruption.
- Be careful when working with large arrays, as they can consume a significant amount of memory, especially on Arduino boards with limited RAM.

MicroPython Syntax Use

```
arrayName = [value1, value2, value3]
```

MicroPython Syntax Explanation
In MicroPython, arrays are typically handled using Python's built-in list type, which can store elements of the same or different types. Lists are dynamic, meaning their size can change, and elements are accessed using index values.

MicroPython Simple Code Example

```
numbers = [10, 20, 30, 40, 50]
for i in range(len(numbers)):
    print(numbers[i])
```

- The first line declares a list *numbers* initialized with 5 elements.
- The *for* loop iterates over the list and prints each element.

Notes

- In MicroPython, lists are dynamic, meaning their size can grow or shrink, unlike arrays in Arduino, where the size is fixed.
- Lists in MicroPython can hold elements of different types, but it's recommended to keep the same type for consistency in numerical operations.

Warnings

- Lists in MicroPython may consume more memory than fixed-size arrays in Arduino, especially when storing large datasets.
- Ensure you handle lists carefully in resource-constrained environments to avoid memory and performance issues.

Chapter 10. Control structure

Chapter Overview

Control structures are essential components of programming, enabling decision-making and looping processes in a program. This chapter focuses on common control structures such as `if`, `else if`, `else`, `switch-case`, and looping structures (`for`, `while`, `do-while`) in Arduino and MicroPython environments. Understanding these structures allows developers to create dynamic programs that respond to changing inputs and conditions.

Chapter Purpose

The purpose of this chapter is to:

- Introduce key control structures for decision-making and iteration.
- Demonstrate how to use `if`, `else if`, and `else` for conditional logic.
- Explore `switch-case` and its alternative in MicroPython.
- Explain looping structures such as `for`, `while`, and `do-while`.
- Provide examples of exiting loops (`break`), skipping iterations (`continue`), and returning values from functions (`return`).
- Highlight differences between Arduino and MicroPython syntax for these control structures.

Chapter Syntax Table

Control Structure	Arduino Syntax	MicroPython Syntax
if	`if (condition) { /* code */ }`	`if condition: # code`
else if / elif	`else if (condition) { /* code */ }`	`elif condition: # code`
else	`else { /* code */ }`	`else: # code`
switch-case	`switch (variable) { case value1: /* code */ }`	`if-elif-else` used instead
for loop	`for (init; condition; increment) { /* code */ }`	`for variable in range(start, stop): # code`
while loop	`while (condition) { /* code */ }`	`while condition: # code`
do-while loop	`do { /* code */ } while (condition);`	`while True: # code with break`
break	`break;`	`break`
continue	`continue;`	`continue`
return	`return;` or `return value;`	`return` or `return value`

if: Conditional Statement

In programming, *if* is a conditional statement that allows the program to execute a block of code only if a specified condition is true. It is one of the most fundamental control structures and is used to make decisions within a program based on the values of variables or expressions.

Use Purpose
The *if* statement is used when you want to execute code only under certain conditions. For example, you may want to turn on an LED only if a sensor value exceeds a threshold or send a message if a button is pressed.

Arduino Syntax Use

```
if (condition) {
// Code to execute if the condition is true
}
```

Arduino Syntax Explanation
In Arduino, the *if* statement checks whether the *condition* inside the parentheses is true. If the condition evaluates to *true*, the code inside the curly braces is executed. If it is *false*, the code is skipped.

- *condition*: A logical expression or comparison that evaluates to *true* or *false*.

Arduino Simple Code Example

```
int sensorValue = analogRead(A0);
if (sensorValue > 500) {
digitalWrite(LED_BUILTIN, HIGH);
}
```

- The *if* statement checks if the sensor value from analog pin A0 is greater than 500. If it is, the built-in LED is turned on.

Notes

- The condition can use comparison operators (e.g., ==, >, <, >=, <=) or logical operators (e.g., && for AND, || for OR).
- If the condition is false, the code inside the *if* block is ignored.

Warnings

- Make sure the condition inside the *if* statement is correctly formed to avoid unintended behavior. A common mistake is using = (assignment) instead of == (comparison).
- The code inside the *if* block is executed only once when the condition becomes true. If you want to repeat the check, you must place the *if* statement inside a loop like *loop()*.

MicroPython Syntax Use

```
if condition:
# Code to execute if the condition is true
```

MicroPython Syntax Explanation

In MicroPython, the *if* statement is similar to Arduino. The condition is followed by a colon (:), and the code block is indented. If the condition evaluates to *true*, the indented code block is executed.

MicroPython Simple Code Example

```
sensor_value = 400
if sensor_value > 300:
print("Sensor value is high")
```

- The *if* statement checks if *sensor_value* is greater than 300. If true, it prints "Sensor value is high."

Notes

- In MicroPython, indentation is crucial to indicate which code belongs inside the *if* block.
- Conditions can include comparisons and logical operators, similar to Arduino.

Warnings

- Ensure proper indentation in MicroPython, as it defines code blocks. Incorrect indentation can lead to syntax errors.
- As with Arduino, be careful when forming conditions. Misuse of assignment = instead of comparison == can lead to unexpected results.

else if: Conditional Statement for Multiple Conditions

In programming, *else if* is used after an initial *if* statement to check additional conditions if the first condition is false. It allows the program to evaluate multiple conditions in sequence and execute the appropriate block of code based on which condition is true. If none of the conditions are met, you can use a final *else* block to execute default code.

Use Purpose
The *else if* statement is used when you need to check multiple conditions and perform different actions based on which condition is true. It helps in situations where you have more than two possible outcomes, such as controlling different device behaviors based on sensor readings.

Arduino Syntax Use

```
if (condition1) {
// Code to execute if condition1 is true
} else if (condition2) {
// Code to execute if condition2 is true
} else {
// Code to execute if none of the conditions are true
}
```

Arduino Syntax Explanation
In Arduino, the *if* statement checks the first condition:

- If *condition1* is true, the first block of code is executed.
- If *condition1* is false but *condition2* is true, the *else if* block is executed.
- If both *condition1* and *condition2* are false, the *else* block is executed.

Arduino Simple Code Example

```
int sensorValue = analogRead(A0);
if (sensorValue > 800) {
digitalWrite(LED_BUILTIN, HIGH);
} else if (sensorValue > 500) {
digitalWrite(LED_BUILTIN, LOW);
} else {
digitalWrite(LED_BUILTIN, LOW);
Serial.println("Low sensor value");
}
```

- The *if* statement checks if *sensorValue* is greater than 800. If true, the LED is turned on.
- If the value is not greater than 800 but greater than 500, the LED is turned off.
- If neither condition is met, the LED is turned off and a message is printed to the serial monitor.

Notes

- You can have multiple *else if* statements to check multiple conditions in a sequence.
- The *else* block is optional and only runs if none of the *if* or *else if* conditions are true.

Warnings

- Make sure your conditions are mutually exclusive if needed, meaning only one should be true at a time. If multiple conditions can be true, the first matching condition will execute, and the remaining conditions will be skipped.
- If no *else* statement is provided and all conditions are false, no code will execute for that condition.

MicroPython Syntax Use

```
if condition1:
# Code to execute if condition1 is true
elif condition2:
# Code to execute if condition2 is true
else:
# Code to execute if none of the conditions are true
```

MicroPython Syntax Explanation

In MicroPython, *elif* is used instead of *else if*. The syntax is similar to Arduino, but indentation is used to define code blocks. Multiple conditions can be checked using *if*, *elif*, and *else*.

MicroPython Simple Code Example

```
sensor_value = 600 if sensor_value > 800:
print("High sensor value")
elif sensor_value > 500:
print("Medium sensor value")
else:
print("Low sensor value")
```

- The *if* statement checks if *sensor_value* is greater than 800. If true, it prints "High sensor value."
- If the value is not greater than 800 but greater than 500, it prints "Medium sensor value."
- If neither condition is met, it prints "Low sensor value."

Notes

- In MicroPython, *elif* serves the same purpose as *else if* in Arduino.
- Indentation is required to group code blocks in MicroPython.

Warnings

- Ensure proper indentation in MicroPython, as it defines the code structure. Incorrect indentation can lead to errors.
- As with Arduino, be mindful of the order of conditions. The first matching condition will execute, and the rest will be ignored.

else: Conditional Statement for Default Case

In programming, *else* is used as the final option in an *if-else* conditional structure. If none of the previous *if* or *else if* conditions are true, the code inside the *else* block will be executed. It acts as a "catch-all" for situations when all other conditions fail.

Use Purpose
The *else* statement is used when you need a default block of code to run if none of the specified conditions in the *if* or *else if* statements are met. This is useful when you want to handle cases where input or values fall outside of the expected conditions.

Arduino Syntax Use

```
if (condition1) {
// Code to execute if condition1 is true
} else {
// Code to execute if condition1 is false
}
```

Arduino Syntax Explanation
In Arduino, the *else* block is executed if the *if* condition is false:

- If *condition1* is true, the first block of code is executed.
- If *condition1* is false, the code inside the *else* block is executed.

Arduino Simple Code Example

```
int temperature = analogRead(A0);
if (temperature > 600) {
Serial.println("High temperature detected!");
} else {
Serial.println("Temperature is normal.");
}
```

- The *if* statement checks if *temperature* is greater than 600. If true, the message "High temperature detected!" is printed.
- If the *temperature* is less than or equal to 600, the *else* block prints "Temperature is normal."

Notes

- The *else* block does not take a condition—it's only executed if the previous *if* or *else if* statements are false.
- The *else* statement is optional; it can be omitted if no default action is needed.

Warnings

- The *else* block should always come after an *if* or *else if* statement.
- Ensure that the *if* condition properly handles all logical possibilities before relying on the *else* block for handling other cases.

MicroPython Syntax Use

```
if condition1:
# Code to execute if condition1 is true
else:
# Code to execute if condition1 is false
```

MicroPython Syntax Explanation

In MicroPython, the *else* block works similarly to Arduino. If the *if* condition is false, the code inside the *else* block is executed.

MicroPython Simple Code Example

```
temperature = 550 if temperature > 600:
print("High temperature detected!")
else:
print("Temperature is normal.")
```

- The *if* statement checks if *temperature* is greater than 600. If true, it prints "High temperature detected!"
- If the temperature is less than or equal to 600, the *else* block prints "Temperature is normal."

Notes

- The *else* block in MicroPython is used as a fallback when none of the preceding *if* conditions are true.
- Python relies on indentation to define code blocks, so make sure the *else* block is indented properly.

Warnings

- Be careful to use correct indentation in MicroPython, as incorrect indentation can cause syntax errors.
- The *else* block will execute only if all prior *if* or *elif* conditions are false, so structure conditions carefully to handle all expected cases.

switch-case: Conditional Statement for Multiple Options

In programming, *switch-case* is a control structure that allows you to test the value of a variable or expression and execute different blocks of code based on that value. Unlike *if-else* statements, which check conditions one by one, *switch-case* is typically used when a variable needs to be compared against multiple constant values, making the code cleaner and easier to maintain.

Use Purpose

The *switch-case* statement is useful when you need to perform different actions based on the value of a single variable, such as controlling different behaviors for different input values, modes, or states. It simplifies the code when there are multiple fixed choices.

Arduino Syntax Use

```
switch (variable) {
case value1:
// Code to execute if variable equals value1
break;
case value2:
// Code to execute if variable equals value2
break;
...
default:
// Code to execute if variable doesn't match any case
break;
}
```

Arduino Syntax Explanation

In Arduino, the *switch-case* statement checks the value of a variable and compares it to predefined cases:

- *variable*: The variable or expression being compared.
- *case value1*: The first case to match the variable's value. If it matches, the code inside this block is executed.
- *break;*: This stops further checking after a match is found. Without *break*, the code will "fall through" to the next case.
- *default*: The code inside the *default* block is executed if no other cases match.

Arduino Simple Code Example

```
int mode = 1;
void setup() {
Serial.begin(9600);
}
void loop() {
switch (mode) {
case 1:
Serial.println("Mode 1: LED on");
break;
case 2:
Serial.println("Mode 2: LED off");
break;
default:
Serial.println("Unknown mode");
break;
}
}
```

- The variable *mode* is compared against different cases. If *mode* equals 1, "Mode 1: LED on" is printed. If *mode* equals 2, "Mode 2: LED off" is printed. If *mode* does not match any case, the *default* case prints "Unknown mode."

Notes

- Each *case* is followed by a *break;* to prevent code from executing the following cases after a match. Without *break;*, the program will continue executing subsequent cases (called "fall through").
- The *default* case is optional but is typically included to handle unexpected values.

Warnings

- Ensure you use the *break;* statement after each case to avoid fall-through behavior, which can cause unwanted results.
- *switch-case* works best for comparing a variable to constant values. It cannot be used for ranges or complex conditions (use *if-else* for that).

MicroPython Syntax Use
MicroPython does not have a native *switch-case* structure. Instead, you can achieve the same functionality using *if-elif-else* statements.

MicroPython Syntax Explanation
In MicroPython, *if-elif-else* is used to mimic *switch-case* functionality. Each *elif* block can act as a case, and *else* acts like the *default* case.

MicroPython Simple Code Example

```
mode = 1 if mode == 1:
print("Mode 1: LED on")
elif mode == 2:
print("Mode 2: LED off")
else:
print("Unknown mode")
```

- The *if* statement checks if *mode* equals 1. If true, it prints "Mode 1: LED on." If *mode* equals 2, it prints "Mode 2: LED off." If neither condition is met, the *else* block prints "Unknown mode."

Notes

- In MicroPython, using *if-elif-else* provides the same functionality as *switch-case*, but with more flexibility since conditions can be more complex.
- Unlike Arduino's *switch-case*, MicroPython can evaluate ranges and conditions in *if* statements.

Warnings

- Since there is no direct *switch-case* structure in MicroPython, ensure that your conditions in *if-elif-else* are mutually exclusive to avoid logic errors.
- In performance-sensitive code, using *if-elif-else* may be slower than *switch-case* when there are many options, though this is generally not an issue for small-scale applications.

for Loop: A Looping Structure for Iteration

A *for loop* is a control structure used to repeat a block of code a specific number of times. It allows you to iterate over a range of values or elements, making it ideal for tasks like counting, iterating through arrays, or performing repetitive operations.

Use Purpose
The *for loop* is used when you know in advance how many times you need to repeat a block of code. It is commonly used for tasks such as iterating through arrays, controlling hardware operations, or executing code based on a counter or sequence.

Arduino Syntax Use

```
for (initialization; condition; increment) {
// Code to execute in each iteration
}
```

Arduino Syntax Explanation
In Arduino, a *for loop* consists of three main components:

- *initialization*: Sets the starting value of the loop counter (e.g., int i = 0).
- *condition*: The loop continues to run as long as this condition is true (e.g., i < 10).
- *increment*: Updates the loop counter after each iteration (e.g., i++).

Arduino Simple Code Example

```
void setup() {
Serial.begin(9600);
for (int i = 0; i < 5; i++) {
Serial.print("Iteration: ");
Serial.println(i);
}
}
```

- The loop starts with *i = 0*, and as long as *i* is less than 5, the code inside the loop prints the current iteration number. After each iteration, *i* is incremented by 1.

Notes

- The *for loop* is often used when the number of iterations is known in advance. It's great for counting or iterating over arrays.
- You can modify any part of the loop (initialization, condition, increment) as needed for specific scenarios, like counting down or skipping values.

Warnings

- Be cautious of infinite loops. If the loop condition is always true (e.g., forgetting to update the loop counter), the program will run indefinitely.
- Ensure that your loop counter does not exceed array bounds when iterating through arrays, as this could lead to memory corruption or unexpected behavior.

MicroPython Syntax Use

```
for variable in range(start, stop):
# Code to execute in each iteration
```

MicroPython Syntax Explanation
In MicroPython, a *for loop* is often used with the *range()* function, which generates a sequence of numbers. The loop runs for each number in the sequence:

- *start*: The starting value (inclusive).
- *stop*: The stopping value (exclusive).

MicroPython Simple Code Example

```
for i in range(0, 5):
print("Iteration:", i)
```

- The loop starts at 0 and runs as long as *i* is less than 5, printing the iteration number for each loop.

Notes

- In MicroPython, *range(start, stop)* generates a sequence of numbers from *start* to *stop-1*. The loop runs for each value in that range.
- You can specify a step value in *range()* if you want to skip numbers (e.g., *range(0, 10, 2)* will count by twos).

Warnings

- Be careful with large ranges, as iterating over very large numbers in MicroPython can slow down your program, especially on resource-constrained devices.
- Make sure to properly define the range to avoid off-by-one errors where the loop runs one time too many or too few.

while Loop: A Looping Structure for Repeated Execution

A *while loop* is a control structure that allows you to repeatedly execute a block of code as long as a specified condition is true. Unlike a *for loop*, the number of iterations in a *while loop* is not known in advance; the loop will continue running until the condition becomes false.

Use Purpose

The *while loop* is used when you need to repeat a block of code but don't know beforehand how many times it will execute. It's useful for scenarios where you wait for a specific condition to be met, like waiting for a sensor value to reach a certain threshold or handling user input.

Arduino Syntax Use

```
while (condition) {
// Code to execute while the condition is true
}
```

Arduino Syntax Explanation

In Arduino, the *while* statement keeps running the loop as long as the *condition* inside the parentheses evaluates to true:

- *condition*: A logical expression that is checked before each iteration. The loop continues as long as this condition is true.

Arduino Simple Code Example

```
int buttonState = 0;
void loop() {
buttonState = digitalRead(2);
while (buttonState == LOW) {
// Wait for the button to be pressed
Serial.println("Waiting for button press...");
buttonState = digitalRead(2);
}
Serial.println("Button pressed!");
}
```

- The loop checks if the button (connected to pin 2) is pressed. If the button is not pressed (*LOW*), the *while* loop keeps printing "Waiting for button press..." until the button is pressed.

Notes

- The condition is evaluated before each iteration, so the loop may never execute if the condition is false at the start.
- Inside the loop, you should modify or update something to eventually make the condition false, otherwise, the loop will run indefinitely (infinite loop).

Warnings

- Ensure that the condition will eventually become false, or you risk creating an infinite loop, which can freeze the program.
- Be cautious when using *while* with input devices or sensors to ensure proper checks and updates are happening inside the loop.

MicroPython Syntax Use

```
while condition:
# Code to execute while the condition is true
```

MicroPython Syntax Explanation

In MicroPython, the *while* loop is similar to Arduino. The loop continues to execute as long as the *condition* is true.

MicroPython Simple Code Example

```
button_state = 0 while button_state == 0:
print("Waiting for button press...")
button_state = machine.Pin(2).value()
print("Button pressed!")
```

- The loop checks if the button (connected to pin 2) is pressed. If the button is not pressed (*button_state* == *0*), the loop keeps printing "Waiting for button press..." until the button is pressed.

Notes

- As in Arduino, the condition is evaluated before each loop iteration, and the loop runs while the condition is true.
- You can exit the loop by ensuring the condition eventually becomes false, usually by updating a variable inside the loop.

Warnings

- Be careful not to create infinite loops by ensuring that the condition will eventually be false.
- Improper handling of the condition may lead to performance issues, especially on resource-constrained devices.

do-while Loop: A Looping Structure that Executes at Least Once

A *do-while loop* is a control structure that allows you to repeatedly execute a block of code at least once, regardless of the condition, and then continue executing the block as long as a specified condition remains true. Unlike the *while loop*, the *do-while loop* checks the condition after executing the block of code, ensuring that the code runs at least once.

Use Purpose
The *do-while loop* is used when you want to ensure that a block of code executes at least once before checking a condition. It's useful when an action needs to be performed first, and then a condition is evaluated to determine if it should be repeated.

Arduino Syntax Use

```
do {
// Code to execute
} while (condition);
```

Arduino Syntax Explanation

In Arduino, the *do-while* loop will execute the block of code once, then check the *condition*:

- The code block between the *do* and *while* is executed first.
- After executing the code block, the *condition* is evaluated. If the *condition* is true, the loop repeats; if false, the loop terminates.

Arduino Simple Code Example

```
int count = 0;
void loop() {
do {
Serial.print("Count: ");
Serial.println(count);
count++;
} while (count < 5);
}
```

- The loop prints the value of *count* starting from 0 and increments it after each iteration. The loop continues as long as *count* is less than 5. The code runs at least once, even if *count* starts at a value of 5 or higher.

Notes

- The key difference from the *while* loop is that the condition is evaluated after the code block, meaning the code inside the loop will always execute at least once.
- The *do-while* loop is less commonly used but is helpful in cases where you want the loop body to execute at least once, such as for input validation or initial data processing.

Warnings

- Be careful with infinite loops, especially if the condition never becomes false. Since the code runs at least once, an infinite loop may occur if the condition remains true.
- Ensure that the condition is properly updated within the loop to eventually terminate it, or you may lock the program into an endless loop.

MicroPython Syntax Use

MicroPython does not have a direct *do-while* loop structure. However, you can simulate a *do-while* loop using a *while True* loop with a conditional *break*.

MicroPython Syntax Explanation

You can mimic a *do-while* loop in MicroPython by using an infinite *while* loop with a condition inside to exit the loop.

MicroPython Simple Code Example

```
count = 0 while True:
print("Count:", count)
count += 1 if count >= 5:
break
```

- The code inside the loop is executed at least once. The loop continues to print the value of *count* and increments it until *count* is greater than or equal to 5, at which point the *break* statement exits the loop.

Notes

- In MicroPython, there is no built-in *do-while* loop, but you can achieve the same effect using a *while True* loop with a conditional *break* statement.
- The loop will always run at least once because the *break* condition is checked only after executing the loop body.

Warnings

- Be careful to ensure that the *break* condition is eventually met, or the loop will run indefinitely.
- Mimicking the *do-while* loop in this way can make code harder to read, so use this pattern only when necessary.

break: Exiting a Loop or Switch-Case

The *break* statement is used to immediately exit a loop or a *switch-case* structure, regardless of the condition or iteration count. When *break* is encountered, the control of the program jumps to the first statement after the loop or *switch-case*.

Use Purpose
The *break* statement is commonly used when you need to prematurely exit a loop or stop a *switch-case* once a matching case has been found. It helps prevent further execution within the loop or case, saving time and avoiding unnecessary operations.

Arduino Syntax Use

```
break;
```

Arduino Syntax Explanation
In Arduino, the *break* statement can be used inside loops (like *for*, *while*, *do-while*) and *switch-case* blocks to exit the structure:

- In loops, *break* immediately terminates the loop and the program continues with the first statement after the loop.
- In *switch-case*, *break* prevents the code from "falling through" to the next case by exiting the *switch-case* block.

Arduino Simple Code Example in a Loop

```
for (int i = 0; i < 10; i++) {
if (i == 5) {
break; // Exit the loop when i is 5
}
Serial.println(i);
}
Serial.println("Loop ended.");
```

- In this example, the loop will run until *i* equals 5, at which point the *break* statement exits the loop. The message "Loop ended." is then printed.

Arduino Simple Code Example in Switch-Case

```
int mode = 2;
switch (mode) {
case 1:
Serial.println("Mode 1 selected.");
break;
case 2:
Serial.println("Mode 2 selected.");
break;
default:
Serial.println("Unknown mode.");
break;
}
```

- The *break* statement ensures that after the case for mode 2 is executed, the program exits the *switch-case* structure and does not execute further cases.

Notes

- In a loop, *break* is useful when you need to stop the loop based on a condition.
- In a *switch-case*, *break* prevents the execution of the code for subsequent cases.

Warnings

- Using *break* inside loops without careful consideration can lead to unintended behavior, such as skipping important parts of the loop.
- Failing to use *break* in a *switch-case* can cause "fall-through," where multiple cases are executed unintentionally.

MicroPython Syntax Use

```
break
```

MicroPython Syntax Explanation
In MicroPython, *break* works similarly to Arduino. It is used inside loops to exit the loop prematurely or inside *switch-case*-like structures (though Python uses *if-elif-else* rather than *switch-case*).

MicroPython Simple Code Example in a Loop

```
for i in range(10):
if i == 5:
break # Exit the loop when i is 5
print(i)
print("Loop ended.")
```

- In this example, the loop will run until *i* equals 5, and then the *break* statement exits the loop. The message "Loop ended." is printed after the loop.

Notes

- *break* is typically used in loops like *for* and *while* to exit the loop based on a condition.
- Python does not have a native *switch-case* structure, so *break* is not used in *if-elif-else* blocks, but it can still be used in loops.

Warnings

- Use *break* carefully in loops to avoid prematurely exiting important iterations.
- In MicroPython, as with Arduino, misusing *break* can cause unexpected behavior if not handled properly in loops.

continue: Skip the Current Iteration of a Loop

The *continue* statement is used inside loops to skip the remaining code in the current iteration and move on to the next iteration of the loop. It allows the loop to continue running, but the current iteration's execution is interrupted.

Use Purpose
The *continue* statement is used when you want to skip certain iterations of a loop based on a condition without exiting the loop entirely. It's useful for ignoring specific cases while still continuing to process the rest of the loop.

Arduino Syntax Use

```
continue;
```

Arduino Syntax Explanation
In Arduino, the *continue* statement works inside loops (*for*, *while*, or *do-while*):

- When *continue* is encountered, the loop immediately jumps to the next iteration, skipping any code after the *continue* statement within that iteration.
- In a *for loop*, this means the increment step is executed, and in *while* loops, the condition is re-evaluated.

Arduino Simple Code Example

```
for (int i = 0; i < 10; i++) {
if (i == 5) {
continue; // Skip the iteration when i is 5
}
Serial.println(i);
}
```

- In this example, the loop prints the value of *i* from 0 to 9, but when *i* equals 5, the *continue* statement skips that iteration. As a result, the number 5 is not printed.

Notes

- The *continue* statement only skips the current iteration of the loop. The loop itself continues to run.
- It's useful when you want to avoid certain values or conditions during a loop without breaking out of the loop entirely.

Warnings

- Using *continue* too frequently or inappropriately can make the code harder to follow. Make sure to use it only when necessary.
- In nested loops, *continue* only affects the current loop, not outer loops.

MicroPython Syntax Use

```
continue
```

MicroPython Syntax Explanation

In MicroPython, the *continue* statement works the same way as in Arduino. It is used inside loops to skip the rest of the current iteration and jump to the next iteration of the loop.

MicroPython Simple Code Example

```
for i in range(10):
if i == 5:
continue # Skip the iteration when i is 5
print(i)
```

- In this example, the loop prints the values from 0 to 9, but skips the value 5 due to the *continue* statement.

Notes

- In Python, the *continue* statement behaves exactly the same as in Arduino, allowing you to skip specific iterations of the loop without breaking the loop entirely.

Warnings

- Be careful when using *continue*, especially in complex loops, as it can make the logic harder to understand.
- Like in Arduino, using *continue* in nested loops only affects the loop where it is used.

return: Exiting a Function and Returning a Value

The *return* statement is used to exit a function and optionally return a value to the calling function. When *return* is encountered, the function stops executing, and control is passed back to the part of the program that called the function. The *return* statement can also send a value back to the caller.

Use Purpose
The *return* statement is used to end a function's execution early or to send a value from a function back to the part of the program that called it. It is essential for functions that perform calculations or make decisions and need to provide results.

Arduino Syntax Use

```
return;
return value;
```

Arduino Syntax Explanation

In Arduino, the *return* statement can be used in two ways:

- *return;* exits the function without returning a value. This is used in *void* functions (which don't return values).
- *return value;* exits the function and returns a value. This is used in functions that specify a return type (e.g., *int*, *float*).

Arduino Simple Code Example

Example 1: Function with no return value (void function)

```
void printMessage() {
Serial.println("Hello, World!");
return; // Function exits here
}
```

- In this example, the *return* statement exits the function after printing the message. Since the function has a *void* return type, no value is returned.

Example 2: Function with a return value

```
int addNumbers(int a, int b) {
int result = a + b;
return result; // Return the result of the addition
}
```

- Here, the function *addNumbers()* takes two integers as arguments, adds them together, and returns the result to the caller.

Notes

- The *return* statement can appear anywhere in a function. Once it is encountered, the function immediately stops executing.
- In *void* functions (those that do not return a value), *return;* is optional. The function will automatically exit when the last statement is executed, but you can use *return;* to exit early if needed.

Warnings

- A function with a non-void return type must use *return* to send a value back. If you forget to return a value in such functions, the compiler may give a warning or error.
- In functions that return values, ensure the correct data type is returned (e.g., returning a float in an int function may cause unexpected behavior).

MicroPython Syntax Use

```
return value
return
```

MicroPython Syntax Explanation
In MicroPython, the *return* statement behaves similarly to Arduino. It is used to exit a function and optionally return a value to the caller.

MicroPython Simple Code Example

Example 1: Function with no return value

```
def print_message():
    print("Hello, World!")
    return
```

- In this example, the function *print_message()* prints a message, and the *return* statement is used to exit the function, even though it is not required.

Example 2: Function with a return value

```
def add_numbers(a, b):
    result = a + b
    return result
```

- The function *add_numbers()* takes two arguments, adds them, and returns the result to the caller.

Notes

- Like in Arduino, the *return* statement in Python is optional in functions that don't return a value, but it can be used to exit the function early.
- Python functions can return multiple values by separating them with commas (e.g., *return a, b*).

Warnings

- Ensure that the correct data type is returned, especially when expecting specific types in calculations.
- In Python, if a function does not explicitly use *return*, it automatically returns *None* when it finishes executing.

Chapter -11 . Characters and Strings

Chapter Overview:

Characters and strings are essential elements in programming for handling text and symbolic data. In Arduino, characters are stored as char types, while MicroPython manages characters as strings of length 1. This chapter explores how to declare, manipulate, and use characters and strings in Arduino and MicroPython. Understanding these concepts is crucial for tasks like processing text, user input, and communication through serial interfaces.

Chapter Purpose
The purpose of this chapter is to:

- Introduce the char data type in Arduino for handling individual characters.
- Explain how to declare and manipulate characters in both Arduino and MicroPython.
- Show how MicroPython uses strings to represent individual characters.
- Highlight differences in how characters and strings are handled between Arduino and MicroPython.

Chapter Syntax Table

Data Type	Arduino Syntax	MicroPython Syntax
char	`char variableName = 'A';`	`variableName = 'A'` (treated as a string of length 1)
ASCII value	`char variableName = ASCII_value;`	Not applicable (no ASCII-specific handling)
Strings	`String variableName = "text";`	`variableName = "text"`

Characters (char): 8-bit Signed Character

In Arduino, *char* is an 8-bit data type used to store a single character or a small integer value. It can represent a character from the ASCII table, such as a letter, number, or symbol. Since *char* is a signed data type, it can hold values between -128 and 127. Each character is stored as a corresponding ASCII value.

Use Purpose

The *char* data type is commonly used to store and manipulate individual characters. It is also used when handling text or when you need to work with small integers in a limited range. For example, it's useful for storing user input or transmitting characters via serial communication.

Arduino Syntax Use

```
char variableName = 'character';
char variableName = ASCII_value;
```

Arduino Syntax Explanation

In Arduino, the *char* keyword is used to declare a variable that holds a single character:

- *variableName*: The name of the variable.
- *'character'*: A single character enclosed in single quotes (e.g., 'A').
- *ASCII_value*: A numerical value representing the character's ASCII code (e.g., 65 for 'A').

Arduino Simple Code Example

```
char letter = 'A';
char numberChar = '5';
void setup() {
Serial.begin(9600);
Serial.print("Letter: ");
Serial.println(letter);
Serial.print("Character 5 as ASCII: ");
Serial.println(numberChar);
}
```

- The first line declares a *char* variable called *letter* and assigns it the value 'A'.
- The second line declares a *char* variable *numberChar* and assigns it the character '5'.
- The *Serial.print()* statements output the values stored in the *char* variables to the serial monitor.

Notes
- Each *char* variable takes up 1 byte of memory.
- The value of a *char* can be a character (e.g., 'A') or its ASCII equivalent (e.g., 65 for 'A'). You can switch between them easily since characters are stored as their ASCII values.

Warnings
- When dealing with numeric characters (e.g., '5'), remember that the character '5' is different from the integer 5. The character '5' has an ASCII value of 53, whereas the integer 5 is just the number 5.
- Always enclose characters in single quotes. Using double quotes will treat the value as a string (an array of characters), not a single character.

MicroPython Syntax Use

```
variableName = 'character'
```

MicroPython Syntax Explanation
In MicroPython, *char* does not exist as a specific data type. Instead, characters are handled as strings with a length of 1. A single character in MicroPython is stored and manipulated as a string of length 1.

MicroPython Simple Code Example

```
letter = 'A'
number_char = '5'
print("Letter:", letter)
print("Character 5:", number_char)
```

- In MicroPython, characters like 'A' and '5' are simply treated as strings with a length of 1.

Notes

- In MicroPython, there is no separate *char* data type. Characters are handled as strings.
- Python's *str* type can store individual characters, and you can use string functions to manipulate them.

Warnings

- Since MicroPython treats characters as strings, they cannot be directly used in arithmetic operations as in C-based languages.
- Be mindful of character encoding and the difference between characters and their integer (ASCII) representations when working with text and numerical data.

Chapter 12. Data Conversion Techniques

Chapter Overview

Data conversion techniques are essential in programming for converting data types from one form to another, such as converting strings to integers, integers to strings, and floats to strings. These conversions are frequently required when handling inputs, outputs, or communication between devices. This chapter explains how to perform these conversions in both Arduino and MicroPython, highlighting the different syntax and methods available for each platform.

Chapter Purpose

The purpose of this chapter is to:

- Explain how to convert strings to integers and integers to strings in Arduino and MicroPython.
- Provide methods for converting floating-point numbers to strings for both platforms.
- Highlight the importance of data conversion in programming, especially when dealing with input/output operations and communication protocols.
- Offer simple code examples and warnings about potential issues related to data conversions.

Chapter Syntax Table

Conversion	Arduino Syntax	MicroPython Syntax
String to Integer	`int variable = stringVariable.toInt();`	`variable = int(stringVariable)`
Integer to String	`String variable = String(intVariable);`	`variable = str(intVariable)`
Float to String	`String variable = String(floatVariable, decimalPlaces);`	`variable = "{:.2f}".format(floatVariable)`

String to Integer Conversion

In Arduino and MicroPython, converting a string to an integer means taking a sequence of characters (usually representing numbers) and converting it into an actual integer data type. This is often done when you receive input in the form of a string but need to perform mathematical operations with the data.

Use Purpose
String-to-integer conversion is useful when dealing with input data that comes as text, such as from a sensor, a keypad, or user input, but you need to process it as a number. For example, when reading numbers from a serial input or a web server, the data is often received as a string and needs to be converted into an integer for calculations.

Arduino: String to Integer Conversion

Arduino Syntax Use

```
int variableName = stringVariable.toInt();
```

Arduino Syntax Explanation
In Arduino, you can convert a *String* object to an integer using the *toInt()* function. This method reads the numeric characters in the string and converts them into an integer value.

Arduino Simple Code Example

```
String numberString = "1234";
int number = 0;
void setup() {
Serial.begin(9600);
number = numberString.toInt(); // Convert String to integer
Serial.print("Converted number: ");
Serial.println(number);
}
```

- The *numberString* holds the string "1234".
- The *toInt()* method converts the string "1234" into the integer 1234 and stores it in the *number* variable.
- The result is printed to the serial monitor.

Notes

- The *toInt()* method only works for valid numeric strings. If the string contains non-numeric characters, it returns 0.
- It ignores leading whitespace and stops converting at the first non-numeric character.

Warnings

- If the string contains characters other than digits, the conversion may not work as expected and return 0.
- Be cautious of empty strings, as they will also return 0.

MicroPython: String to Integer Conversion

MicroPython Syntax Use

```
variableName = int(stringVariable)
```

MicroPython Syntax Explanation
In MicroPython, the built-in *int()* function is used to convert a string into an integer. This function reads the numeric characters in the string and converts them to an integer.

MicroPython Simple Code Example

```
number_string = "1234"
number = int(number_string)
print("Converted number:", number)
```

- The *number_string* holds the string "1234".
- The *int()* function converts the string "1234" into the integer 1234.

Notes

- The *int()* function will raise an error if the string contains non-numeric characters (except for leading/trailing spaces, which are ignored).
- It's more strict than Arduino's *toInt()* as it doesn't silently return 0 for invalid input.

Warnings

- Be sure the string represents a valid integer. If the string contains non-numeric characters (except whitespace), a *ValueError* will be raised.
- Using *int()* on empty strings will also cause an error, so handle invalid input properly with try/except or validation.

Integer to String Conversion

Integer-to-string conversion is the process of taking an integer (a whole number) and converting it into a string (a sequence of characters). This is useful when you need to display numbers as text or send them as strings in communication protocols.

Use Purpose
Converting an integer to a string is commonly used in situations where you need to send a number as text, display it on an LCD screen, or concatenate it with other strings. For example, when you want to print a number with additional text, it needs to be converted to a string first.

Arduino: Integer to String Conversion

Arduino Syntax Use

```
String stringVariable = String(intVariable);
```

Arduino Syntax Explanation
In Arduino, you can convert an integer to a string using the *String()* constructor. This method takes the integer value and converts it into a string.

Arduino Simple Code Example
```
int number = 1234;
String numberString;
void setup() {
Serial.begin(9600);
numberString = String(number); // Convert integer to String
Serial.print("Converted String: ");
Serial.println(numberString);
}
```

- The *String()* constructor converts the integer *number* (1234) into a string and stores it in the *numberString* variable.
- The string is then printed to the serial monitor.

Notes

- The *String()* constructor is the simplest way to convert an integer into a string in Arduino.
- You can also use *itoa()* (integer-to-ascii) function for manual conversion, but *String()* is more beginner-friendly.

Warnings

- Be cautious when using the *String()* object in memory-constrained environments (like small Arduino boards) because dynamic memory allocation may cause fragmentation.

MicroPython: Integer to String Conversion

MicroPython Syntax Use

```
stringVariable = str(intVariable)
```

MicroPython Syntax Explanation
In MicroPython, the *str()* function is used to convert an integer into a string. This function reads the integer and converts it to a string representation.

MicroPython Simple Code Example

```
number = 1234
number_string = str(number)
print("Converted String:", number_string)
```

- The *str()* function converts the integer *number* (1234) into a string and stores it in the *number_string* variable.

Notes

- In MicroPython, *str()* is the simplest and most common way to convert integers into strings. It works similarly to the *String()* constructor in Arduino.
- You can concatenate strings and integers easily once converted.

Warnings

- Ensure that the variable being converted is a valid integer; otherwise, using *str()* on non-integer types could produce unexpected results.

Float to String Conversion

Float-to-string conversion is the process of converting a floating-point number (a number with decimals) into a string (a sequence of characters). This is useful when you want to display or send a float value as text, such as printing sensor data or combining a float value with other strings.

Use Purpose
Converting a float to a string is often necessary when you need to display the floating-point number as text (e.g., on an LCD or serial monitor) or when you need to transmit it as part of a message (e.g., over a network or serial communication).

Arduino: Float to String Conversion

Arduino Syntax Use

```
String stringVariable = String(floatVariable, decimalPlaces);
dtostrf(floatVariable, width, decimalPlaces, buffer); // Alternative method
```

Arduino Syntax Explanation

In Arduino, you can use the *String()* function to convert a float to a string, specifying the number of decimal places you want to keep. Alternatively, you can use the *dtostrf()* function to control the formatting more precisely.

- *floatVariable*: The float value you want to convert.
- *decimalPlaces*: The number of decimal places to display in the resulting string.

Arduino Simple Code Example

```
float temperature = 23.4567;
String temperatureString;
void setup() {
Serial.begin(9600);
temperatureString = String(temperature, 2); // Convert float to String with 2 decimal places
Serial.print("Temperature as String: ");
Serial.println(temperatureString);
}
```

- The *String()* constructor converts the float *temperature* (23.4567) into a string with 2 decimal places (resulting in "23.46") and stores it in the *temperatureString* variable.

Alternative Method (Using `dtostrf`)

```
char buffer[10];
dtostrf(temperature, 6, 2, buffer);
Serial.println(buffer);
```

- This method uses *dtostrf()* to format the float into a string with 6 characters wide and 2 decimal places. The result is stored in the *buffer* array.

Notes

- *String()* is simpler for beginners, but *dtostrf()* provides more control over the formatting (like padding with spaces).
- *dtostrf()* stands for "double to string representation of float", but it works for float values as well.

Warnings

- Avoid excessive use of the *String()* object on memory-constrained boards, as it may lead to memory fragmentation.
- Be careful with the number of decimal places—more places require more memory.

MicroPython: Float to String Conversion

MicroPython Syntax Use

```
stringVariable = "{:.2f}".format(floatVariable)
stringVariable = str(floatVariable) // Simple conversion
```

MicroPython Syntax Explanation
In MicroPython, you can convert a float to a string using the *str()* function for simple conversions or *format()* for more control over decimal places.

- *floatVariable*: The float value you want to convert.
- *"{:.2f}"*: This is a format string that specifies 2 decimal places.

MicroPython Simple Code Example (Using `format()`)

```
temperature = 23.4567
temperature_string = "{:.2f}".format(temperature)
print("Temperature as String:", temperature_string)
```

- This example converts the float *temperature* (23.4567) into a string with 2 decimal places (resulting in "23.46").

Simple Conversion (Using `str()`)

```
temperature_string = str(temperature)
print("Temperature as String:", temperature_string)
```

- The *str()* function converts the float *temperature* directly into a string, retaining as many decimal places as the original value.

Notes

- Using *format()* gives you control over how many decimal places to show, making it a preferred method when precision is required.
- *str()* provides a quick and easy way to convert a float to a string without worrying about formatting.

Warnings

- Be mindful of the number of decimal places to display—showing too many can consume more memory and make the output harder to read.
- Ensure that your float values are within the precision limits of the device to avoid rounding errors.

Chapter 13. Communication Protocols

Chapter Overview

In embedded systems, communication protocols are essential for enabling data transfer between devices, sensors, and peripherals. This chapter focuses on the most common communication protocols used in Arduino and MicroPython: UART, SPI, I2C, and Bluetooth. Each protocol serves different use cases, from wired to wireless communication, and understanding how to implement them ensures smooth and efficient data exchange in your projects.

Chapter Purpose

The purpose of this chapter is to:

- Explain how to set up and use common communication protocols (UART, SPI, I2C, and Bluetooth) in both Arduino and MicroPython.
- Provide syntax and examples to demonstrate real-world applications of each protocol.
- Highlight differences between Arduino and MicroPython when working with these protocols.
- Offer tips and warnings to avoid common communication issues.

Chapter Syntax Table

Protocol	Arduino Syntax	MicroPython Syntax
UART	Serial.begin(baudrate); Serial.print(data); Serial.read();	uart = UART(1, baudrate=9600); uart.write(data); uart.read();
SPI	SPI.begin(); SPI.transfer(data); SPI.end();	spi = machine.SPI(1, baudrate=500000); spi.write(data); spi.read(size);
I2C	Wire.begin(); Wire.write(data); Wire.read();	i2c = machine.I2C(1, scl=Pin(22), sda=Pin(21), freq=400000); i2c.writeto(addr, data); i2c.readfrom(addr, nbytes);
Bluetooth	Serial.begin(baudrate); Serial.write(data); Serial.read();	uart = UART(1, baudrate=9600); uart.write(data); uart.read();

UART (Serial Communication)

UART (Universal Asynchronous Receiver/Transmitter) is a hardware communication protocol used for serial communication between devices. It allows for data transmission between two devices, like a microcontroller and a computer, by sending bits sequentially over a communication line. UART is widely used for communication in embedded systems.

Use Purpose
UART is used to send and receive data between two devices. It's commonly used for debugging, data exchange with sensors, or interfacing with hardware components. It's an asynchronous protocol, meaning no clock signal is required, making it simpler for many applications.

Arduino Syntax Use

```
Serial.begin(baudrate);
Serial.print(data);
Serial.read();
```

Arduino Syntax Explanation

- *Serial.begin(baudrate);*: Starts serial communication at a specified baud rate (e.g., 9600).
- *Serial.print(data);*: Sends data to another device via the serial port.
- *Serial.read();*: Reads incoming data from the serial port.

Arduino Simple Code Example

```
void setup() {
Serial.begin(9600); // Start serial communication
}
void loop() {
Serial.println("Hello, World!"); // Send data
delay(1000); // Wait 1 second
}
```

In this example, the Arduino sends "Hello, World!" to the serial monitor every second.

Notes

- The baud rate must match on both communicating devices (e.g., Arduino and computer).
- A common baud rate is 9600, but faster options, such as 115200, are also available.

Warnings

- Mismatched baud rates can lead to communication failures and data corruption.
- Always initialize communication with *Serial.begin()* before transmitting data.

MicroPython Syntax Use

```
uart = machine.UART(1, baudrate=9600)
uart.write(data)
uart.read()
```

MicroPython Syntax Explanation

- *uart = machine.UART(1, baudrate=9600)*: Initializes UART on channel 1 with a baud rate of 9600.
- *uart.write(data)*: Sends data over the UART port.
- *uart.read()*: Reads incoming data from the UART port.

MicroPython Simple Code Example

```
from machine import UART
uart = UART(1, baudrate=9600)
uart.write('Hello, World!')
data = uart.read()
```

In this example, the MicroPython device sends "Hello, World!" via UART and reads any incoming data.

Notes

- Ensure the correct UART pins are connected for successful communication.
- The baud rate needs to be consistent across both devices for reliable communication.

Warnings

- Incorrect baud rate settings may lead to data errors or communication failures.
- Ensure proper pin configuration and UART channel selection before using UART communication.

SPI (Serial Peripheral Interface)

SPI (Serial Peripheral Interface) is a communication protocol used to transfer data between a microcontroller and peripheral devices like sensors, displays, and memory modules. It's a synchronous protocol, meaning it uses a clock signal to synchronize data transmission between devices.

Use Purpose

SPI is used when high-speed data communication is needed between a master (like a microcontroller) and one or more peripheral devices (slaves). It's often used in embedded systems to connect components like sensors, SD cards, or displays that require fast, continuous data transfer.

Arduino Syntax Use

```
SPI.begin();
SPI.transfer(data);
SPI.end();
```

Arduino Syntax Explanation

- *SPI.begin();*: Initializes SPI communication and sets up the necessary pins for the SPI bus.
- *SPI.transfer(data);*: Sends data through the SPI bus and receives data from the slave device.
- *SPI.end();*: Ends SPI communication and releases the SPI bus.

Arduino Simple Code Example

```
#include <SPI.h> void setup() {
SPI.begin(); // Start SPI communication
}
void loop() {
byte receivedData = SPI.transfer(0x01); // Send data and receive
response
delay(1000); // Wait 1 second
}
```

In this example, the Arduino sends a byte of data (0x01) to the SPI slave and stores the received byte in the variable *receivedData*.

Notes

- SPI uses four main connections: MISO (Master In Slave Out), MOSI (Master Out Slave In), SCK (Serial Clock), and SS (Slave Select).
- Data transfer is full-duplex, meaning data is sent and received simultaneously.

Warnings

- Ensure proper pin connections for SPI communication: MOSI to MOSI, MISO to MISO, and so on.
- Be careful with voltage levels between devices; mismatched voltages can damage components.

MicroPython Syntax Use

```
spi = machine.SPI(1, baudrate=500000)
spi.write(data)
spi.read(size)
```

MicroPython Syntax Explanation

- *spi = machine.SPI(1, baudrate=500000)*: Initializes SPI communication on bus 1 with a baud rate of 500kHz.
- *spi.write(data)*: Sends data to the SPI bus.
- *spi.read(size)*: Reads a specific amount of data (in bytes) from the SPI bus.

MicroPython Simple Code Example

```
from machine import SPI
spi = SPI(1, baudrate=500000)
spi.write(b'Hello') # Send data
received = spi.read(5) # Read 5 bytes
```

In this example, the MicroPython device sends "Hello" via SPI and reads 5 bytes of data in response.

Notes

- Like Arduino, SPI in MicroPython requires connections for MOSI, MISO, SCK, and SS.
- SPI is typically faster than other communication protocols like I2C.

Warnings

- Ensure that all devices share a common ground (GND) to avoid communication issues.
- Set appropriate baud rates for the devices being used to prevent data loss or corruption.

I2C (Inter-Integrated Circuit)

I2C (Inter-Integrated Circuit) is a communication protocol commonly used to transfer data between a microcontroller (master) and multiple peripheral devices (slaves) over just two wires. It's a synchronous protocol, meaning it relies on a clock signal for timing, and it allows for multiple devices to share the same bus.

Use Purpose

I2C is typically used to connect microcontrollers to low-speed peripherals like sensors, displays, or EEPROMs. It is well-suited for applications where multiple devices need to be connected using minimal wiring.

Arduino Syntax Use

```
Wire.begin();
Wire.beginTransmission(address);
Wire.write(data);
Wire.endTransmission();
Wire.requestFrom(address, quantity);
Wire.read();
```

Arduino Syntax Explanation

- *Wire.begin();*: Initializes the I2C communication on the master device.
- *Wire.beginTransmission(address);*: Begins communication with the slave device at the specified address.
- *Wire.write(data);*: Sends data to the slave device.
- *Wire.endTransmission();*: Ends the transmission to the slave device.
- *Wire.requestFrom(address, quantity);*: Requests data from the slave device.
- *Wire.read();*: Reads incoming data from the slave device.

Arduino Simple Code Example

```
#include <Wire.h> void setup() {
Wire.begin(); // Start I2C communication
}
void loop() {
Wire.beginTransmission(0x40); // Begin communication with the device at address 0x40
Wire.write(0x01); // Send a byte of data
Wire.endTransmission(); // End the transmission
Wire.requestFrom(0x40, 1); // Request 1 byte from the device at 0x40
if (Wire.available()) {
int data = Wire.read(); // Read the incoming byte
}
delay(1000); // Wait 1 second
}
```

In this example, the Arduino sends a byte to the I2C device at address 0x40 and requests one byte in return.

Notes

- I2C requires two lines: SDA (Serial Data) and SCL (Serial Clock). Both must be connected between the master and all slaves.
- Each I2C device has a unique 7-bit address, allowing multiple devices to share the same bus.

Warnings

- Incorrect device addresses can lead to communication failures, so ensure each device's address is correct.
- I2C uses pull-up resistors on the SDA and SCL lines. If missing, the communication may fail.

MicroPython Syntax Use

```
i2c = machine.I2C(1, scl=Pin(22), sda=Pin(21), freq=400000)
i2c.writeto(addr, data)
i2c.readfrom(addr, nbytes)
```

MicroPython Syntax Explanation

- *i2c = machine.I2C(1, scl=Pin(22), sda=Pin(21), freq=400000)*: Initializes I2C communication on bus 1 with specified clock (SCL) and data (SDA) pins, and a frequency of 400kHz.
- *i2c.writeto(addr, data)*: Sends data to the device at the specified address.
- *i2c.readfrom(addr, nbytes)*: Reads the specified number of bytes from the device.

MicroPython Simple Code Example

```
from machine import I2C, Pin
i2c = I2C(1, scl=Pin(22), sda=Pin(21), freq=400000)
i2c.writeto(0x40, b'\x01') # Write byte to the device
data = i2c.readfrom(0x40, 1) # Read 1 byte
```

In this example, the MicroPython device writes a byte to the I2C device at address 0x40 and reads one byte back.

Notes

- Like Arduino, I2C in MicroPython uses two pins (SDA and SCL), which must be configured for each device.
- The *readfrom()* and *writeto()* methods are used to communicate with I2C devices.

Warnings

- Ensure proper wiring and device addresses for successful communication.
- Use appropriate pull-up resistors for SDA and SCL lines to avoid communication issues.

Bluetooth

Bluetooth is a wireless communication protocol that allows short-range data exchange between devices. It is commonly used in microcontroller projects to enable wireless communication between a microcontroller and other Bluetooth-enabled devices, such as smartphones, computers, or sensors.

Use Purpose

Bluetooth is used in applications where wireless communication is needed, such as home automation, remote control, data logging, and wearable devices. It allows for the transmission of data without requiring physical connections.

Arduino Syntax Use

```
Serial.begin(baudrate);
Serial.write(data);
Serial.read();
```

Arduino Syntax Explanation

- *Serial.begin(baudrate);*: Initializes serial communication (often over Bluetooth) at the specified baud rate (e.g., 9600).
- *Serial.write(data);*: Sends data through the Bluetooth module to a connected device.
- *Serial.read();*: Reads incoming data from the Bluetooth module.

Arduino Simple Code Example

```
void setup() {
Serial.begin(9600); // Start Bluetooth communication
}
void loop() {
if (Serial.available()) {
char data = Serial.read(); // Read incoming data
Serial.write(data); // Send data back (echo)
}
}
```

In this example, the Arduino reads data from the Bluetooth module and sends it back to the connected device (acting as an echo).

Notes

- Most Bluetooth modules (like HC-05 or HC-06) connect via serial communication to the microcontroller, requiring the TX (Transmit) and RX (Receive) pins.
- Ensure the baud rate is set to match the Bluetooth module's communication speed.

Warnings

- Incorrect TX/RX wiring can prevent proper communication. TX from the Bluetooth module should be connected to RX on the microcontroller, and vice versa.
- Ensure that the correct voltage levels are used, as some Bluetooth modules operate at 3.3V, while microcontrollers like Arduino may operate at 5V.

MicroPython Syntax Use

```
uart = machine.UART(1, baudrate=9600)
uart.write(data)
uart.read()
```

MicroPython Syntax Explanation

- *uart = machine.UART(1, baudrate=9600)*: Initializes UART communication on bus 1 with a baud rate of 9600, often used for Bluetooth communication.
- *uart.write(data)*: Sends data via Bluetooth to a connected device.
- *uart.read()*: Reads incoming data from the Bluetooth module.

MicroPython Simple Code Example

```
from machine import
UART uart = UART(1, baudrate=9600)
uart.write('Hello') # Send data
data = uart.read() # Read incoming data
```

In this example, the MicroPython device sends "Hello" via Bluetooth and reads incoming data from the Bluetooth module.

Notes

- MicroPython typically communicates with Bluetooth modules using UART, just like in Arduino.
- Use the correct pins for TX and RX, and ensure the baud rate is set correctly.

Warnings

- Make sure the Bluetooth module's voltage levels match the microcontroller's to avoid damage.
- Double-check TX and RX connections between the Bluetooth module and the microcontroller for correct data transmission.

Section Project in Programming Fundamentals section

Foundations of Computing and I/O

Project: LED Blink using ESP32/ESP8266

Objective
Make an LED blink on and off at regular intervals using an ESP32 or ESP8266 microcontroller. This is the simplest project to understand how to control an output pin and is designed for absolute beginner-friendliness.

Programming Fundamentals
Brief description of **Digital Write** and **Input/Output Declaration**:

- **Digital Write**: A command used to send an ON or OFF signal to a device like an LED.
- **Input/Output Declaration**: Configuring a pin as either input or output.

Requirement Components

- **ESP32** or **ESP8266** microcontroller
- **Breadboard**
- **LED** (1 piece)
- **220-ohm resistor** (to protect the LED)
- **Jumper wires**
- **USB cable**
- **Computer with Arduino IDE or MicroPython IDE installed**

Circuit Diagram

Circuit Connection

1. Connect the **positive leg** of the LED (longer leg) to **GPIO2** (or any other GPIO pin) of the ESP32/ESP8266.
2. Connect the **negative leg** (shorter leg) of the LED to one side of a **220-ohm resistor**.
3. Connect the other side of the resistor to **GND** (ground) on the ESP32/ESP8266.

Arduino Programming Section

Arduino Syntax:

- *pinMode(pin, mode)*: Sets a pin to behave as input or output.
- *digitalWrite(pin, value)*: Sets the pin to HIGH (ON) or LOW (OFF).

Arduino Code:

```
void setup() {
  pinMode(2, OUTPUT);   // Set GPIO2 as an output pin.
}

void loop() {
  digitalWrite(2, HIGH);  // Turn LED on.
  delay(1000);            // Wait 1 second.
  digitalWrite(2, LOW);   // Turn LED off.
  delay(1000);            // Wait 1 second.
}
```

Steps to Upload:

1. Open the **Arduino IDE** and connect your ESP32 or ESP8266 to your computer via USB.
2. Copy and paste the code into a new sketch.
3. In **Tools > Board**, select **ESP32** or **ESP8266** and the correct COM port.
4. Click **Upload** to transfer the code to the board.

Check Output:
The LED should blink on and off every second.

MicroPython Programming Section
MicroPython Syntax:
- *pin = machine.Pin(pin_number, mode)*: Sets a pin as an input or output.
- *pin.value(state)*: Sets the pin to HIGH (1) or LOW (0).

MicroPython Code:

```python
from machine import Pin
from time import sleep

led = Pin(2, Pin.OUT)   # Set GPIO2 as output.

while True:
    led.value(1)    # Turn LED on.
    sleep(1)        # Wait 1 second.
    led.value(0)    # Turn LED off.
    sleep(1)        # Wait 1 second.
```

Steps to Upload:
1. Open your **MicroPython IDE** (such as Thonny) and connect the ESP32/ESP8266 via USB.
2. Copy and paste the code into the editor.
3. Click **Run** to upload the code to the board.

Check Output:
The LED should blink on and off every second.

Troubleshooting Tips

- **LED not blinking**: Ensure correct connections and that the positive leg of the LED is connected to the GPIO pin.
- **Code not uploading**: Check that the correct board and COM port are selected in the IDE.
- **LED too dim or bright**: Ensure you're using the correct 220-ohm resistor.

Further Exploration

- **Change Blink Speed**: Modify the `delay(1000)` (Arduino) or `sleep(1)` (MicroPython) to make the LED blink faster or slower.
- **Multiple LEDs**: Try connecting more LEDs to different GPIO pins and create different blinking patterns.
- **Button Control**: Add a button to control when the LED blinks, introducing user interaction.

Note
This project provides an easy introduction to working with ESP32/ESP8266 microcontrollers and understanding basic input/output operations. It serves as a great starting point for further exploration in electronics and programming.

Project: Button-Controlled LED using ESP32/ESP8266

Objective
Use a push button to turn an LED on and off. This project helps you learn how to read input from a button and control the output to an LED using ESP32 or ESP8266 microcontroller.

Programming Fundamentals
Brief description of **Digital Write**, **Digital Read**, and **Input/Output Declaration**:

- **Digital Write**: Sends an ON or OFF signal to an output device like an LED.
- **Digital Read**: Reads the current state of an input device, such as a button (pressed or not pressed).
- **Input/Output Declaration**: Configures pins as either input or output to manage components.

Requirement Components

- **ESP32** or **ESP8266** microcontroller
- **Breadboard**
- **LED** (1 piece)

- **220-ohm resistor** (to protect the LED)
- **Push button**
- **10k-ohm resistor** (for the button)
- **Jumper wires**
- **USB cable**
- **Computer with Arduino IDE or MicroPython IDE installed**

Circuit Diagram

Circuit Connection
1. Connect the **positive leg** of the LED (longer leg) to **GPIO2** (or any other GPIO pin) of the ESP32/ESP8266.
2. Connect the **negative leg** (shorter leg) of the LED to one side of a **220-ohm resistor**.
3. Connect the other side of the resistor to **GND** (ground).
4. Connect one leg of the **push button** to **GPIO4**.
5. Connect the other leg of the push button to **GND**.

6. Use a **10k-ohm resistor** between **GPIO4** and **3.3V** to act as a pull-up resistor for the button.

Arduino Programming Section
Arduino Syntax:
- *pinMode(pin, mode)*: Sets a pin to behave as input or output.
- *digitalWrite(pin, value)*: Sets the pin to HIGH (ON) or LOW (OFF).
- *digitalRead(pin)*: Reads the state (HIGH or LOW) of a pin.

Arduino Code:

```
void setup() {
  pinMode(2, OUTPUT);   // Set GPIO2 as output for the LED.
  pinMode(4, INPUT_PULLUP);   // Set GPIO4 as input for the button with pull-up resistor.
}

void loop() {
  int buttonState = digitalRead(4);   // Read the button state.

  if (buttonState == LOW) {   // If button is pressed (LOW)
    digitalWrite(2, HIGH);   // Turn LED on.
  } else {
    digitalWrite(2, LOW);   // Turn LED off.
  }
}
```

Steps to Upload:

1. Open the **Arduino IDE** and connect your ESP32 or ESP8266 to your computer via USB.
2. Copy and paste the code into a new sketch.
3. In **Tools > Board**, select **ESP32** or **ESP8266** and the correct COM port.
4. Click **Upload** to transfer the code to the board.

Check Output:
Pressing the button should turn the LED on, and releasing the button should turn the LED off.

MicroPython Programming Section

MicroPython Syntax:

- *pin = machine.Pin(pin_number, mode)*: Sets a pin as an input or output.
- *pin.value(state)*: Sets the pin to HIGH (1) or LOW (0).
- *pin.value()*: Reads the state of the input pin.

MicroPython Code:

```python
from machine import Pin
from time import sleep

led = Pin(2, Pin.OUT)   # Set GPIO2 as output for the LED.
button = Pin(4, Pin.IN, Pin.PULL_UP)   # Set GPIO4 as input for the button with pull-up resistor.

while True:
    if button.value() == 0:   # If button is pressed (LOW)
        led.value(1)   # Turn LED on.
    else:
        led.value(0)   # Turn LED off.
    sleep(0.1)   # Small delay for button debounce.
```

Steps to Upload:

1. Open your **MicroPython IDE** (such as Thonny) and connect the ESP32/ESP8266 via USB.
2. Copy and paste the code into the editor.
3. Click **Run** to upload the code to the board.

Check Output:
Pressing the button should turn the LED on, and releasing the button should turn the LED off.

Troubleshooting Tips

- **Button not working**: Ensure the button is connected correctly and that the pull-up resistor is in place.
- **LED not lighting up**: Check that the LED is connected correctly and the pin assignments are accurate.
- **Code not uploading**: Make sure the correct board and COM port are selected in the IDE.

Further Exploration

- **Toggle Functionality**: Modify the code so that pressing the button once toggles the LED on or off, instead of holding it.
- **Add Multiple Buttons**: Control multiple LEDs or add more buttons to create different patterns or interactions.
- **Use Interrupts**: Implement button interrupts to handle button presses more efficiently without continuously checking for input.

Note

This project is an excellent way to learn about digital input and output using ESP32/ESP8266. It demonstrates how to interact with physical components like buttons and LEDs, giving you a strong foundation for more advanced projects.

Project: Analog Temperature Sensor with LED using ESP32/ESP8266

Objective

Use an analog temperature sensor (like the LM35) to read the temperature and turn an LED on when it reaches a certain threshold. This project introduces reading analog values and controlling digital outputs.

Programming Fundamentals

Brief description of **Analog Read**, **Digital Write**, and **Input/Output Declaration**:

- **Analog Read**: Reads the value from an analog sensor (e.g., temperature sensor) as a voltage.
- **Digital Write**: Sends an ON or OFF signal to an output device like an LED.
- **Input/Output Declaration**: Configuring pins as input (for sensors) or output (for components like LEDs).

Requirement Components

- **ESP32 or ESP8266** microcontroller
- **Breadboard**
- **LM35 temperature sensor**
- **LED** (1 piece)
- **220-ohm resistor** (to protect the LED)
- **Jumper wires**
- **USB cable**
- **Computer with Arduino IDE or MicroPython IDE installed**

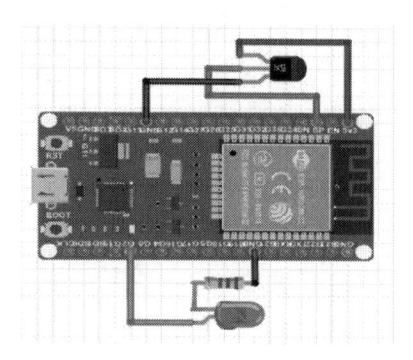

Circuit Diagram

Circuit Connection

1. Connect the **Vout pin** of the LM35 sensor to **GPIO36 (ADC1)** of the ESP32/ESP8266.

2. Connect the **Vcc pin** of the LM35 sensor to **3.3V** on the ESP32/ESP8266.
3. Connect the **GND pin** of the LM35 sensor to **GND** on the ESP32/ESP8266.
4. Connect the **positive leg** of the LED to **GPIO2**.
5. Connect the **negative leg** of the LED to one side of a **220-ohm resistor**.
6. Connect the other side of the resistor to **GND**.

Arduino Programming Section

Arduino Syntax:

- *analogRead(pin)*: Reads the analog value (voltage) from a pin.
- *digitalWrite(pin, value)*: Sets the pin to HIGH (ON) or LOW (OFF).***Arduino Code:***

```
const int tempPin = 36;   // Analog pin for LM35
const int ledPin = 2;     // GPIO pin for LED
float temperature;

void setup() {
  pinMode(ledPin, OUTPUT);   // Set LED pin as output
  Serial.begin(9600);   // Begin serial communication for monitoring temperature
}

void loop() {
  int sensorValue = analogRead(tempPin);   // Read analog value from LM35
  temperature = sensorValue * (3.3 / 4095.0) * 100;   // Convert to temperature in Celsius
  Serial.println(temperature);   // Print temperature to the serial monitor

  if (temperature > 30) {   // If temperature exceeds 30°C
    digitalWrite(ledPin, HIGH);   // Turn LED on
  } else {
    digitalWrite(ledPin, LOW);   // Turn LED off
  }

  delay(1000);   // Wait 1 second before next reading
}
```

Steps to Upload:

1. Open the **Arduino IDE** and connect your ESP32 or ESP8266 to your computer via USB.
2. Copy and paste the code into a new sketch.
3. In **Tools > Board**, select **ESP32** or **ESP8266** and the correct COM port.
4. Click **Upload** to transfer the code to the board.

Check Output:

The temperature will be printed in the serial monitor, and the LED will turn on when the temperature exceeds 30°C.

MicroPython Programming Section

MicroPython Syntax:

- *adc = machine.ADC(Pin(pin_number))*: Reads the analog value from the sensor pin.
- *pin.value(state)*: Sets the pin to HIGH (1) or LOW (0).

MicroPython Code:

```python
from machine import Pin, ADC
from time import sleep

temp_sensor = ADC(Pin(36))   # Set ADC pin for LM35
temp_sensor.width(ADC.WIDTH_12BIT)   # Set ADC resolution to 12 bits
temp_sensor.atten(ADC.ATTN_11DB)   # Set attenuation for full-scale voltage of 3.3V
led = Pin(2, Pin.OUT)   # Set GPIO2 as output for LED

def read_temperature():
    sensor_value = temp_sensor.read()   # Read analog value
    voltage = sensor_value * (3.3 / 4095)   # Convert to voltage
    temperature = voltage * 100   # Convert to temperature in Celsius
    return temperature

while True:
    temp = read_temperature()
    print("Temperature: {:.2f} C".format(temp))   # Print temperature
    
    if temp > 30:   # If temperature exceeds 30°C
        led.value(1)   # Turn LED on
```

```
else:
    led.value(0)  # Turn LED off

sleep(1)  # Wait 1 second before next reading
```

Steps to Upload:

1. Open your **MicroPython IDE** (such as Thonny) and connect the ESP32/ESP8266 via USB.
2. Copy and paste the code into the editor.
3. Click **Run** to upload the code to the board.

Check Output:
The temperature will be printed in the terminal, and the LED will turn on when the temperature exceeds 30°C.

Troubleshooting Tips

- **Incorrect temperature readings**: Ensure the LM35 sensor is correctly connected and powered.
- **LED not turning on**: Verify the pin connections for the LED and ensure the threshold temperature is set correctly.
- **Code not uploading**: Check that the correct board and COM port are selected in the IDE.

Further Exploration

- **Adjust Temperature Threshold**: Modify the threshold temperature at which the LED turns on or off.
- **Multiple Sensors**: Add more sensors (e.g., humidity or pressure) and integrate them into the project for more complex outputs.
- **Display Readings**: Use an OLED display to show the temperature readings directly on the device.

Note
This project demonstrates how to work with analog sensors and digital outputs, providing a great foundation for projects involving temperature control, data logging, and environmental monitoring.

Project: PWM LED Brightness Control with Potentiometer using ESP32/ESP8266

Objective
Use a potentiometer (analog input) to adjust the brightness of an LED using PWM (Pulse Width Modulation). This project teaches how to use analog inputs to control digital outputs.

Programming Fundamentals
Brief description of **PWM Support**, **Analog Read**, and **Digital Write**:

- **PWM (Pulse Width Modulation)**: Controls the brightness of an LED by adjusting the amount of time the LED is on during each cycle.
- **Analog Read**: Reads the value from the potentiometer to get a voltage level.
- **Digital Write**: Sends a PWM signal to control the LED brightness.

Requirement Components

- **ESP32** or **ESP8266** microcontroller
- **Breadboard**
- **Potentiometer**
- **LED** (1 piece)
- **220-ohm resistor** (to protect the LED)
- **Jumper wires**

- USB cable
- Computer with Arduino IDE or MicroPython IDE installed

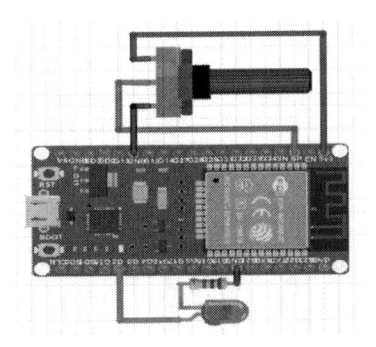

Circuit Diagram

Circuit Connection

1. Connect the **middle leg** of the potentiometer to **GPIO36 (ADC1)** on the ESP32/ESP8266.
2. Connect one of the other legs of the potentiometer to **3.3V** and the remaining leg to **GND**.
3. Connect the **positive leg** of the LED to **GPIO2**.
4. Connect the **negative leg** of the LED to one side of a **220-ohm resistor**.
5. Connect the other side of the resistor to **GND**.

Arduino Programming Section

Arduino Syntax:

- *analogRead(pin)*: Reads the analog value (voltage) from a pin.
- *analogWrite(pin, value)*: Sends a PWM signal to a pin to control output intensity.

Arduino Code:

```
const int potPin = 36;   // Potentiometer connected to GPIO36
const int ledPin = 2;    // LED connected to GPIO2

void setup() {
  pinMode(ledPin, OUTPUT);   // Set LED pin as output
}

void loop() {
  int potValue = analogRead(potPin);   // Read potentiometer value
  int ledBrightness = map(potValue, 0, 4095, 0, 255);   // Map the value to a PWM range (0-255)
  analogWrite(ledPin, ledBrightness);   // Set LED brightness using PWM
}
```

Steps to Upload:

1. Open the **Arduino IDE** and connect your ESP32 or ESP8266 to your computer via USB.
2. Copy and paste the code into a new sketch.
3. In **Tools > Board**, select **ESP32** or **ESP8266** and the correct COM port.
4. Click **Upload** to transfer the code to the board.

Check Output:
Turning the potentiometer will adjust the brightness of the LED.

MicroPython Programming Section

MicroPython Syntax:

- *adc = machine.ADC(Pin(pin_number))*: Reads the analog value from the potentiometer.
- *pwm = machine.PWM(Pin(pin_number), freq)*: Sends a PWM signal to control the brightness of the LED.

MicroPython Code:

```python
from machine import Pin, ADC, PWM
from time import sleep

pot = ADC(Pin(36))   # Potentiometer connected to GPIO36
pot.width(ADC.WIDTH_12BIT)   # Set ADC resolution to 12 bits
pot.atten(ADC.ATTN_11DB)   # Set attenuation for full-scale voltage of 3.3V
led = PWM(Pin(2), freq=5000)   # LED connected to GPIO2, PWM frequency at 5kHz

while True:
    pot_value = pot.read()   # Read potentiometer value
    led.duty(pot_value // 16)   # Set LED brightness (duty cycle between 0-255)
    sleep(0.1)
```

Steps to Upload:

1. Open your **MicroPython IDE** (such as Thonny) and connect the ESP32/ESP8266 via USB.
2. Copy and paste the code into the editor.
3. Click **Run** to upload the code to the board.

Check Output:
Turning the potentiometer will adjust the brightness of the LED.

Troubleshooting Tips

- **LED not dimming/brightening**: Ensure the potentiometer is connected properly and the LED is receiving PWM signals.
- **Incorrect brightness levels**: Check that the map or scaling of the potentiometer value is correct.
- **Code not uploading**: Verify the correct board and COM port are selected in the IDE.

Further Exploration

- **Change PWM Frequency**: Adjust the PWM frequency in the code to see how it affects the smoothness of the brightness control.
- **Add Multiple LEDs**: Control multiple LEDs with different potentiometers to create a light show.
- **Use Different Sensors**: Replace the potentiometer with other sensors (like a light sensor) to control the brightness based on environmental conditions.

Note

This project provides an excellent introduction to using PWM and analog inputs to control digital outputs. It's a great starting point for exploring more advanced projects like motor control or sensor-based automation.

Programming Fundamentals (Operators and Math)

Project: Simple Calculator using ESP32/ESP8266

Objective
Create a simple calculator that takes two numbers as input and

performs basic arithmetic operations such as addition, subtraction, multiplication, division, and modulus.

Programming Fundamentals

Brief description of **Addition**, **Subtraction**, **Multiplication**, **Division**, and **Modulus** operations:

- **Addition (+)**: Adds two numbers.
- **Subtraction (-)**: Subtracts the second number from the first.
- **Multiplication (*)**: Multiplies two numbers.
- **Division (/)**: Divides the first number by the second.
- **Modulus (%)**: Returns the remainder of division between two numbers.

Requirement Components

- **ESP32** or **ESP8266** microcontroller
- **Breadboard**
- **Jumper wires**
- **USB cable**
- **Computer with Arduino IDE or MicroPython IDE installed**

Circuit Diagram

(There's no specific circuit for this project since it's a software-only calculator.)

Circuit Connection

This project doesn't require any physical circuit connection. All calculations are performed in the code.

Arduino Programming Section

Arduino Syntax:

- *Serial.begin(baud_rate)*: Initializes serial communication with the specified baud rate.
- *Serial.print(), Serial.println()*: Displays output to the Serial Monitor.

- *Serial.readStringUntil(character)*: Reads input from the Serial Monitor until a specific character is detected.

Arduino Code:

```
float num1, num2, result;
char operation;
void setup() {
  Serial.begin(9600);  // Start serial communication at 9600 baud rate
  Serial.println("Simple Calculator");
  Serial.println("Enter operation: +, -, *, /, %");
}
void loop() {
  if (Serial.available() > 0) {
    operation = Serial.read();  // Read operation

    Serial.println("Enter first number: ");
    while (Serial.available() == 0) {}  // Wait for user input
    num1 = Serial.parseFloat();  // Read first number

    Serial.println("Enter second number: ");
    while (Serial.available() == 0) {}  // Wait for user input
    num2 = Serial.parseFloat();  // Read second number

    switch (operation) {
      case '+':
        result = num1 + num2;
        Serial.print("Result: ");
        Serial.println(result);
        break;
      case '-':
        result = num1 - num2;
        Serial.print("Result: ");
        Serial.println(result);
        break;
      case '*':
        result = num1 * num2;
        Serial.print("Result: ");
        Serial.println(result);
        break;
      case '/':
        if (num2 != 0) {
          result = num1 / num2;
          Serial.print("Result: ");
          Serial.println(result);
        } else {
          Serial.println("Error: Division by zero");
        }
        break;
      case '%':
        if (num2 != 0) {
          result = int(num1) % int(num2);
          Serial.print("Result: ");
          Serial.println(result);
        } else {
          Serial.println("Error: Division by zero");
        }
        break;
      default:
        Serial.println("Invalid operation");
    }
  }
}
```

Steps to Upload:
1. Open the **Arduino IDE** and connect your ESP32 or ESP8266 to your computer via USB.
2. Copy and paste the code into a new sketch.
3. In **Tools > Board**, select **ESP32** or **ESP8266** and the correct COM port.
4. Click **Upload** to transfer the code to the board.

Check Output:
You can enter the numbers and operations via the Serial Monitor, and the result will be displayed in the Serial Monitor.

MicroPython Programming Section
MicroPython Syntax:
- *input()*: Reads input from the user.
- *print()*: Displays output to the console.
- *if-elif* structure: Used for making decisions based on the operation input.

MicroPython Code:

```python
def calculator():
    print("Simple Calculator")
    num1 = float(input("Enter first number: "))
    operation = input("Enter operation (+, -, *, /, %): ")
    num2 = float(input("Enter second number: "))

    if operation == '+':
        result = num1 + num2
    elif operation == '-':
        result = num1 - num2
    elif operation == '*':
        result = num1 * num2
    elif operation == '/':
        if num2 != 0:
            result = num1 / num2
        else:
            result = "Error: Division by zero"
    elif operation == '%':
        if num2 != 0:
            result = num1 % num2
        else:
            result = "Error: Division by zero"
    else:
        result = "Invalid operation"

    print("Result:", result)

while True:
    calculator()
```

Steps to Upload:

1. Open your **MicroPython IDE** (such as Thonny) and connect the ESP32/ESP8266 via USB.
2. Copy and paste the code into the editor.
3. Click **Run** to execute the calculator.
4. You can enter numbers and operations through the terminal interface.

Check Output:
The program will display the result of the calculation in the terminal.

Troubleshooting Tips
- **No response from Serial Monitor**: Ensure that the correct baud rate (9600) is selected in the Serial Monitor.
- **Division by zero error**: Make sure the second number is not zero for division and modulus operations.
- **Invalid operation**: Ensure you input valid operations like +, - , *, /, and %.

Further Exploration
- **Add more functions**: Expand the calculator to include more complex functions such as square roots, powers, or logarithms.
- **Create a user-friendly interface**: Implement a physical interface with buttons for input and an LCD to display results.
- **Store and recall values**: Add functionality to store results in memory and recall them later for further calculations.

Note
This project is a great introduction to performing arithmetic operations using an ESP32/ESP8266. It demonstrates how to take inputs from the user and perform calculations, providing a foundation for more advanced mathematical and scientific applications.

Project: Area and Perimeter of a Rectangle using ESP32/ESP8266

Objective
Write a program to calculate the area and perimeter of a rectangle given its length and width. This helps practice basic arithmetic operations like multiplication and addition.

Programming Fundamentals
Brief description of **Multiplication** and **Addition**:

- **Multiplication**: Used to calculate the area of the rectangle (length * width).
- **Addition**: Used to calculate the perimeter of the rectangle (2 * (length + width)).

Requirement Components

- **ESP32 or ESP8266 microcontroller**
- **Breadboard**
- **Jumper wires**
- **USB cable**
- **Computer with Arduino IDE or MicroPython IDE installed**

Circuit Diagram
(No specific circuit needed for this software-only program.)

Circuit Connection
This project is software-only and does not require any hardware connection.

Arduino Programming Section

Arduino Syntax:

- *Serial.begin(baud_rate)*: Initializes serial communication with the specified baud rate.
- *Serial.print(), Serial.println()*: Displays output to the Serial Monitor.
- *Serial.readStringUntil(character)*: Reads input from the Serial Monitor until a specific character is detected.

Arduino Code:

```
float length, width, area, perimeter;

void setup() {
  Serial.begin(9600);   // Start serial communication at 9600 baud rate
  Serial.println("Calculate Area and Perimeter of a Rectangle");
}

void loop() {
  Serial.println("Enter the length of the rectangle: ");
  while (Serial.available() == 0) {}  // Wait for input
  length = Serial.parseFloat();   // Read length input

  Serial.println("Enter the width of the rectangle: ");
  while (Serial.available() == 0) {}  // Wait for input
  width = Serial.parseFloat();   // Read width input

  area = length * width;   // Calculate area
  perimeter = 2 * (length + width);   // Calculate perimeter

  Serial.print("Area: ");
  Serial.println(area);
  Serial.print("Perimeter: ");
  Serial.println(perimeter);

  delay(1000);   // Delay before next calculation
}
```

Steps to Upload:
1. Open the **Arduino IDE** and connect your ESP32 or ESP8266 to your computer via USB.
2. Copy and paste the code into a new sketch.
3. In **Tools > Board**, select **ESP32** or **ESP8266** and the correct COM port.
4. Click **Upload** to transfer the code to the board.

Check Output:
You can enter the length and width of the rectangle via the Serial Monitor, and the program will display the area and perimeter.

MicroPython Programming Section

MicroPython Syntax:

- *input()*: Reads input from the user.
- *print()*: Displays output to the console.

MicroPython Code:

```python
def calculate_area_perimeter():
    length = float(input("Enter the length of the rectangle: "))
    width = float(input("Enter the width of the rectangle: "))

    area = length * width   # Calculate area
    perimeter = 2 * (length + width)   # Calculate perimeter

    print("Area:", area)
    print("Perimeter:", perimeter)

while True:
    calculate_area_perimeter()
```

Steps to Upload:

1. Open your **MicroPython IDE** (such as Thonny) and connect the ESP32/ESP8266 via USB.
2. Copy and paste the code into the editor.
3. Click **Run** to execute the program.

Check Output:
The program will display the area and perimeter of the rectangle based on the input values you provide.

Troubleshooting Tips

- **Incorrect values in Serial Monitor**: Ensure you are entering valid numerical values for length and width.
- **No response from the board**: Ensure the correct baud rate is set in the Serial Monitor (9600).
- **Code not uploading**: Verify that the correct board and COM port are selected in the IDE.

Further Exploration

- **Different Shapes**: Expand the program to calculate the area and perimeter of other shapes, such as circles or triangles.
- **User-friendly Interface**: Add an OLED or LCD display to show the results directly on the screen, making the program more interactive.
- **Data Logging**: Store the area and perimeter calculations in an SD card or cloud for data analysis.

Note
This project provides a simple introduction to using ESP32/ESP8266 for arithmetic operations, making it a great starting point for learning about basic programming and mathematical applications.

Project: Exponentiation Calculator using ESP32/ESP8266

Objective
Create a program that calculates the power of a number (exponentiation) using the ^ operator or a built-in function. This project helps beginners understand how exponentiation works in programming.

Programming Fundamentals

Brief description of **Exponentiation**:

- **Exponentiation**: The process of raising a base number to the power of an exponent (base^exponent). It can be done using the pow( ) function or ** operator in most programming languages.

Requirement Components

- **ESP32 or ESP8266** microcontroller
- **Breadboard**
- **Jumper wires**
- **USB cable**
- **Computer with Arduino IDE or MicroPython IDE installed**

Circuit Diagram

(No specific circuit needed for this software-only program.)

Circuit Connection

This is a software-only program and doesn't require any hardware connection.

Arduino Programming Section

Arduino Syntax:

- *Serial.begin(baud_rate)*: Initializes serial communication with the specified baud rate.
- *Serial.print(), Serial.println()*: Displays output to the Serial Monitor.
- *Serial.readStringUntil(character)*: Reads input from the Serial Monitor until a specific character is detected.
- *pow(base, exponent)*: A function that returns the base raised to the power of the exponent.

Arduino Code:

```
float base, exponent, result;

void setup() {
  Serial.begin(9600);   // Start serial communication at 9600 baud rate
  Serial.println("Exponentiation Calculator");
}

void loop() {
  Serial.println("Enter the base number: ");
  while (Serial.available() == 0) {}  // Wait for input
  base = Serial.parseFloat();  // Read base input

  Serial.println("Enter the exponent: ");
  while (Serial.available() == 0) {}  // Wait for input
  exponent = Serial.parseFloat();  // Read exponent input

  result = pow(base, exponent);  // Calculate base^exponent

  Serial.print("Result: ");
  Serial.println(result);

  delay(1000);  // Delay before the next calculation
}
```

Steps to Upload:

1. Open the **Arduino IDE** and connect your ESP32 or ESP8266 to your computer via USB.
2. Copy and paste the code into a new sketch.
3. In **Tools > Board**, select **ESP32** or **ESP8266** and the correct COM port.
4. Click **Upload** to transfer the code to the board.

Check Output:

You can enter the base and exponent values via the Serial Monitor, and the program will display the result of the exponentiation.

MicroPython Programming Section

MicroPython Syntax:

- *input()*: Reads input from the user.
- *pow(base, exponent)*: A built-in function that returns the base raised to the power of the exponent.
- *print()*: Displays output to the console.

MicroPython Code:

```python
def exponentiation_calculator():
    base = float(input("Enter the base number: "))
    exponent = float(input("Enter the exponent: "))
    
    result = pow(base, exponent)    # Calculate base^exponent
    print("Result:", result)

while True:
    exponentiation_calculator()
```

Steps to Upload:

1. Open your **MicroPython IDE** (such as Thonny) and connect the ESP32/ESP8266 via USB.
2. Copy and paste the code into the editor.
3. Click **Run** to execute the program.

Check Output:
The program will ask for the base and exponent values, and it will display the result of the exponentiation in the terminal.

Troubleshooting Tips

- **No response from Serial Monitor**: Ensure the correct baud rate (9600) is selected in the Serial Monitor.
- **Incorrect values**: Ensure you're entering valid numbers for both base and exponent.
- **Code not uploading**: Verify that the correct board and COM port are selected in the IDE.

Further Exploration

- **Negative Exponents**: Modify the program to handle negative exponents and calculate fractional results.
- **Exponentiation of Complex Numbers**: Expand the program to include operations with complex numbers.
- **User-Friendly Interface**: Add an OLED or LCD display to show the base, exponent, and result directly on the screen.

Note
This project introduces exponentiation in programming using ESP32/ESP8266. It's a perfect exercise to understand how to perform mathematical operations programmatically, laying the foundation for more complex arithmetic and scientific calculations.

Project: Trigonometric Calculator using ESP32/ESP8266

Objective
Build a simple trigonometric calculator that computes the sine, cosine, and tangent of an angle provided by the user. This project introduces the basic trigonometric functions in programming.

Programming Fundamentals
Brief description of **Sine**, **Cosine**, and **Tangent**:

- **Sine (sin)**: Computes the sine of an angle (in radians).
- **Cosine (cos)**: Computes the cosine of an angle (in radians).
- **Tangent (tan)**: Computes the tangent of an angle (in radians).

Requirement Components
- **ESP32** or **ESP8266** microcontroller
- **Breadboard**
- **Jumper wires**
- **USB cable**
- **Computer with Arduino IDE or MicroPython IDE installed**

Circuit Diagram
(No specific circuit needed for this software-only program.)

Circuit Connection
This project is software-only and does not require any hardware connections.

Arduino Programming Section
Arduino Syntax:
- *Serial.begin(baud_rate)*: Initializes serial communication with the specified baud rate.
- *Serial.print(), Serial.println()*: Displays output to the Serial Monitor.
- *sin(angle), cos(angle), tan(angle)*: Functions that return the sine, cosine, and tangent of an angle (in radians).

Arduino Code:
```
float angle, result;
void setup() {
  Serial.begin(9600);   // Start serial communication at 9600 baud rate
  Serial.println("Trigonometric Calculator");
}

void loop() {
  Serial.println("Enter the angle in degrees: ");
  while (Serial.available() == 0) {}  // Wait for input
  angle = Serial.parseFloat();   // Read angle input
  angle = angle * 3.14159 / 180;  // Convert degrees to radians

  Serial.print("Sine: ");
  result = sin(angle);   // Compute sine
  Serial.println(result);

  Serial.print("Cosine: ");
  result = cos(angle);   // Compute cosine
  Serial.println(result);

  Serial.print("Tangent: ");
  result = tan(angle);   // Compute tangent
  Serial.println(result);

  delay(1000);   // Delay before next calculation
}
```

Steps to Upload:

1. Open the **Arduino IDE** and connect your ESP32 or ESP8266 to your computer via USB.
2. Copy and paste the code into a new sketch.
3. In **Tools > Board**, select **ESP32** or **ESP8266** and the correct COM port.
4. Click **Upload** to transfer the code to the board.

Check Output:
You can enter an angle (in degrees) via the Serial Monitor, and the program will compute the sine, cosine, and tangent of the given angle.

MicroPython Programming Section

MicroPython Syntax:

- *input()*: Reads input from the user.
- *sin(angle), cos(angle), tan(angle)*: Functions that return the sine, cosine, and tangent of an angle (in radians).
- *math.radians(angle)*: Converts degrees to radians.

MicroPython Code:

```
import math

def trigonometric_calculator():
    angle = float(input("Enter the angle in degrees: "))
    angle_in_radians = math.radians(angle)  # Convert degrees to radians

    sine = math.sin(angle_in_radians)
    cosine = math.cos(angle_in_radians)
    tangent = math.tan(angle_in_radians)

    print("Sine: {:.4f}".format(sine))
    print("Cosine: {:.4f}".format(cosine))
    print("Tangent: {:.4f}".format(tangent))

while True:
    trigonometric_calculator()
```

Steps to Upload:

1. Open your **MicroPython IDE** (such as Thonny) and connect the ESP32/ESP8266 via USB.
2. Copy and paste the code into the editor.
3. Click **Run** to execute the program.

Check Output:
The program will ask for an angle in degrees and display the sine, cosine, and tangent values of that angle in the terminal.

Troubleshooting Tips

- **No response from Serial Monitor**: Ensure that the correct baud rate (9600) is selected in the Serial Monitor.
- **Incorrect trigonometric values**: Make sure you're entering the angle in degrees. The program automatically converts it to radians for calculations.
- **Code not uploading**: Verify that the correct board and COM port are selected in the IDE.

Further Exploration
- **Inverse Trigonometric Functions**: Extend the program to include inverse functions such as arcsin, arccos, and arctan.
- **Hyperbolic Functions**: Add hyperbolic trigonometric functions (sinh, cosh, tanh) to the calculator.
- **Graphical Output**: Connect the ESP32/ESP8266 to a display and plot the sine, cosine, and tangent graphs based on user inputs.

Note
This project is an easy introduction to trigonometric functions in programming using the ESP32/ESP8266. It helps to understand how these functions work and is a great foundation for more complex mathematical and scientific calculations.

Variables, Data Types, and Control Structures

Project : Temperature Conversion Program using ESP32/ESP8266

Objective
Write a program to convert temperatures between Celsius and Fahrenheit. This project helps practice variables, data types, and conditional statements to control the flow of the program.

Programming Fundamentals
Brief description of **int**, **float**, **if-else**, and **return**:

- **int**: A data type used to store integers.
- **float**: A data type used to store decimal numbers.
- **if-else**: A conditional statement that helps in controlling the flow of the program based on conditions.
- **return**: A statement used to return values from a function.

Requirement Components

- **ESP32** or **ESP8266** microcontroller
- **Breadboard**
- **Jumper wires**
- **USB cable**
- **Computer with Arduino IDE or MicroPython IDE installed**

Circuit Diagram
(No specific circuit is needed for this software-only program.)

Circuit Connection
This project is software-only and does not require any hardware connection.

Arduino Programming Section
Arduino Syntax:
- *Serial.begin(baud_rate)*: Initializes serial communication with the specified baud rate.
- *Serial.print(), Serial.println()*: Displays output to the Serial Monitor.
- *if-else*: Controls the flow based on whether the condition is true or false.
- *return*: Sends a value back from a function.

Arduino Code:

```
float celsiusToFahrenheit(float celsius) {
  return (celsius * 9.0 / 5.0) + 32.0;
}
float fahrenheitToCelsius(float fahrenheit) {
  return (fahrenheit - 32.0) * 5.0 / 9.0;
}
void setup() {
  Serial.begin(9600);   // Start serial communication at 9600 baud rate
  Serial.println("Temperature Conversion Program");
}
void loop() {
  char option;
  float temp, result;
  Serial.println("Enter 'C' to convert Celsius to Fahrenheit or 'F' to convert Fahrenheit to Celsius:");
  while (Serial.available() == 0) {}  // Wait for user input
  option = Serial.read();   // Read user input

  if (option == 'C' || option == 'c') {
    Serial.println("Enter temperature in Celsius: ");
    while (Serial.available() == 0) {}  // Wait for user input
    temp = Serial.parseFloat();   // Read temperature input
    result = celsiusToFahrenheit(temp);   // Convert to Fahrenheit
    Serial.print("Temperature in Fahrenheit: ");
    Serial.println(result);
  }
  else if (option == 'F' || option == 'f') {
    Serial.println("Enter temperature in Fahrenheit: ");
    while (Serial.available() == 0) {}  // Wait for user input
    temp = Serial.parseFloat();   // Read temperature input
    result = fahrenheitToCelsius(temp);   // Convert to Celsius
    Serial.print("Temperature in Celsius: ");
    Serial.println(result);
  }
  else {
    Serial.println("Invalid option");
  }

  delay(2000);   // Delay before the next calculation
}
```

Steps to Upload:

1. Open the **Arduino IDE** and connect your ESP32 or ESP8266 to your computer via USB.
2. Copy and paste the code into a new sketch.
3. In **Tools > Board**, select **ESP32** or **ESP8266** and the correct COM port.
4. Click **Upload** to transfer the code to the board.

Check Output:
You can enter either 'C' or 'F' in the Serial Monitor to convert temperatures between Celsius and Fahrenheit.

MicroPython Programming Section
MicroPython Syntax:
- *input()*: Reads input from the user.
- *if-else*: Controls the flow based on whether the condition is true or false.
- *return*: Sends a value back from a function.

MicroPython Code:

```python
def celsius_to_fahrenheit(celsius):
    return (celsius * 9.0 / 5.0) + 32.0
def fahrenheit_to_celsius(fahrenheit):
    return (fahrenheit - 32.0) * 5.0 / 9.0
def temperature_conversion():
    option = input("Enter 'C' to convert Celsius to Fahrenheit or 'F' to convert Fahrenheit to Celsius: ")

    if option == 'C' or option == 'c':
        temp = float(input("Enter temperature in Celsius: "))
        result = celsius_to_fahrenheit(temp)
        print("Temperature in Fahrenheit: {:.2f}".format(result))
    elif option == 'F' or option == 'f':
        temp = float(input("Enter temperature in Fahrenheit: "))
        result = fahrenheit_to_celsius(temp)
        print("Temperature in Celsius: {:.2f}".format(result))
    else:
        print("Invalid option")

while True:
    temperature_conversion()
```

Steps to Upload:

1. Open your **MicroPython IDE** (such as Thonny) and connect the ESP32/ESP8266 via USB.
2. Copy and paste the code into the editor.
3. Click **Run** to execute the program.

Check Output:
The program will ask whether to convert temperatures between Celsius and Fahrenheit, and it will display the result accordingly.

Troubleshooting Tips

- **Invalid or no input**: Ensure you are entering valid temperature values and selecting the correct conversion option (C or F).
- **No response from the board**: Make sure the Serial Monitor is set to the correct baud rate (9600).
- **Code not uploading**: Verify that the correct board and COM port are selected in the IDE.

Further Exploration

- **Kelvin Conversion**: Add options to convert between Celsius, Fahrenheit, and Kelvin.
- **User Interface**: Use an OLED or LCD display to show the input and results in real-time.
- **Data Logging**: Store conversion history on an SD card or send it to a cloud service for monitoring.

Note
This project helps beginners practice basic concepts like conditional statements, variables, and data types while learning how to work with serial communication in ESP32/ESP8266.

Project: Simple ATM System using ESP32/ESP8266

Objective
Create a simple ATM-like system where the user can withdraw, deposit, or check their balance using a switch-case structure and loops. The system will practice the use of global and local variables, `unsigned int`, and various programming constructs like loops and conditionals.

Programming Fundamentals
Brief description of **Global Variables**, **Local Variables**, **unsigned int**, **switch-case**, **while loop**, and **break**:

- **Global Variables**: Variables that can be accessed by any function in the program.
- **Local Variables**: Variables that are only accessible within the function where they are declared.
- **unsigned int**: A data type used to store non-negative integer values.
- **switch-case**: A control statement that chooses between multiple options based on the value of a variable.
- **while loop**: A loop that continues executing as long as a specified condition is true.
- **break**: A statement used to exit loops or switch-case structures.

Requirement Components

- **ESP32** or **ESP8266** microcontroller
- **Breadboard**
- **Jumper wires**
- **USB cable**
- **Computer with Arduino IDE or MicroPython IDE installed**

Circuit Diagram

(No specific circuit needed for this software-only program.)

Circuit Connection

This project is software-only and does not require any hardware connection.

Arduino Programming Section

Arduino Syntax:

- *Serial.begin(baud_rate)*: Initializes serial communication with the specified baud rate.
- *Serial.print(), Serial.println()*: Displays output to the Serial Monitor.
- *switch-case*: Used to handle multiple options based on the value of a variable.
- *while loop*: Executes code repeatedly while the condition is true.
- *break*: Exits the current loop or switch structure.

Arduino Code:

```
unsigned int balance = 1000;  // Global variable to store the user's balance
void setup() {
  Serial.begin(9600);  // Start serial communication at 9600 baud rate
  Serial.println("Welcome to the ATM System");
}
void loop() {
  char option;
  unsigned int amount;
  Serial.println("\nSelect an option:");
  Serial.println("1. Check Balance");
  Serial.println("2. Deposit Money");
  Serial.println("3. Withdraw Money");
  Serial.println("4. Exit");
  while (Serial.available() == 0) {}  // Wait for user input
  option = Serial.read();  // Read user option
  switch (option) {
    case '1':  // Check balance
      Serial.print("Your current balance is: ");
      Serial.println(balance);
      break;
    case '2':  // Deposit money
      Serial.println("Enter amount to deposit: ");
      while (Serial.available() == 0) {}  // Wait for user input
      amount = Serial.parseInt();  // Read deposit amount
      balance += amount;
      Serial.print("Amount deposited: ");
      Serial.println(amount);
      Serial.print("New balance: ");
      Serial.println(balance);
      break;
    case '3':  // Withdraw money
      Serial.println("Enter amount to withdraw: ");
      while (Serial.available() == 0) {}  // Wait for user input
      amount = Serial.parseInt();  // Read withdrawal amount
      if (amount <= balance) {
        balance -= amount;
        Serial.print("Amount withdrawn: ");
        Serial.println(amount);
        Serial.print("New balance: ");
        Serial.println(balance);
      } else {
        Serial.println("Insufficient balance.");
      }
      break;
    case '4':  // Exit
      Serial.println("Thank you for using the ATM.");
      while (true) {}  // Stop the program
      break;
    default:  // Invalid option
      Serial.println("Invalid option. Please try again.");
      break;
  }
  delay(2000);  // Delay before showing the menu again
}
```

Steps to Upload:
1. Open the **Arduino IDE** and connect your ESP32 or ESP8266 to your computer via USB.
2. Copy and paste the code into a new sketch.
3. In **Tools > Board**, select **ESP32** or **ESP8266** and the correct COM port.
4. Click **Upload** to transfer the code to the board.

Check Output:
You can use the Serial Monitor to select options like checking balance, depositing, withdrawing, or exiting. The balance will be updated accordingly based on the transactions.

MicroPython Programming Section
MicroPython Syntax:
- *input()*: Reads input from the user.
- *switch-case* (Python equivalent: *if-elif*): Allows the program to choose among multiple options based on user input.
- *while loop*: Continually runs code while the condition is true.
- *break*: Used to exit the loop.

MicroPython Code:

```python
balance = 1000   # Global variable to store the user's balance

def atm_system():
    while True:
        print("\nATM System Menu:")
        print("1. Check Balance")
        print("2. Deposit Money")
        print("3. Withdraw Money")
        print("4. Exit")
        option = input("Choose an option: ")
        if option == '1':   # Check balance
            print(f"Your current balance is: {balance}")
        elif option == '2':   # Deposit money
            amount = int(input("Enter amount to deposit: "))
            global balance
            balance += amount
            print(f"Amount deposited: {amount}")
            print(f"New balance: {balance}")
        elif option == '3':   # Withdraw money
            amount = int(input("Enter amount to withdraw: "))
            if amount <= balance:
                balance -= amount
                print(f"Amount withdrawn: {amount}")
                print(f"New balance: {balance}")
            else:
                print("Insufficient balance.")
        elif option == '4':   # Exit
            print("Thank you for using the ATM.")
            break
        else:
            print("Invalid option. Please try again.")
while True:
    atm_system()
```

Steps to Upload:

1. Open your **MicroPython IDE** (such as Thonny) and connect the ESP32/ESP8266 via USB.
2. Copy and paste the code into the editor.
3. Click **Run** to execute the program.

Check Output:
The program will prompt you to choose options for balance inquiry, deposit, withdrawal, or exiting. You can interact with it via the terminal and the balance will update as transactions are made.

Troubleshooting Tips

- **Invalid input**: Ensure you are entering valid numeric values for deposits and withdrawals.
- **Insufficient balance**: Make sure the withdrawal amount doesn't exceed the available balance.
- **No response from the board**: Verify that the Serial Monitor is set to the correct baud rate (9600).
- **Code not uploading**: Ensure that the correct board and COM port are selected in the IDE.

Further Exploration

- **Pin Authentication**: Add a feature to authenticate the user with a PIN before allowing transactions.
- **Transaction History**: Implement a system to record and display the last few transactions (deposits and withdrawals).
- **Multiple Accounts**: Allow the system to manage multiple user accounts with different balances.

Note
This project is a great introduction to ATM systems, using global and local variables, control structures, and loops. It helps beginners understand how to use conditionals and loops to create interactive programs with ESP32/ESP8266.

Project : Sum and Average of Array Elements using ESP32/ESP8266

Objective
Build a program to input a collection of numbers into an array and then calculate the sum and average using loops. This project focuses on handling arrays and using control structures to iterate over the elements.

Programming Fundamentals
Brief description of **Array**, **for loop**, **int**, and **float**:

- **Array**: A collection of data items (of the same type) stored at contiguous memory locations.
- **for loop**: A control structure that allows repetitive execution of a block of code over a collection or a range.
- **int**: A data type used to store whole numbers.
- **float**: A data type used to store numbers with fractional parts (decimal numbers).

Requirement Components

- **ESP32** or **ESP8266** microcontroller
- **Breadboard**
- **Jumper wires**
- **USB cable**
- **Computer with Arduino IDE or MicroPython IDE installed**

Circuit Diagram
(No specific circuit needed for this software-only program.)
Circuit Connection
This is a software-only program and does not require any hardware connection.

Arduino Programming Section
Arduino Syntax:
- *Serial.begin(baud_rate)*: Initializes serial communication with the specified baud rate.
- *Serial.print(), Serial.println()*: Displays output to the Serial Monitor.
- *for loop*: Iterates over the elements of an array.
- *int, float*: Data types used to store integers and floating-point numbers.

Arduino Code:

```
int numbers[5];  // Array to hold 5 numbers
int sum = 0;
float average;

void setup() {
  Serial.begin(9600);  // Start serial communication at 9600 baud rate
  Serial.println("Sum and Average Calculator");

  // Input numbers into the array
  for (int i = 0; i < 5; i++) {
    Serial.print("Enter number ");
    Serial.print(i + 1);
    Serial.println(":");
    while (Serial.available() == 0) {}  // Wait for input
    numbers[i] = Serial.parseInt();  // Read input and store in array
  }

  // Calculate the sum of the array elements
  for (int i = 0; i < 5; i++) {
    sum += numbers[i];
  }
  // Calculate the average of the array elements
  average = sum / 5.0;
  // Print the sum and average to the Serial Monitor
  Serial.print("Sum: ");
  Serial.println(sum);
  Serial.print("Average: ");
  Serial.println(average);
}
void loop() {
  // Empty loop since no continuous process is needed
}
```

Steps to Upload:

1. Open the **Arduino IDE** and connect your ESP32 or ESP8266 to your computer via USB.
2. Copy and paste the code into a new sketch.
3. In **Tools > Board**, select **ESP32** or **ESP8266** and the correct COM port.
4. Click **Upload** to transfer the code to the board.

Check Output:

The program will prompt the user to input 5 numbers via the Serial Monitor. Once entered, it will calculate and display the sum and average of the numbers.

MicroPython Programming Section

MicroPython Syntax:

- *input()*: Reads input from the user.
- *for loop*: Iterates over a collection or range of numbers.
- *int, float*: Data types used to store integer and floating-point numbers.

MicroPython Code:

```python
numbers = []   # Array to store numbers
sum = 0

# Input numbers into the array
for i in range(5):
    num = int(input(f"Enter number {i + 1}: "))
    numbers.append(num)
# Calculate sum of array elements
for num in numbers:
    sum += num
# Calculate average of array elements
average = sum / len(numbers)

# Print sum and average
print("Sum:", sum)
print("Average:", average)
```

Steps to Upload:

1. Open your **MicroPython IDE** (such as Thonny) and connect the ESP32/ESP8266 via USB.
2. Copy and paste the code into the editor.
3. Click **Run** to execute the program.

Check Output:
The program will ask the user to input 5 numbers, then it will calculate and display the sum and average of those numbers.

Troubleshooting Tips

- **Invalid Input**: Ensure you are entering valid integer values when prompted for input.
- **Incorrect Sum/Average**: Ensure the correct number of inputs (5) is entered before performing the calculations.
- **No response from Serial Monitor**: Verify that the Serial Monitor is set to the correct baud rate (9600).

Further Exploration

- **Dynamic Array Size**: Modify the program to accept a dynamic number of inputs rather than a fixed number.
- **Real-time Calculation**: Allow the sum and average to be displayed in real-time as each new number is entered.
- **Range Calculation**: Add additional functionality to compute the minimum, maximum, or range of the array elements.

Note
This project provides a simple introduction to handling arrays, using loops, and performing arithmetic operations. It is a great foundational project for beginners to learn how to handle collections of data and iterate over them programmatically.

Project : LED Control with User Input (Digital Pin) using ESP32/ESP8266

Objective
Use a boolean variable to control the state of an LED (on/off) based on user input. This project is a great way to learn control structures and boolean logic in programming.

Programming Fundamentals
Brief description of **boolean, while loop,** and **if-else**:

- **boolean**: A data type that represents one of two values: `true` or `false`. Used to control the LED state (on/off).
- **while loop**: Repeatedly executes a block of code as long as the condition is true.
- **if-else**: A conditional statement used to execute different code blocks based on whether a condition is `true` or `false`.

Requirement Components

- **ESP32** or **ESP8266** microcontroller
- **Breadboard**
- **LED**
- **220-ohm resistor**
- **Jumper wires**
- **USB cable**
- **Computer with Arduino IDE or MicroPython IDE installed**

Circuit Diagram
Visual aid showing the LED connected to the ESP32/ESP8266 through a digital pin. The positive leg of the LED connects to the GPIO pin, and the negative leg connects through a 220-ohm resistor to the ground (GND).

Circuit Connection
1. Connect the **positive leg** of the LED to **GPIO2** of the ESP32/ESP8266.
2. Connect the **negative leg** of the LED to one side of the **220-ohm resistor**.
3. Connect the other side of the resistor to **GND**.

Arduino Programming Section
Arduino Syntax:
- *pinMode(pin, mode)*: Configures a digital pin as input or output.
- *digitalWrite(pin, value)*: Sets the pin to HIGH (on) or LOW (off).
- *boolean*: A data type used to hold `true` or `false` values.

Arduino Code:
```
boolean ledState = false;   // Variable to store LED state

void setup() {
  pinMode(2, OUTPUT);   // Set GPIO2 as output
  Serial.begin(9600);   // Start serial communication
  Serial.println("Enter '1' to turn LED on or '0' to turn LED off:");
}
void loop() {
  if (Serial.available() > 0) {
    char input = Serial.read();   // Read user input
    if (input == '1') {
      ledState = true;   // Turn LED on
    } else if (input == '0') {
      ledState = false;   // Turn LED off
    } else {
      Serial.println("Invalid input. Please enter '1' or '0'.");
    }
    // Set the LED state based on user input
    digitalWrite(2, ledState ? HIGH : LOW);
    // Display the LED state to the user
    Serial.print("LED is ");
    Serial.println(ledState ? "ON" : "OFF");
```

```
    }
}
```

Steps to Upload:

1. Open the **Arduino IDE** and connect your ESP32 or ESP8266 to your computer via USB.
2. Copy and paste the code into a new sketch.
3. In **Tools > Board**, select **ESP32** or **ESP8266** and the correct COM port.
4. Click **Upload** to transfer the code to the board.

Check Output:
You can enter '1' to turn the LED on or '0' to turn it off using the Serial Monitor. The current state of the LED will also be displayed.

MicroPython Programming Section
MicroPython Syntax:

- *pin = machine.Pin(pin_number, mode)*: Configures a digital pin as input or output.
- *pin.value(state)*: Sets the pin to HIGH (1) or LOW (0).
- *boolean*: Represents True or False.

MicroPython Code:

```
from machine import Pin
import time
led = Pin(2, Pin.OUT)  # Set GPIO2 as output
led_state = False  # Boolean variable to store LED state
while True:
    user_input = input("Enter '1' to turn LED on or '0' to turn LED off: ")

    if user_input == '1':
        led_state = True   # Turn LED on
    elif user_input == '0':
        led_state = False  # Turn LED off
    else:
        print("Invalid input. Please enter '1' or '0'.")
        continue
    # Set the LED state based on user input
    led.value(1 if led_state else 0)

    # Display the LED state
```

```
print(f"LED is {'ON' if led_state else 'OFF'}")
```

Steps to Upload:

1. Open your **MicroPython IDE** (such as Thonny) and connect the ESP32/ESP8266 via USB.
2. Copy and paste the code into the editor.
3. Click **Run** to execute the program.

Check Output:

Enter '1' to turn the LED on or '0' to turn it off through the terminal. The LED state will be updated, and the program will display the current state.

Troubleshooting Tips

- **LED not turning on/off**: Ensure the LED is properly connected to the correct GPIO pin.
- **Invalid input**: Ensure you are entering '1' or '0' in the Serial Monitor or terminal.
- **No response from Serial Monitor**: Verify that the correct baud rate is selected (9600) in the Serial Monitor.
- **Code not uploading**: Check if the correct board and COM port are selected in the IDE.

Further Exploration

- **Toggle Functionality**: Modify the program to allow toggling the LED on and off with the same input.
- **Multiple LEDs**: Expand the program to control multiple LEDs using different inputs.
- **PWM for Brightness Control**: Use PWM to control the brightness of the LED instead of just turning it on and off.

Note

This project introduces basic control structures, boolean logic, and user interaction using ESP32/ESP8266. It's a great way for beginners to get familiar with handling user input, controlling hardware components like LEDs, and applying boolean logic in programming.

Working with Data and Characters

Project Title: User Input Validation using ESP32/ESP8266

Objective
Create a program where the user inputs characters or strings, and the program validates the input (e.g., checking if it's a valid name or email). This helps in working with strings and character handling.

Programming Fundamentals
Brief description of **Characters (char)**, **String**, and **if-else**:

- **char**: A data type that stores a single character.
- **String**: A sequence of characters used to represent text.
- **if-else**: A conditional statement that executes different blocks of code depending on whether a condition is true or false.

Requirement Components

- **ESP32** or **ESP8266** microcontroller
- **Breadboard**
- **Jumper wires**
- **USB cable**
- **Computer with Arduino IDE or MicroPython IDE installed**

Circuit Diagram
(No specific circuit needed for this software-only program.)

Circuit Connection
This is a software-only project, so no hardware connections are required.

Arduino Programming Section
Arduino Syntax:
- *Serial.begin(baud_rate)*: Initializes serial communication with the specified baud rate.
- *Serial.read(), Serial.print()*: Reads and prints characters from the Serial Monitor.
- *if-else*: Conditional statements used for input validation.

Arduino Code:

```
String input;

void setup() {
  Serial.begin(9600);  // Start serial communication at 9600 baud rate
  Serial.println("Input Validation Program");
  Serial.println("Enter a valid name or email:");
}

void loop() {
  if (Serial.available() > 0) {
    input = Serial.readString();  // Read input from the user

    // Check if the input is a valid name (only alphabetic characters)
    if (isValidName(input)) {
      Serial.print("Valid name: ");
      Serial.println(input);
    }
    // Check if the input is a valid email (contains '@' and '.')
    else if (isValidEmail(input)) {
      Serial.print("Valid email: ");
      Serial.println(input);
    }
    else {
      Serial.println("Invalid input. Please enter a valid name or email.");
    }
  }
  delay(1000);  // Small delay before next input
}

bool isValidName(String str) {
  for (int i = 0; i < str.length(); i++) {
    if (!isAlpha(str.charAt(i))) {
      return false;  // If any character is not alphabetic, it's not a valid name
    }
  }
  return true;
}
bool isValidEmail(String str) {
  return (str.indexOf('@') > 0 && str.indexOf('.') > str.indexOf('@') + 1);
}
```

```
}
```

Steps to Upload:
1. Open the **Arduino IDE** and connect your ESP32 or ESP8266 to your computer via USB.
2. Copy and paste the code into a new sketch.
3. In **Tools > Board**, select **ESP32** or **ESP8266** and the correct COM port.
4. Click **Upload** to transfer the code to the board.

Check Output:
You can enter a name or an email address via the Serial Monitor. The program will validate if it is a valid name (all alphabetic characters) or a valid email (contains '@' and '.').

MicroPython Programming Section
MicroPython Syntax:
- *input()*: Reads input from the user.
- *if-else*: Conditional statements used for input validation.
- *find()*: Used to locate characters or substrings in a string.

MicroPython Code:
```python
def is_valid_name(name):
    return name.isalpha()  # Check if the input contains only alphabetic characters

def is_valid_email(email):
    return '@' in email and '.' in email[email.index('@'):]  # Check if email contains '@' and '.'

def input_validation():
    user_input = input("Enter a valid name or email: ")

    if is_valid_name(user_input):
        print(f"Valid name: {user_input}")
    elif is_valid_email(user_input):
        print(f"Valid email: {user_input}")
    else:
        print("Invalid input. Please enter a valid name or email.")

while True:
    input_validation()
```

Steps to Upload:

1. Open your **MicroPython IDE** (such as Thonny) and connect the ESP32/ESP8266 via USB.
2. Copy and paste the code into the editor.
3. Click **Run** to execute the program.

Check Output:
You will be prompted to enter a name or an email, and the program will validate whether the input is a valid name or email.

Troubleshooting Tips
- **Invalid name or email**: Ensure the input is correctly formatted with only alphabetic characters for names and a valid format for emails (including '@' and '.').
- **No response from Serial Monitor**: Ensure the correct baud rate (9600) is selected in the Serial Monitor.
- **Code not uploading**: Check if the correct board and COM port are selected in the IDE.

Further Exploration

- **Phone Number Validation**: Extend the program to validate phone numbers.
- **Password Validation**: Implement a password validation system that checks for minimum length and special characters.
- **User Registration System**: Combine input validation with data storage to create a simple user registration system.

Note
This project provides a simple introduction to handling user input and validating strings. It's an excellent way for beginners to practice working with strings, characters, and conditionals in programming using the ESP32/ESP8266.

Project: String to Integer Converter using ESP32/ESP8266

Objective
Build a program that converts a string input (e.g., a number entered as text) into an integer for mathematical operations. This project introduces data conversion techniques.

Programming Fundamentals
Brief description of **String to Integer Conversion**, **if-else**, and **Serial Communication**:

- **String to Integer Conversion**: This involves converting a string (text) that represents a number into an integer data type for mathematical operations.
- **if-else**: A conditional statement that helps execute different blocks of code based on the condition being true or false.
- **Serial Communication**: Allows communication between the microcontroller and the user via the Serial Monitor (in Arduino) or console (in MicroPython).

Requirement Components

- **ESP32** or **ESP8266** microcontroller
- **Breadboard**
- **Jumper wires**
- **USB cable**
- **Computer with Arduino IDE or MicroPython IDE installed**

Circuit Diagram
(No specific circuit needed for this software-only program.)

Circuit Connection
This is a software-only project, so no hardware connections are required.

Arduino Programming Section

Arduino Syntax:

- *Serial.begin(baud_rate)*: Initializes serial communication with the specified baud rate.
- *Serial.readString(), parseInt(), toInt()*: Functions used to read input and convert strings to integers.

Arduino Code:

```
String input;  // Variable to store the string input
int number;    // Variable to store the converted integer

void setup() {
  Serial.begin(9600);  // Start serial communication at 9600 baud rate
  Serial.println("String to Integer Converter");
  Serial.println("Enter a number:");
}

void loop() {
  if (Serial.available() > 0) {
    input = Serial.readString();  // Read input from user

    // Convert the string to an integer
    number = input.toInt();

    // Output the converted integer
    Serial.print("Converted Integer: ");
    Serial.println(number);

    // Perform an operation with the integer (e.g., addition)
    int result = number + 10;
    Serial.print("Adding 10 to the number: ");
    Serial.println(result);
  }
  delay(1000);  // Delay before accepting next input
}
```

Steps to Upload:

1. Open the **Arduino IDE** and connect your ESP32 or ESP8266 to your computer via USB.
2. Copy and paste the code into a new sketch.
3. In **Tools > Board**, select **ESP32** or **ESP8266** and the correct COM port.
4. Click **Upload** to transfer the code to the board.

Check Output:
Enter a number as a string via the Serial Monitor, and the program will convert it into an integer. It will also add 10 to the number and display the result.

MicroPython Programming Section

MicroPython Syntax:

- *input()*, *int()*, *print()*: Functions used to read input, convert a string to an integer, and display output.

MicroPython Code:

```
def string_to_integer_converter():
    user_input = input("Enter a number: ")  # Read input from the user

    try:
        # Convert the string to an integer
        number = int(user_input)
        print("Converted Integer:", number)

        # Perform an operation with the integer (e.g., addition)
        result = number + 10
        print("Adding 10 to the number:", result)
    except ValueError:
        print("Invalid input. Please enter a valid number.")

while True:
    string_to_integer_converter()
```

Steps to Upload:

1. Open your **MicroPython IDE** (such as Thonny) and connect the ESP32/ESP8266 via USB.
2. Copy and paste the code into the editor.
3. Click **Run** to execute the program.

Check Output:
The program will prompt you to enter a number as a string, convert it to an integer, and then add 10 to the number and display the result.

Troubleshooting Tips

- **Invalid input**: Ensure that the input is a valid number in string format to avoid conversion errors.
- **No response from Serial Monitor**: Verify the correct baud rate (9600) is selected in the Serial Monitor.
- **Code not uploading**: Check that the correct board and COM port are selected in the IDE.

Further Exploration

- **Float Conversion**: Modify the program to handle floating-point numbers by converting strings to float data type.
- **Negative Numbers**: Add functionality to validate and handle negative numbers.
- **Multiple Operations**: Extend the program to perform multiple operations (addition, subtraction, multiplication, etc.) on the converted integer.

Note

This project introduces data type conversion from strings to integers, which is crucial when working with user inputs in text form. It's a foundational project for handling input validation and performing mathematical operations using ESP32/ESP8266.

Project: Basic Calculator with String Input using ESP32/ESP8266

Objective

Create a simple calculator that takes user input as a string (numbers and operators), converts them to integers, performs the operations, and converts the result back to a string for display. This project covers both string manipulation and data conversion.

Programming Fundamentals

Brief description of **String to Integer Conversion, Integer to String Conversion**, and **Arithmetic Operations**:

- **String to Integer Conversion**: Converts a string containing numbers into an integer for performing calculations.
- **Integer to String Conversion**: Converts the result of a calculation back into a string for display.
- **Arithmetic Operations**: Includes basic operations like addition, subtraction, multiplication, and division.

Requirement Components

- **ESP32** or **ESP8266** microcontroller
- **Breadboard**
- **Jumper wires**
- **USB cable**
- **Computer with Arduino IDE or MicroPython IDE installed**

Circuit Diagram

(No specific circuit needed for this software-only program.)

Circuit Connection

This is a software-only project, so no hardware connections are required.

Arduino Programming Section

Arduino Syntax:

- *Serial.begin(baud_rate)*: Initializes serial communication with the specified baud rate.
- *Serial.readString(), toInt(), toFloat()*: Functions used to read and convert strings to integers or floats for calculations.

Arduino Code:

```
String input;
int num1, num2;
char operation;
String result;

void setup() {
  Serial.begin(9600);   // Start serial communication at 9600 baud rate
  Serial.println("Basic Calculator with String Input");
  Serial.println("Enter the operation in this format: num1 operator num2 (e.g., 5 + 3):");
}

void loop() {
  if (Serial.available() > 0) {
    input = Serial.readString();   // Read input from user

    // Split the input string into numbers and operator
    int firstSpace = input.indexOf(' ');
    int secondSpace = input.lastIndexOf(' ');

    num1 = input.substring(0, firstSpace).toInt();
    operation = input.charAt(firstSpace + 1);
    num2 = input.substring(secondSpace + 1).toInt();

    // Perform the appropriate operation
    switch (operation) {
      case '+':
        result = String(num1 + num2);
        break;
      case '-':
        result = String(num1 - num2);
        break;
      case '*':
        result = String(num1 * num2);
        break;
      case '/':
        if (num2 != 0) {
          result = String((float)num1 / num2);
        } else {
          result = "Error: Division by zero";
        }
        break;
      default:
        result = "Invalid operator";
        break;
    }

    // Display the result
    Serial.print("Result: ");
    Serial.println(result);
  }
  delay(1000);   // Small delay before next input
}
```

Steps to Upload:
1. Open the **Arduino IDE** and connect your ESP32 or ESP8266 to your computer via USB.
2. Copy and paste the code into a new sketch.
3. In **Tools > Board**, select **ESP32** or **ESP8266** and the correct COM port.
4. Click **Upload** to transfer the code to the board.

Check Output:
You can input a mathematical operation like 5 + 3 via the Serial Monitor, and the program will display the result.

MicroPython Programming Section
MicroPython Syntax:
- *input()*, *int()*, *float()*, *print()*: Functions used to read input, convert between data types, and display results.

MicroPython Code:

```python
def basic_calculator():
    user_input = input("Enter the operation (e.g., 5 + 3): ")
    
    # Split the input into numbers and operator
    components = user_input.split()
    num1 = int(components[0])
    operator = components[1]
    num2 = int(components[2])
    
    # Perform the operation
    if operator == '+':
        result = num1 + num2
    elif operator == '-':
        result = num1 - num2
    elif operator == '*':
        result = num1 * num2
    elif operator == '/':
        if num2 != 0:
            result = num1 / num2
        else:
            result = "Error: Division by zero"
    else:
        result = "Invalid operator"
    
    # Display the result
    print("Result:", result)

while True:
    basic_calculator()
```

Steps to Upload:

1. Open your **MicroPython IDE** (such as Thonny) and connect the ESP32/ESP8266 via USB.
2. Copy and paste the code into the editor.
3. Click **Run** to execute the program.

Check Output:
The program will prompt you to enter a mathematical operation like 5 + 3, and it will display the result.

Troubleshooting Tips

- **Invalid input format**: Ensure the input is in the correct format (e.g., 5 + 3).
- **Division by zero**: Ensure the divisor is not zero when performing division.
- **No response from Serial Monitor**: Verify that the correct baud rate (9600) is selected in the Serial Monitor.

Further Exploration

- **Floating-point Numbers**: Modify the program to handle floating-point numbers for more precise calculations.
- **Advanced Operations**: Add support for more complex operations like exponents or modulus.
- **User Interface**: Integrate a small display or keypad for user input and output, making the calculator more interactive.

Note
This project introduces both string manipulation and data conversion techniques, allowing for the creation of a simple but functional calculator using ESP32/ESP8266. It demonstrates how to parse user input and perform basic arithmetic operations in a user-friendly way.

Operators and Logical Flow

Project: Number Comparison Game using ESP32/ESP8266

Objective
Create a number guessing game where the program generates a random number, and the user has to guess it. The program will give hints using comparison operators (greater than, less than, equal to).

Programming Fundamentals
Brief description of **Comparison Operators (==, !=, >, <, >=, <=)** and **if-else**:

- **Comparison Operators**: These are used to compare two values (e.g., if one number is greater than another or if two numbers are equal).
- **if-else**: A conditional statement that helps to decide what action to take based on the result of the comparison.

Requirement Components

- **ESP32** or **ESP8266** microcontroller
- **Breadboard**
- **Jumper wires**
- **USB cable**
- **Computer with Arduino IDE or MicroPython IDE installed**

Circuit Diagram
(No specific circuit needed for this software-only program.)

Circuit Connection
This is a software-only project, so no hardware connections are required.

Arduino Programming Section

Arduino Syntax:

- *randomSeed(), random()*: Functions used to generate a random number.
- *if-else*: Conditional statements used to compare the guessed number with the target number.

Arduino Code:

```
int targetNumber;   // The number the user has to guess
int userGuess;

void setup() {
  Serial.begin(9600);   // Start serial communication at 9600 baud rate
  randomSeed(analogRead(0));   // Generate a seed for the random number generator
  targetNumber = random(1, 101);   // Generate a random number between 1 and 100

  Serial.println("Number Comparison Game");
  Serial.println("Guess the number between 1 and 100:");
}

void loop() {
  if (Serial.available() > 0) {
    userGuess = Serial.parseInt();   // Read user's guess

    // Compare user's guess with the target number
    if (userGuess == targetNumber) {
      Serial.println("Congratulations! You guessed the correct number.");
      Serial.println("Generating a new number. Try again!");
      targetNumber = random(1, 101);   // Generate a new random number
    }
    else if (userGuess < targetNumber) {
      Serial.println("Too low! Try again.");
    }
    else if (userGuess > targetNumber) {
      Serial.println("Too high! Try again.");
    }
  }
  delay(1000);   // Small delay before the next guess
}
```

Steps to Upload:

1. Open the **Arduino IDE** and connect your ESP32 or ESP8266 to your computer via USB.
2. Copy and paste the code into a new sketch.
3. In **Tools > Board**, select **ESP32** or **ESP8266** and the correct COM port.
4. Click **Upload** to transfer the code to the board.

Check Output:
You can guess a number via the Serial Monitor, and the program will give feedback on whether your guess is too high, too low, or correct.

MicroPython Programming Section
MicroPython Syntax:
- *random.randint(), if-else, input(), print()*: Functions and structures used to generate random numbers, compare values, and interact with the user.

MicroPython Code:

```python
import random
def number_comparison_game():
    target_number = random.randint(1, 100)   # Generate a random number between 1 and 100
    print("Number Comparison Game")
    print("Guess the number between 1 and 100:")

    while True:
        try:
            user_guess = int(input("Enter your guess: "))

            if user_guess == target_number:
                print("Congratulations! You guessed the correct number.")
                break   # End the game when the correct number is guessed
            elif user_guess < target_number:
                print("Too low! Try again.")
            elif user_guess > target_number:
                print("Too high! Try again.")
        except ValueError:
            print("Invalid input. Please enter a number.")
while True:
    number_comparison_game()
    if input("Play again? (y/n): ").lower() != 'y':
        break
```

Steps to Upload:

1. Open your **MicroPython IDE** (such as Thonny) and connect the ESP32/ESP8266 via USB.
2. Copy and paste the code into the editor.
3. Click **Run** to execute the program.

Check Output:
The program will generate a random number, and you can guess it via the terminal. The program will give feedback on whether your guess is too high, too low, or correct.

Troubleshooting Tips

- **Invalid input**: Ensure the input is a valid integer number.
- **No response from Serial Monitor**: Ensure the correct baud rate (9600) is selected in the Serial Monitor.
- **Random number not generating**: Verify that the random seed is properly initialized using `randomSeed()` or `random.randint()`.

Further Exploration

- **Score System**: Add a score system that tracks how many guesses it takes to get the correct answer.
- **Difficulty Levels**: Implement different difficulty levels by adjusting the range of random numbers (e.g., 1 to 50 for easy, 1 to 100 for hard).
- **Timer**: Add a timer to see how quickly the user can guess the correct number.

Note
This project helps beginners understand how to use comparison operators and conditionals to create a game-like environment. The number guessing game is simple but illustrates how to interact with user inputs and give meaningful feedback using ESP32/ESP8266.

Project: Simple Bitwise Calculator using ESP32/ESP8266

Objective
Write a program that allows the user to input two numbers and perform bitwise operations like AND, OR, XOR, and NOT on them. The result will be displayed using bitwise logic.

Programming Fundamentals
Brief description of **Bitwise Operators (&, |, ^, ~)**:

- **& (AND)**: Compares each bit of two numbers and returns 1 if both bits are 1, otherwise returns 0.
- **| (OR)**: Compares each bit of two numbers and returns 1 if either bit is 1, otherwise returns 0.
- **^ (XOR)**: Compares each bit of two numbers and returns 1 if the bits are different, otherwise returns 0.
- **~ (NOT)**: Inverts all the bits of a number (turns 0 to 1 and vice versa).

Requirement Components

- **ESP32 or ESP8266 microcontroller**
- **Breadboard**
- **Jumper wires**
- **USB cable**
- **Computer with Arduino IDE or MicroPython IDE installed**

Circuit Diagram
(No specific circuit needed for this software-only program.)

Circuit Connection
This is a software-only project, so no hardware connections are required.

Arduino Programming Section
Arduino Syntax:
- *Serial.begin(baud_rate)*: Initializes serial communication with the specified baud rate.
- *Serial.readString(), Serial.print()*: Functions used to read input and display output via the Serial Monitor.
- *bitwise operators (&, |, ^, ~)*: Performs bitwise calculations.

Arduino Code:
```
int num1, num2;
String input;
char operation;
void setup() {
  Serial.begin(9600);  // Start serial communication at 9600 baud rate
  Serial.println("Simple Bitwise Calculator");
  Serial.println("Enter two numbers followed by a bitwise operator (&, |, ^, ~):");
}
void loop() {
  if (Serial.available() > 0) {
    input = Serial.readString();  // Read input from user
    // Split the input into numbers and operator
    int firstSpace = input.indexOf(' ');
    int secondSpace = input.lastIndexOf(' ');
    num1 = input.substring(0, firstSpace).toInt();
    operation = input.charAt(firstSpace + 1);
    // Perform the bitwise operation
    int result;
    switch (operation) {
      case '&':
        num2 = input.substring(secondSpace + 1).toInt();
        result = num1 & num2;
        break;
      case '|':
        num2 = input.substring(secondSpace + 1).toInt();
        result = num1 | num2;
        break;
      case '^':
        num2 = input.substring(secondSpace + 1).toInt();
        result = num1 ^ num2;
        break;
      case '~':
        result = ~num1;
        break;
      default:
        Serial.println("Invalid operator. Use &, |, ^, or ~.");
        return;
    }
    // Display the result
    Serial.print("Result: ");
    Serial.println(result);
  }
  delay(1000);  // Delay for next input
}
```

Steps to Upload:
1. Open the **Arduino IDE** and connect your ESP32 or ESP8266 to your computer via USB.
2. Copy and paste the code into a new sketch.
3. In **Tools > Board**, select **ESP32** or **ESP8266** and the correct COM port.
4. Click **Upload** to transfer the code to the board.

Check Output:
You can input two numbers and a bitwise operator via the Serial Monitor, and the program will display the result of the bitwise operation.

MicroPython Programming Section
MicroPython Syntax:
- *input(), int(), print()*: Functions used to read input, convert numbers, and display results.
- *bitwise operators (&, |, ^, ~)*: Performs bitwise calculations.

MicroPython Code:

```python
def bitwise_calculator():
    user_input = input("Enter two numbers followed by a bitwise operator (&, |, ^, ~): ")

    # Split the input into numbers and operator
    components = user_input.split()
    num1 = int(components[0])
    operator = components[1]

    # Perform the bitwise operation
    if operator == '&':
        num2 = int(components[2])
        result = num1 & num2
    elif operator == '|':
        num2 = int(components[2])
        result = num1 | num2
    elif operator == '^':
        num2 = int(components[2])
        result = num1 ^ num2
    elif operator == '~':
        result = ~num1
    else:
        result = "Invalid operator. Use &, |, ^, or ~."

    # Display the result
    print("Result:", result)

while True:
    bitwise_calculator()
```

Steps to Upload:

1. Open your **MicroPython IDE** (such as Thonny) and connect the ESP32/ESP8266 via USB.
2. Copy and paste the code into the editor.
3. Click **Run** to execute the program.

Check Output:
The program will ask for two numbers and a bitwise operator. You can input numbers and a bitwise operator (like &, |, ^, ~), and it will display the result.

Troubleshooting Tips

- **Invalid operator**: Ensure you are using one of the valid bitwise operators (&, |, ^, ~).
- **Invalid input**: Ensure the numbers are entered correctly, and check for any spaces or incorrect format.
- **No response from Serial Monitor**: Verify the correct baud rate (9600) is selected in the Serial Monitor.

Further Exploration
- **Bit Shifting Operations**: Add support for bit shifting operators like << (left shift) and >> (right shift).
- **Binary Representation**: Modify the program to display the binary representation of the numbers and the result.
- **Multiple Bitwise Operations**: Allow the user to input more complex expressions involving multiple bitwise operations.

Note
This project helps beginners understand how bitwise operations work and how to manipulate bits in integers. It's a good introduction to low-level programming concepts using ESP32/ESP8266 and provides a practical understanding of bitwise logic.

Project: Logical Flow Light Control using ESP32/ESP8266

Objective
Build a program that simulates a smart lighting system where two sensors (e.g., motion and light sensors) control an LED. The LED should only turn on when specific conditions are met, such as when it's dark and motion is detected.

Programming Fundamentals
Brief description of **Boolean Operators (&&, ||, !)** and **if-else**:

- **&& (AND)**: Returns true if both conditions are true.
- **|| (OR)**: Returns true if at least one of the conditions is true.
- **! (NOT)**: Reverses the boolean value, true becomes false and vice versa.
- **if-else**: A conditional statement that checks if conditions are met to perform specific actions (e.g., turning on/off the LED).

Requirement Components

- **ESP32** or **ESP8266** microcontroller
- **LED**
- **Motion sensor (PIR)**
- **Light sensor (LDR or photoresistor)**
- **220-ohm resistor**
- **Breadboard**
- **Jumper wires**
- **USB cable**
- **Computer with Arduino IDE or MicroPython IDE installed**

Circuit Diagram
Visual aid showing the LED connected to GPIO2, the motion sensor connected to a digital input pin (e.g., GPIO12), and the light sensor connected to an analog input pin (e.g., A0).

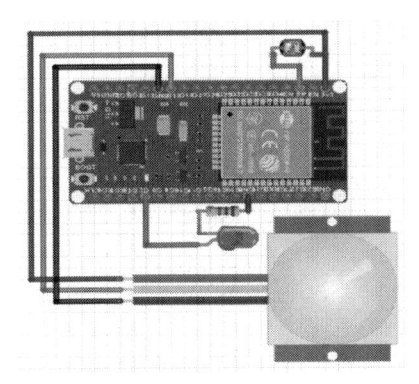

Circuit Connection

1. Connect the **LED** to GPIO2, with a 220-ohm resistor between the LED and ground.
2. Connect the **motion sensor (PIR)** output pin to GPIO12.
3. Connect the **light sensor (LDR)** between 3.3V and a voltage divider connected to A0 (analog input pin).
4. Connect the ground pins of all components to the GND pin of the ESP32/ESP8266.

Arduino Programming Section

Arduino Syntax:

- *digitalRead(pin)*: Reads the value (HIGH/LOW) from a digital pin.
- *analogRead(pin)*: Reads the analog value from a pin.
- *digitalWrite(pin, value)*: Sets the pin to HIGH (on) or LOW (off).
- *boolean operators (&&, ||, !)*: Used to control logical flow.

Arduino Code:

```
int ledPin = 2;              // LED connected to GPIO2
int motionSensorPin = 12;    // PIR motion sensor connected to GPIO12
int lightSensorPin = A0;     // Light sensor (LDR) connected to A0 (analog)

void setup() {
  pinMode(ledPin, OUTPUT);             // Set LED as output
  pinMode(motionSensorPin, INPUT);     // Set motion sensor as input
  Serial.begin(9600);                  // Start serial communication for debugging
}

void loop() {
  int motionDetected = digitalRead(motionSensorPin);   // Read motion sensor
  int lightLevel = analogRead(lightSensorPin);         // Read light sensor

  // Assume a threshold for the light sensor: lower values mean it is dark
  if (lightLevel < 500 && motionDetected == HIGH) {  // Dark and motion detected
    digitalWrite(ledPin, HIGH);    // Turn on the LED
    Serial.println("LED ON: Motion detected in darkness.");
  } else {
    digitalWrite(ledPin, LOW);    // Turn off the LED
    Serial.println("LED OFF: No motion or too much light.");
  }

  delay(1000);  // Small delay before checking again
}
```

Steps to Upload:

1. Open the **Arduino IDE** and connect your ESP32 or ESP8266 to your computer via USB.
2. Copy and paste the code into a new sketch.
3. In **Tools > Board**, select **ESP32** or **ESP8266** and the correct COM port.
4. Click **Upload** to transfer the code to the board.

Check Output:

The LED will turn on when the room is dark and motion is detected. The Serial Monitor will display the current status of the LED and the sensor readings.

MicroPython Programming Section

MicroPython Syntax:

- *Pin()*: Configures a pin as input or output.
- *machine.ADC()*: Reads the analog value from the light sensor.
- *if-else*: Conditional statements for controlling the flow.

MicroPython Code:

```python
from machine import Pin, ADC
import time

# Configure pins
led = Pin(2, Pin.OUT)              # LED connected to GPIO2
motion_sensor = Pin(12, Pin.IN)    # Motion sensor (PIR) connected to GPIO12
light_sensor = ADC(Pin(36))        # Light sensor (LDR) connected to GPIO36 (A0 on ESP32)

# Light sensor threshold for darkness (adjust based on your environment)
light_threshold = 500

while True:
    motion_detected = motion_sensor.value()   # Read the motion sensor (1: motion, 0: no motion)
    light_level = light_sensor.read()         # Read the light sensor (0-4095)

    if light_level < light_threshold and motion_detected:   # Dark and motion detected
        led.value(1)  # Turn on the LED
        print("LED ON: Motion detected in darkness.")
    else:
        led.value(0)  # Turn off the LED
        print("LED OFF: No motion or too much light.")

    time.sleep(1)  # Wait for 1 second before checking again
```

Steps to Upload:

1. Open your **MicroPython IDE** (such as Thonny) and connect the ESP32/ESP8266 via USB.
2. Copy and paste the code into the editor.
3. Click **Run** to execute the program.

Check Output:
The LED will turn on when the room is dark and motion is detected, just like the Arduino version. The console will display the status of the LED and the sensor readings.

Troubleshooting Tips

- **LED not turning on**: Ensure the motion sensor and light sensor are correctly connected, and check the sensor thresholds.
- **Incorrect light detection**: Adjust the light threshold in the code based on your specific lighting conditions.
- **No response from Serial Monitor**: Ensure the correct baud rate (9600) is selected in the Serial Monitor.

Further Exploration

- **Adjustable Thresholds**: Add potentiometers or buttons to dynamically adjust the light sensitivity threshold.
- **Multiple LEDs**: Control more than one LED in different locations, each responding to its own motion and light sensors.
- **Wireless Control**: Add Wi-Fi functionality to control the light system remotely through a web interface.

Note
This project introduces basic boolean logic and conditionals using sensors to create a smart lighting system. It's an excellent way to learn how to integrate multiple sensors and control devices like LEDs using ESP32/ESP8266.

Project: Grade Calculator with Compound Operators using ESP32/ESP8266

Objective
Create a program where the user inputs test scores. Use compound operators to calculate the total and average, then display a grade based on comparison operators (e.g., >= 90 for an A, >= 80 for a B).

Programming Fundamentals
Brief description of *Compound Operators (+=, -=, =, /=, %=) and **Comparison Operators**:

- **Compound Operators**: These are shorthand versions of common mathematical operations (e.g., += adds and assigns a value).
- **Comparison Operators**: Used to compare values (e.g., >=, <=, ==, !=) to decide the grade based on test scores.

Requirement Components

- **ESP32** or **ESP8266** microcontroller
- **USB cable**
- **Computer with Arduino IDE or MicroPython IDE installed**

Circuit Diagram
(No specific circuit needed for this software-only program.)

Arduino Programming Section
Arduino Syntax:

- *Serial.begin(baud_rate)*: Initializes serial communication with the specified baud rate.
- *Serial.readString(), toInt()*: Functions to read input from the user and convert it to an integer.
- *Compound operators (+=, -=, =, /=)*: Used to perform calculations.
- *Comparison operators*: Used to determine grades based on average scores.

Arduino Code:

```
int totalScore = 0;
int numTests = 0;
int score;
float average;
char grade;
void setup() {
  Serial.begin(9600);   // Start serial communication at 9600 baud rate
  Serial.println("Grade Calculator");
  Serial.println("Enter the test scores one by one. Type '-1' to finish:");
}
void loop() {
  if (Serial.available() > 0) {
    score = Serial.parseInt();   // Read input and convert to integer

    if (score == -1) {
      // Calculate the average
      if (numTests > 0) {
        average = totalScore / (float)numTests;
        // Determine the grade based on average score
        if (average >= 90) {
          grade = 'A';
        } else if (average >= 80) {
          grade = 'B';
        } else if (average >= 70) {
          grade = 'C';
        } else if (average >= 60) {
          grade = 'D';
        } else {
          grade = 'F';
        }
        // Display the total, average, and grade
        Serial.print("Total Score: ");
        Serial.println(totalScore);
        Serial.print("Average Score: ");
        Serial.println(average);
        Serial.print("Grade: ");
        Serial.println(grade);
      } else {
        Serial.println("No tests were entered.");
      }
      totalScore = 0;
      numTests = 0;
      delay(2000);   // Wait before starting again
      Serial.println("Enter new test scores or '-1' to finish:");
    } else {
      // Add the score to the total and increment the number of tests
      totalScore += score;
      numTests += 1;
      Serial.print("Score added: ");
      Serial.println(score);
    }
  }
}
```

Steps to Upload:

1. Open the **Arduino IDE** and connect your ESP32 or ESP8266 to your computer via USB.
2. Copy and paste the code into a new sketch.
3. In **Tools > Board**, select **ESP32** or **ESP8266** and the correct COM port.
4. Click **Upload** to transfer the code to the board.

Check Output:

You can input test scores one by one via the Serial Monitor. The program will display the total score, average, and grade when you type -1 to finish.

MicroPython Programming Section

MicroPython Syntax:

- *input(), int(), print()*: Functions to read input from the user, convert values to integers, and display output.
- *Compound operators (+=, -=, =, /=)*: Used to perform calculations.
- *Comparison operators*: Used to compare the average score with grading criteria.

MicroPython Code:

```python
def grade_calculator():
    total_score = 0
    num_tests = 0

    while True:
        try:
            score = int(input("Enter test score (or -1 to finish): "))

            if score == -1:
                break  # Stop entering scores

            total_score += score  # Use compound operator to add to total
            num_tests += 1  # Increment the number of tests

        except ValueError:
            print("Invalid input. Please enter a valid number.")

    if num_tests > 0:
        average = total_score / num_tests

        # Determine grade
        if average >= 90:
            grade = 'A'
        elif average >= 80:
            grade = 'B'
        elif average >= 70:
            grade = 'C'
        elif average >= 60:
            grade = 'D'
        else:
            grade = 'F'

        # Display the results
        print(f"Total Score: {total_score}")
        print(f"Average Score: {average:.2f}")
        print(f"Grade: {grade}")
    else:
        print("No test scores were entered.")

# Run the grade calculator
grade_calculator()
```

Steps to Upload:

1. Open your **MicroPython IDE** (such as Thonny) and connect the ESP32/ESP8266 via USB.
2. Copy and paste the code into the editor.
3. Click **Run** to execute the program.

Check Output:
The program will prompt you to input test scores. Once you enter -1, it will calculate the total score, average, and grade.

Troubleshooting Tips

- **Invalid input**: Ensure that the scores entered are numeric values.
- **No response from Serial Monitor**: Ensure the correct baud rate (9600) is selected in the Serial Monitor.
- **Incorrect grade**: Verify that the comparison logic is correct for calculating grades based on the average.

Further Exploration

- **Weighted Grades**: Add a feature that allows for different weightings for each test score.
- **Multiple Subjects**: Allow input for different subjects, and calculate averages for each subject individually.
- **Grade Summary**: Store and display the highest and lowest scores along with the average and grade.

Note

This project introduces the use of compound operators and comparison logic to perform mathematical operations on test scores and determine grades. It's an excellent practice for handling user input and performing calculations using ESP32/ESP8266.

Chapter 14 ESP Deep Sleep

Chapter Overview:

In this chapter, we'll explore the different wake-up features of the ESP32 and how to leverage these features to optimize power consumption in projects using deep sleep mode. This chapter is especially useful for those building battery-powered IoT devices or applications that need to conserve power while maintaining functionality. The focus will be on utilizing Timer Wake-up, Touchpad Wake-up, and External GPIO Wake-up in both Arduino and MicroPython environments.

Chapter Purpose:

The purpose of this chapter is to introduce and explain the different wake-up methods available on the ESP32, provide practical examples for implementing these methods, and guide developers in creating energy-efficient systems using deep sleep mode. By the end of this chapter, you will be able to:

- Understand the various wake-up mechanisms supported by the ESP32.
- Implement Timer Wake-up, Touchpad Wake-up, and External GPIO Wake-up using Arduino and MicroPython.
- Use deep sleep mode effectively to extend battery life in IoT applications.
- Troubleshoot common issues associated with wake-up methods in both Arduino and MicroPython.

Syntax Table:

Topic	Arduino Syntax	MicroPython Syntax
Deep Sleep Mode	`esp_deep_sleep_start()`	`machine.deepsleep(time_in_ms)`
Timer Wake-up	`esp_sleep_enable_timer_wakeup(uint64_t time_in_us)`	`machine.deepsleep(time_in_ms)`
Touchpad Wake-up	`esp_sleep_enable_touchpad_wakeup()`	`esp32.wake_on_touch(True)`
External GPIO Wake-up	`esp_sleep_enable_ext0_wakeup(gpio_num_t gpio_num, int level)`	`esp32.wake_on_ext0(pin, level)`

1. Timer Wake-up

Timer Wake-up is a feature that lets the ESP32 go to sleep and wake up after a certain amount of time. It's like setting an alarm clock. The ESP32 goes to "sleep" to save power and "wakes up" when the timer goes off.

Use Purpose:

The purpose of using Timer Wake-up is to save battery or power in projects where the ESP32 doesn't need to be awake all the time. It's useful in projects like weather stations, where the ESP32 only needs to turn on once in a while to check the data.

Arduino Syntax Use:

```
esp_sleep_enable_timer_wakeup(uint64_t time_in_us);
```

Arduino Syntax Explanation:

- **time_in_us**: This is the amount of time you want the ESP32 to sleep, measured in microseconds. For example, `1,000,000` microseconds equals 1 second.

Arduino Simple Code Example:

This example makes the ESP32 sleep for 10 seconds, then wake up.

```
void setup() {
  Serial.begin(115200);
  esp_sleep_enable_timer_wakeup(10 * 1000000);   // Sleep for 10 seconds
  Serial.println("Going to sleep for 10 seconds...");
  esp_deep_sleep_start();   // Go to deep sleep
}

void loop() {
  // This code will only run after the ESP32 wakes up
}
```

Notes:

- **Deep sleep mode** saves a lot of power and is very useful in battery-powered projects.
- Use this when you want the ESP32 to wake up at regular intervals to do something, like checking a sensor.

Warnings:

- The time is set in microseconds (1 second = 1,000,000 microseconds), so be careful with the number.
- Timer wake-up is not super precise. It might be off by a few seconds.

MicroPython Syntax Use:

```
machine.deepsleep(time_in_ms)
```

MicroPython Syntax Explanation:

- **time_in_ms**: This is the time you want the ESP32 to sleep, measured in milliseconds. For example, `10,000` milliseconds equals 10 seconds.

MicroPython Simple Code Example:

This example puts the ESP32 to sleep for 10 seconds.

```
import machine

print("Going to sleep for 10 seconds...")
machine.deepsleep(10000)   # Sleep for 10,000 milliseconds (10 seconds)
```

Notes:

- In MicroPython, deep sleep works the same as in Arduino, saving power by putting the ESP32 to sleep.
- You can wake it up after a specific time, just like setting an alarm.

Warnings:

- Be careful to use milliseconds (`1,000 milliseconds = 1 second`) when setting the time in MicroPython.
- Deep sleep is good for saving power, but the ESP32 can't do anything while it's asleep.

Project: ESP32 Wakes Up Every 10 Seconds to Read a Sensor Value

Objective
The goal of this project is to create a power-efficient system where the ESP32 wakes up every 10 seconds, reads sensor data (e.g., temperature and humidity from a DHT11 sensor), and then goes back into deep sleep to save battery power. The collected data can also be sent to a cloud service if needed.

Programming Fundamentals

- Utilize **deep sleep mode** to conserve battery life.
- Use **Timer Wake-up** to wake the ESP32 every 10 seconds.
- Read sensor data, such as temperature and humidity, during each wake-up cycle.
- Optionally send data to a cloud service like ThingsBoard or AWS IoT.

Required Components

- ESP32 development board
- DHT11/DHT22 (Temperature & Humidity Sensor)
- Jumper wires
- Breadboard
- USB cable for programming

Circuit Connection

- DHT11 Sensor:
    - VCC to 3.3V on ESP32
    - GND to GND on ESP32
    - Data pin to GPIO 4 on ESP32

Arduino Programming Section

Arduino Syntax

- `esp_sleep_enable_timer_wakeup(uint64_t time_in_us)`
- `esp_deep_sleep_start()`

Arduino Code

```
#include <DHT.h>

#define DHTPIN 4      // Pin connected to the sensor
#define DHTTYPE DHT11 // DHT11 sensor type
DHT dht(DHTPIN, DHTTYPE);

void setup() {
  Serial.begin(115200);
  dht.begin();

  // Wake up every 10 seconds
  esp_sleep_enable_timer_wakeup(10 * 1000000);
}

void loop() {
  // Read temperature and humidity
  float humidity = dht.readHumidity();
  float temperature = dht.readTemperature();

  // Check if readings are valid
  if (isnan(humidity) || isnan(temperature)) {
    Serial.println("Failed to read from DHT sensor!");
  } else {
    Serial.print("Temperature: ");
    Serial.print(temperature);
    Serial.print("°C, Humidity: ");
    Serial.print(humidity);
    Serial.println("%");
  }

  // Sleep for 10 seconds
  esp_deep_sleep_start();
}
```

Steps to Upload

1. Connect the ESP32 to your computer using a USB cable.
2. Open Arduino IDE and select your ESP32 board under **Tools > Board**.
3. Paste the code into a new sketch and click **Upload**.

Check Output
Open the Serial Monitor to see the temperature and humidity readings every 10 seconds.

MicroPython Programming Section

MicroPython Syntax

```
machine.deepsleep(time_in_ms)
```

MicroPython Code

```python
import machine
import dht
import time

# Pin for DHT11 sensor
sensor = dht.DHT11(machine.Pin(4))

while True:
    sensor.measure()
    temp = sensor.temperature()
    hum = sensor.humidity()

    print('Temperature:', temp, 'C')
    print('Humidity:', hum, '%')

    # Sleep for 10 seconds
    machine.deepsleep(10000)
```

Steps to Upload

1. Connect the ESP32 to your computer and open Thonny IDE.
2. Paste the MicroPython code and click **Run**.

Check Output
You will see the temperature and humidity readings every 10 seconds in the Thonny Shell.

Troubleshooting Tips

- **No Output?**: Check if the correct COM port is selected in Arduino IDE or Thonny.
- **Sensor Not Responding?**: Verify that the sensor is connected to the right GPIO pin and that the code matches the pin configuration.
- **ESP32 Not Waking Up?**: Ensure the timer is correctly set (in microseconds for Arduino, milliseconds for MicroPython).

Further Exploration

- You can send the collected sensor data to cloud platforms like ThingsBoard or AWS IoT.
- Adjust the sleep duration depending on how often you need the ESP32 to wake up and read the sensor.
- Add other sensors like motion or light sensors for a more complex monitoring system.

Note

This project introduces beginners to using deep sleep mode on the ESP32, which is ideal for battery-powered IoT applications. You can further expand it by adding cloud data transmission or more sensors.

2. Touchpad Wake-up

Touchpad Wake-up is a feature on the ESP32 that allows the device to wake up from deep sleep when a touch sensor is activated. The ESP32 has built-in touch sensor capabilities on certain GPIO pins, which can detect capacitive touch and trigger a wake-up event.

Use Purpose:

Touchpad Wake-up is useful in interactive projects where the ESP32 needs to stay in deep sleep to save power but wake up when a user touches a sensor. Examples include touch-based controls for smart home systems or low-power wake-up triggers for portable devices.

Arduino Syntax Use:

```
esp_sleep_enable_touchpad_wakeup();
```

Arduino Syntax Explanation:

`esp_sleep_enable_touchpad_wakeup()`: This function enables touchpad wake-up. It triggers the ESP32 to wake up from deep sleep when a touch is detected on one of the available touch-enabled pins.

Arduino Simple Code Example:

```
#include "driver/touch_pad.h"

void setup() {
  Serial.begin(115200);

  // Configure touchpad pin
  touchAttachInterrupt(T3, callback, 40); // Using Touchpad 3 (T3)

  // Enable touchpad wakeup
  esp_sleep_enable_touchpad_wakeup();

  Serial.println("Going to sleep now, touch sensor to wake me up.");
  esp_deep_sleep_start();
}

void loop() {}

void callback() {
  Serial.println("Touch detected, waking up!");
}
```

Notes:

Touchpad wake-up is handy for creating user-friendly devices where a simple touch can activate the system.
Touchpad pins are predefined on the ESP32. Make sure you're using the correct GPIO that supports capacitive touch.

Warnings:

The touch sensitivity can vary depending on the environment, humidity, and sensor configuration.
Improper grounding or noisy circuits may cause false wake-ups or missed touches.

MicroPython Syntax Use:

```
esp32.wake_on_touch(True)
```

MicroPython Syntax Explanation:

`esp32.wake_on_touch(True)`: This function enables wake-up on touch for the ESP32 in MicroPython. The ESP32 wakes up from deep sleep when a touch is detected on a touchpad-enabled pin.

MicroPython Simple Code Example:

```python
import machine
import esp32

# Enable touchpad wakeup
esp32.wake_on_touch(True)

# Set up touch sensor on GPIO 15 (Touchpad T3)
touch = machine.TouchPad(machine.Pin(15))

print('Going to sleep. Touch to wake up.')
machine.deepsleep()
```

Notes:

Touchpad wake-up in MicroPython is straightforward to set up and allows for low-power wake-up mechanisms in interactive projects. Like Arduino, only specific GPIO pins support touch functionality on the ESP32.

Warnings:

Ensure that the touch sensor is sensitive enough for the user to trigger the wake-up but not so sensitive that environmental factors cause false triggers.
Be aware of potential power consumption increases when using touchpads in noisy environments, as the ESP32 might wake up unintentionally.

Project: ESP32 Wakes Up When a Touch Sensor is Activated

Objective
The objective of this project is to create a system where the ESP32 wakes up from deep sleep when a touch sensor is activated. This is useful for smart home applications, such as control panels, where touching a panel can wake the device to control lights, appliances, or other systems.

Programming Fundamentals
- Use **Touchpad Wake-up** to detect touch input and wake the ESP32.
- Utilize **deep sleep mode** to save power when the device is inactive.
- The system will remain in low-power mode until the user touches the sensor.

Required Components
- ESP32 development board
- Touch sensor (using ESP32's built-in touch functionality on specific GPIO pins)
- Jumper wires
- Breadboard
- USB cable for programming

Circuit Connection
- Use one of the ESP32's touch-enabled GPIO pins (e.g., GPIO 4 or GPIO 15).
  - Connect the touchpad sensor directly to the appropriate touch pin on the ESP32.
  - Ground the sensor to the **GND** pin on the ESP32.

Arduino Programming Section
Arduino Syntax

```
esp_sleep_enable_touchpad_wakeup()
esp_deep_sleep_start()
```

Arduino Code

```
#include "driver/touch_pad.h"

void setup() {
  Serial.begin(115200);

  // Configure touchpad pin (T3 = GPIO 15)
  touchAttachInterrupt(T3, callback, 40); // Threshold value for touch detection
  // Enable touchpad wakeup
  esp_sleep_enable_touchpad_wakeup();

  Serial.println("Going to sleep now, touch sensor to wake me up.");
  esp_deep_sleep_start();
}
void loop() {}

void callback() {
  Serial.println("Touch detected, waking up!");
}
```

Steps to Upload

1. Connect the ESP32 to your computer using a USB cable.
2. Open Arduino IDE and select your ESP32 board under **Tools > Board**.
3. Paste the code into a new sketch and click **Upload**.

Check Output

1. Open the Serial Monitor in Arduino IDE.
2. The ESP32 will go into deep sleep, and upon touching the sensor, it will wake up and print a message on the Serial Monitor.

MicroPython Programming Section

MicroPython Syntax

```
esp32.wake_on_touch(True)
machine.deepsleep()
```

MicroPython Code

```
import machine
import esp32

# Enable touchpad wakeup
esp32.wake_on_touch(True)

# Set up touch sensor on GPIO 15 (Touchpad T3)
touch = machine.TouchPad(machine.Pin(15))

print('Going to sleep. Touch to wake up.')
machine.deepsleep()
```

Steps to Upload

1. Connect the ESP32 to your computer and open Thonny IDE.
2. Paste the MicroPython code and click **Run**.

Check Output

1. The ESP32 will go into deep sleep.
2. When the touch sensor is activated, the ESP32 will wake up, and a message will appear in the Thonny Shell.

Troubleshooting Tips

- If the ESP32 doesn't wake up, ensure that the correct GPIO pin is used for the touch sensor.
- Check the sensitivity threshold in the Arduino code (`touchAttachInterrupt`). Adjust it if the sensor is too sensitive or not responsive enough.
- Verify the Serial Monitor or Thonny Shell for any errors or debug messages.

Further Exploration

- Integrate this project with a smart home system to control lights or appliances. For example, upon waking up, the ESP32 can trigger a relay to turn on a light or send a signal to another device via Wi-Fi.
- Add multiple touch sensors to control different devices or perform different actions depending on the touched sensor.
- You can expand the project to include cloud integration for logging the activation events.

Note

This project demonstrates how to use the ESP32's touch functionality to wake the device from deep sleep, making it suitable for low-power applications that require interaction, such as smart home panels.

3. External GPIO Wake-up (Single GPIO)

External GPIO Wake-up (Single GPIO) is a feature that allows the ESP32 to wake up from deep sleep when a signal change (high or low) is detected on a specific GPIO pin. This is typically used for waking the ESP32 using a button press, a sensor signal, or other external events.

Use Purpose:

This feature is useful in projects where the ESP32 needs to be in deep sleep mode to conserve power, but it should wake up when triggered by an external event, such as pressing a button, a sensor detecting motion, or any other GPIO input signal.

Arduino Syntax Use:

```
esp_sleep_enable_ext0_wakeup(gpio_num_t gpio_num, int level);
```

Arduino Syntax Explanation:
- **gpio_num**: This specifies the GPIO pin that will trigger the wake-up.
- **level**: This specifies the signal level that will wake up the ESP32, either **LOW** (0) or **HIGH** (1).

Arduino Simple Code Example:

This example sets up the ESP32 to wake up from deep sleep when a button connected to GPIO 13 is pressed.

```
#define BUTTON_PIN 13   // GPIO pin for external button

void setup() {
  Serial.begin(115200);

  // Enable wakeup on GPIO 13 with a LOW signal
  esp_sleep_enable_ext0_wakeup(GPIO_NUM_13, 0);   // 0 means LOW level triggers wakeup

  Serial.println("Going to sleep, press the button to wake me up.");
  esp_deep_sleep_start();   // Enter deep sleep
}

void loop() {
  // This code will run after waking up
  Serial.println("Woke up from sleep!");
}
```

Notes:

- External GPIO wake-up is especially useful in low-power applications where the ESP32 needs to stay in deep sleep and wake only when necessary.
- You can use this feature in battery-powered devices, where power efficiency is a priority, such as IoT sensors or remote monitoring systems.

Warnings:

- The GPIO pin used for wake-up must be properly configured for input. Ensure that the correct pin is specified in the code.
- The wake-up trigger (HIGH or LOW) depends on the external component, so make sure to configure the level properly for the device you are using.

MicroPython Syntax Use:

```
esp32.wake_on_ext0(pin, level)
```

MicroPython Syntax Explanation:

- `pin`: This is the GPIO pin that will trigger the wake-up.
- `level`: This is the signal level (either LOW or HIGH) that will wake the ESP32.

MicroPython Simple Code Example:

This example sets up the ESP32 to wake up when a button connected to GPIO 13 is pressed.

```
import machine
import esp32

# Configure the GPIO pin for external wakeup
button_pin = machine.Pin(13, machine.Pin.IN)

# Enable external wakeup on GPIO 13 with a LOW signal
esp32.wake_on_ext0(pin=button_pin, level=0)

print('Going to sleep, press the button to wake me up.')
machine.deepsleep()
```

Notes:

- In MicroPython, external GPIO wake-up works similarly to Arduino, where the ESP32 can wake up from deep sleep when a signal is detected on a GPIO pin.
- This method is very efficient for projects that need to conserve power, such as motion detectors or remote sensor devices.

Warnings:

- Ensure that the pin is correctly set up as an input before configuring it for wake-up.
- Be mindful of the external circuit; improper configurations could result in false wake-ups or missed triggers.

Project: ESP32 Wakes Up When a Button is Pressed

Objective

The objective of this project is to create a power-efficient system where the ESP32 stays in deep sleep mode and only wakes up when a button is pressed. This is ideal for remote-controlled devices, like a smart doorbell, where power conservation is important, and the device only needs to be active when triggered by the button.

Programming Fundamentals

- Use **External GPIO Wake-up** to detect button presses and wake the ESP32.
- Utilize **deep sleep mode** to save power while the device is inactive.
- The system stays in deep sleep until someone presses the button, triggering the ESP32 to wake up and perform an action (e.g., sending a notification, ringing a bell, or taking a photo).

Required Components

- ESP32 development board
- Push-button switch
- Jumper wires
- Breadboard
- 10kΩ pull-down resistor (optional, depending on button wiring)
- USB cable for programming

Circuit Connection

- **Button Wiring**:
    - One leg of the button to **GPIO 13** (or any other external GPIO pin on the ESP32)
    - The other leg of the button to **GND**
    - (Optional) Connect a **10kΩ pull-down resistor** between **GPIO 13** and **GND** to ensure stable readings.

Arduino Programming Section

Arduino Syntax

```
esp_sleep_enable_ext0_wakeup(gpio_num_t gpio_num, int level)
esp_deep_sleep_start()
```

Arduino Code

This code wakes the ESP32 when a button connected to GPIO 13 is pressed.

```
#define BUTTON_PIN 13  // GPIO pin for the button

void setup() {
  Serial.begin(115200);

  // Enable wakeup on GPIO 13 with a LOW signal
  esp_sleep_enable_ext0_wakeup(GPIO_NUM_13, 0);  // 0 means LOW level triggers wakeup

  Serial.println("Going to sleep. Press the button to wake me up.");
  esp_deep_sleep_start();  // Enter deep sleep
}
void loop() {
  // This code will only run after the ESP32 wakes up
  Serial.println("Woke up from deep sleep!");
}
```

Steps to Upload

1. Connect the ESP32 to your computer using a USB cable.
2. Open Arduino IDE and select your ESP32 board under **Tools > Board**.
3. Paste the code into a new sketch and click **Upload**.

Check Output

1. Open the Serial Monitor in Arduino IDE.

2. The ESP32 will enter deep sleep mode, and upon pressing the button, it will wake up and print a message to the Serial Monitor.

MicroPython Programming Section

MicroPython Syntax

```
esp32.wake_on_ext0(pin, level)
machine.deepsleep()
```

MicroPython Code

This MicroPython code wakes the ESP32 when a button connected to GPIO 13 is pressed.

```python
import machine
import esp32

# Set up the button pin as input
button_pin = machine.Pin(13, machine.Pin.IN)

# Enable external wakeup on GPIO 13 with a LOW signal
esp32.wake_on_ext0(pin=button_pin, level=0)

print('Going to sleep. Press the button to wake me up.')
machine.deepsleep()
```

Steps to Upload
1. Connect the ESP32 to your computer and open Thonny IDE.
2. Paste the MicroPython code into Thonny and click **Run**.

Check Output
1. The ESP32 will go into deep sleep.
2. Press the button connected to GPIO 13 to wake the ESP32 and print the message in the Thonny Shell.

Troubleshooting Tips

- **No Response When Pressing the Button?**: Make sure you are using the correct GPIO pin for the button and check the wiring. Also, ensure the button pulls the pin low when pressed.

- **False Wake-ups**: If the ESP32 wakes up without pressing the button, verify the button wiring and consider adding a pull-down resistor if one is not present.
- **Not Waking Up**: Ensure the button wiring is properly set and the GPIO pin is configured correctly for input.

Further Exploration

- **Triggering Actions After Wake-up**: After the ESP32 wakes up from the button press, it can perform different tasks, such as sending a notification, turning on a light, or ringing a doorbell.
- **Adding Sensors or Other Inputs**: You can expand the project by adding sensors or other inputs that also wake the ESP32, giving the device multiple trigger points.
- **Cloud Integration**: Send a notification to a cloud platform (such as Firebase or AWS IoT) when the button is pressed, allowing remote monitoring or control.

Note

This project demonstrates how to use **External GPIO Wake-up** in the ESP32 to create a power-efficient system that stays in deep sleep mode until a button is pressed, making it ideal for remote-controlled devices like smart doorbells or interactive home automation systems.

4.Starting Sleep Modes

Deep Sleep Mode is a low-power state in which the ESP32 turns off most of its components, including the CPU and peripherals, while keeping a few essential functions (like the RTC – Real-Time Clock) active. In this mode, the ESP32 uses minimal power, making it ideal for battery-powered projects. It can wake up from deep sleep based on certain triggers such as timers, external GPIO signals, or touch sensors.

Use Purpose:

The primary purpose of Deep Sleep Mode is to significantly reduce power consumption in applications where the ESP32 doesn't need to be running all the time. It's used in projects like remote IoT sensors, data loggers, and smart devices that need to be operational for long periods on battery power.

Arduino Syntax Use:

```
esp_deep_sleep_start();
```

Arduino Syntax Explanation:

- **esp_deep_sleep_start()**: This function initiates deep sleep mode on the ESP32. Once the ESP32 enters deep sleep, the only way to wake it up is through a pre-configured wake-up source (such as a timer, touchpad, or GPIO pin).

Arduino Simple Code Example:

This code puts the ESP32 into deep sleep mode for 10 seconds and then wakes up to perform a task.

```
void setup() {
  Serial.begin(115200);

  // Set the timer to wake up after 10 seconds
  esp_sleep_enable_timer_wakeup(10 * 1000000);  // 10 seconds in microseconds

  Serial.println("Going to sleep for 10 seconds...");
  esp_deep_sleep_start();  // Enter deep sleep mode
}

void loop() {
  // This code will only run after the ESP32 wakes up
  Serial.println("Woke up from deep sleep!");
}
```

Notes:

- Deep Sleep Mode is excellent for conserving battery power, especially for projects where the ESP32 doesn't need to be continuously active.
- The ESP32 retains some memory during deep sleep, allowing it to resume specific tasks upon waking up.

Warnings:

- After entering deep sleep, the ESP32 will lose its current state, and the program will restart upon waking up, so you may need to use non-volatile memory (like RTC memory) to store important data.
- Ensure that the wake-up source is properly configured, as the ESP32 will remain in deep sleep until it detects a trigger.

MicroPython Syntax Use:

```
machine.deepsleep(time_in_ms)
```

MicroPython Syntax Explanation:

- **machine.deepsleep(time_in_ms)**: This function puts the ESP32 into deep sleep mode for a specified amount of time, measured in milliseconds. After the specified duration, the ESP32 wakes up automatically.

MicroPython Simple Code Example:

This code puts the ESP32 into deep sleep mode for 10 seconds.

```
import machine

print("Going to sleep for 10 seconds...")
machine.deepsleep(10000)  # 10 seconds in milliseconds
```

Notes:

- In MicroPython, deep sleep is as simple as calling the `deepsleep()` function. You can configure the ESP32 to wake up after a set period or based on other wake-up sources.
- Like in Arduino, the ESP32 restarts upon waking up, so consider storing important information in non-volatile memory.

Warnings:

- Deep sleep consumes minimal power, but make sure the wake-up source (like a timer or GPIO pin) is correctly configured to bring the ESP32 out of sleep.
- The ESP32 will lose its current state when it enters deep sleep. Be sure to store critical data in memory that persists through sleep, such as RTC memory or flash.

Project: Battery-powered Weather Station Using ESP32 with Deep Sleep

Objective
The objective of this project is to build a battery-powered weather station that collects temperature and humidity data using the ESP32 and a sensor like DHT11/DHT22. The ESP32 enters deep sleep mode to conserve battery power, waking up periodically (e.g., every hour) to read the sensor values and send the data to a server or log it.

Programming Fundamentals

- Utilize **Deep Sleep Mode** on the ESP32 to reduce power consumption.
- Use **Timer Wake-up** to periodically wake the ESP32 and collect data from the temperature and humidity sensor.
- Send data to a cloud service or log it locally before returning to deep sleep, ensuring long battery life.

Required Components

- ESP32 development board
- DHT11/DHT22 Temperature & Humidity Sensor
- Jumper wires
- Breadboard
- USB cable for programming
- Battery for powering the ESP32

Circuit Connection

- **DHT11/DHT22 Sensor**:
    - VCC to **3.3V** on ESP32
    - GND to **GND** on ESP32

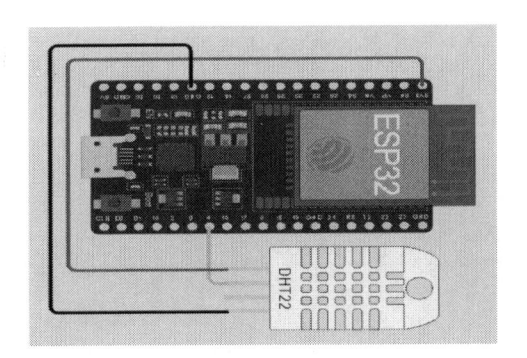

    - Data pin to **GPIO 4** on ESP32

Arduino Programming Section

Arduino Syntax

```
esp_sleep_enable_timer_wakeup(uint64_t time_in_us)
esp_deep_sleep_start()
```

Arduino Code

This code wakes up the ESP32 every hour, reads the temperature and humidity, prints the values, and then goes back to deep sleep.

```
#include <DHT.h>

#define DHTPIN 4      // Pin connected to the sensor
#define DHTTYPE DHT11 // DHT11 sensor type
DHT dht(DHTPIN, DHTTYPE);

void setup() {
  Serial.begin(115200);
  dht.begin();

  // Set the timer to wake up after 1 hour (3600 seconds)
  esp_sleep_enable_timer_wakeup(3600 * 1000000);  // 1 hour in microseconds

  // Read temperature and humidity
  float temperature = dht.readTemperature();
  float humidity = dht.readHumidity();

  // Check if readings are valid
  if (isnan(temperature) || isnan(humidity)) {
    Serial.println("Failed to read from DHT sensor!");
  } else {
    Serial.print("Temperature: ");
    Serial.print(temperature);
    Serial.println(" °C");
    Serial.print("Humidity: ");
    Serial.print(humidity);
    Serial.println(" %");
  }

  // Enter deep sleep
  Serial.println("Going to sleep now for 1 hour...");
  esp_deep_sleep_start();
}

void loop() {
  // This code will only run after the ESP32 wakes up
}
```

Steps to Upload

1. Connect the ESP32 to your computer using a USB cable.
2. Open Arduino IDE and select your ESP32 board under **Tools > Board**.
3. Paste the code into a new sketch and click **Upload**.

Check Output

1. Open the Serial Monitor in Arduino IDE.
2. The ESP32 will wake up, read the temperature and humidity values, print them to the Serial Monitor, and go back into deep sleep. It will wake up again after an hour to repeat the process.

MicroPython Programming Section

MicroPython Syntax

```
machine.deepsleep(time_in_ms)
```

MicroPython Code
This code puts the ESP32 into deep sleep for one hour, reads temperature and humidity from the DHT sensor, and prints the values before going back to sleep.

```python
import machine
import dht
import time

# Set up DHT11 sensor
sensor = dht.DHT11(machine.Pin(4))

# Measure temperature and humidity
sensor.measure()
temperature = sensor.temperature()
humidity = sensor.humidity()

# Print readings
print('Temperature: {} °C'.format(temperature))
print('Humidity: {} %'.format(humidity))

# Sleep for 1 hour (3600 seconds)
print('Going to sleep for 1 hour...')
machine.deepsleep(3600000)  # 1 hour in milliseconds
```

Steps to Upload

1. Connect the ESP32 to your computer and open Thonny IDE.
2. Paste the MicroPython code into Thonny and click **Run**.

Check Output

1. The ESP32 will wake up, read temperature and humidity, print the values, and then go back into deep sleep.
2. The ESP32 will wake up again after an hour and repeat the process.

Troubleshooting Tips

- **Incorrect Readings from DHT Sensor**: Ensure that the sensor is properly wired and that the correct GPIO pin is used in the code.
- **ESP32 Not Waking Up**: Double-check the timer wake-up configuration and ensure the sleep duration is set correctly.
- **No Output on Serial Monitor**: Ensure the correct COM port is selected in Arduino IDE or Thonny.

Further Exploration

- **Cloud Data Logging**: Send the collected temperature and humidity data to a cloud platform like ThingsBoard, Firebase, or AWS IoT for remote monitoring.
- **Adding More Sensors**: Expand the project by adding more sensors, such as pressure or air quality sensors, and include them in the data collection cycle.
- **Adjust Wake-up Interval**: Modify the deep sleep duration based on the application requirements, such as waking up every 30 minutes instead of an hour.

Note

This project demonstrates how to create a battery-powered weather station using the ESP32 with Deep Sleep Mode to conserve power. By waking up periodically to collect data, the ESP32 can operate for extended periods on a single battery charge, making it suitable for remote or portable IoT applications.

Section- Getting started with IoT in esp32 /esp8266

Chapter 15. WiFi Network

Chapter Overview:

In this chapter, we will cover how to use the WiFi functionality of Arduino and ESP32-based devices to connect to networks, create access points, and manage advanced network settings. This chapter will guide you through setting up WiFi connections, scanning for networks, managing WiFi modes, and optimizing network performance. It will also cover both Arduino and MicroPython environments.

Chapter Purpose:

This chapter aims to:

- Teach how to connect to WiFi networks, create access points, and switch between WiFi modes.
- Explain how to manage WiFi connections by checking status, retrieving IP addresses, and adjusting transmission power.
- Demonstrate how to use both Arduino and MicroPython for basic and advanced WiFi management in ESP32 and IoT projects.
- Provide examples for scanning WiFi networks and configuring static IPs.

Syntax Table:

Topic	Arduino Syntax	MicroPython Syntax
Connecting to WiFi	`WiFi.begin(ssid, password);`	`sta_if.connect('ssid', 'password')`
Creating an Access Point	`WiFi.softAP(ssid, password);`	`ap_if.config(essid='ssid', password='password')`
Disconnecting from WiFi	`WiFi.disconnect();`	`sta_if.disconnect()`
Checking Connection Status	`WiFi.status();`	`sta_if.status()`
Getting Local IP Address	`WiFi.localIP();`	`sta_if.ifconfig()[0]`
WiFi Mode: Station	`WiFi.mode(WIFI_STA);`	`sta_if.active(True)`
WiFi Mode: Access Point	`WiFi.mode(WIFI_AP);`	`ap_if.active(True)`
WiFi Mode: AP + Station	`WiFi.mode(WIFI_AP_STA);`	`ap_sta_if.active(True)`
Scanning for Networks	`WiFi.scanNetworks();`	`sta_if.scan()`

Setting Static IP	`WiFi.config(ip, gateway, subnet);`	`sta_if.ifconfig((ip, gateway, subnet, dns))`
Setting Hostname	`WiFi.setHostname(name);`	`sta_if.config(dhcp_hostname=name)`
Adjusting WiFi Power	`WiFi.setTxPower(power);`	`sta_if.config(txpower=power)`
Disabling WiFi Sleep Mode	`WiFi.setSleep(false);`	`sta_if.config(ps_mode=network.WIFI_PS_NONE)`

Basic Wi-Fi Setup

Connecting to WiFi

WiFi.begin(ssid, password) is a function that connects your Arduino or ESP-based device to a specific WiFi network using the provided SSID (network name) and password.

Use Purpose

The function allows your IoT device to connect to a WiFi network, enabling it to access the internet and communicate with other network devices, sensors, or servers.

Arduino Syntax Use

```
WiFi.begin(ssid, password);
```

Arduino Syntax Explanation

- *ssid*: The name of the WiFi network you want to connect to. This should be a string.

- *password*: The password of the WiFi network, provided as a string.

When this function is executed, the Arduino device will attempt to connect to the specified WiFi network.

Arduino Simple Code Example

```
WiFi.begin("YourNetworkName", "YourNetworkPassword");
```

Notes

- The connection process can take some time, so it's common to check the status in a loop and wait until the device successfully connects to the network.
- Make sure the network name (SSID) and password are correct to avoid connection issues.

Warnings

- If the SSID or password is incorrect, the connection will fail, and your device won't be able to access the network.
- WiFi.begin is a blocking function, which means it will stop the code execution until the connection is successful or times out.

MicroPython Syntax Use

```
sta_if = network.WLAN(network.STA_IF)
sta_if.active(True)
sta_if.connect('ssid', 'password')
```

MicroPython Syntax Explanation
- *network.WLAN(network.STA_IF)*: Sets up the device in station mode (to act as a client).
- *sta_if.active(True)*: Activates the WiFi interface.
- *sta_if.connect('ssid', 'password')*: Connects the device to the specified WiFi network.

MicroPython Simple Code Example

```
sta_if.connect('YourNetworkName', 'YourNetworkPassword')
```

Notes

- Check the connection status using *sta_if.isconnected()* to know when the connection is established.
- Station mode (STA) is used when you want the device to connect to an existing WiFi network.

Warnings

- Ensure that the SSID and password are correct, as incorrect values will prevent the device from connecting.
- The connection process might take a few seconds, so it's important to include checks to see if the device has connected successfully.

Creating an Access Point

WiFi.softAP(ssid, password) is a function that turns your Arduino or ESP-based device into a WiFi access point. It creates a new WiFi network that other devices can connect to, using the specified SSID (network name) and password.

Use Purpose

This function is useful when you want your device to act as a WiFi hotspot, allowing other devices to connect directly to it for communication or control without needing an external router.

Arduino Syntax Use

```
WiFi.softAP(ssid, password);
```

Arduino Syntax Explanation

- *ssid*: The name of the WiFi network you want to create. It should be provided as a string.
- *password*: The password for the WiFi network. This should also be provided as a string.

When this function is called, the device creates a WiFi network that other devices can connect to.

Arduino Simple Code Example

```
WiFi.softAP("MyAccessPoint", "MyPassword");
```

Notes

- This function creates an access point, meaning other devices can connect to your Arduino or ESP-based device directly.
- You can optionally leave the password empty for an open network, but it is recommended to use a password for security reasons.

Warnings

- An access point without a password can be insecure, allowing anyone within range to connect.
- The network range and connection speed will depend on the device's capabilities.

MicroPython Syntax Use

```
ap_if = network.WLAN(network.AP_IF)
ap_if.active(True)
ap_if.config(essid='ssid', password='password')
```

MicroPython Syntax Explanation

- *network.WLAN(network.AP_IF)*: Sets the device to Access Point (AP) mode.
- *ap_if.active(True)*: Activates the access point.
- *ap_if.config(essid='ssid', password='password')*: Configures the access point with the given SSID and password.

MicroPython Simple Code Example

```
ap_if.config(essid='MyAccessPoint', password='MyPassword')
```

Notes

- Ensure you activate the access point before configuring it.
- The access point will remain active until manually turned off.

Warnings

- If you do not set a password, the network will be open, making it vulnerable to unwanted connections.

Disconnecting from WiFi

WiFi.disconnect() is a function that disconnects your Arduino or ESP-based device from the currently connected WiFi network. It stops the device from accessing the network or internet.

Use Purpose

This function is useful when you need to disconnect the device from a WiFi network either to reset the connection, switch networks, or simply stop WiFi communication.

Arduino Syntax Use

```
WiFi.disconnect();
```

Arduino Syntax Explanation

- *disconnect()*: This command disconnects the device from the WiFi network it is currently connected to.

Arduino Simple Code Example

```
WiFi.disconnect();
```

Notes

- After calling this function, the device will no longer be connected to any WiFi network and won't have access to the internet.
- It can be useful if you want to stop communication temporarily or change networks.

Warnings

- Disconnecting from the network will stop all ongoing communication, so ensure that no critical data transfer is happening before using this function.
- You will need to reconnect to the WiFi manually using *WiFi.begin(ssid, password)* if you want to re-establish a connection.

MicroPython Syntax Use

```
sta_if.disconnect()
```

MicroPython Syntax Explanation

- *disconnect()*: Disconnects the device from the currently connected WiFi network.

MicroPython Simple Code Example

```
sta_if.disconnect()
```

Notes

- Once disconnected, the device will no longer have WiFi access until reconnected.

Warnings

- Be cautious when disconnecting during critical operations, as it will terminate any ongoing WiFi communication.
- You will need to call *sta_if.connect()* again to reconnect to the WiFi network.

Project: ESP32 Wi-Fi Connection

Objective
Connect the ESP32 to your home Wi-Fi and display the connection status on the serial monitor.

Programming Fundamentals
This project teaches how to use the Wi-Fi capabilities of the ESP32 to connect to a Wi-Fi network and display the connection status using the Serial Monitor.

Requirement Components

- **ESP32 microcontroller**
- **USB cable**
- **Computer with Arduino IDE or MicroPython IDE installed**

Circuit Diagram
This is a software-only project, so no additional circuits are required.

Circuit Connection

1. Connect the **ESP32** to your computer using the USB cable.
2. Ensure that your ESP32 drivers are properly installed to allow communication with the IDE.

Arduino Programming Section

Arduino Syntax:

- *WiFi.begin(ssid, password)*: Initializes the Wi-Fi connection with the specified SSID and password.
- *WiFi.status()*: Checks the connection status.
- *WiFi.localIP()*: Retrieves the ESP32's local IP address after connecting.
- *Serial.print() / Serial.println()*: Displays output on the Serial Monitor.

Arduino Code:

```
#include <WiFi.h>

// Replace with your network credentials
const char* ssid = "your_SSID";
const char* password = "your_PASSWORD";

void setup() {
  Serial.begin(115200);  // Start the serial monitor
  delay(1000);

  Serial.println("Connecting to Wi-Fi...");

  WiFi.begin(ssid, password);  // Connect to Wi-Fi

  // Wait until connected
  while (WiFi.status() != WL_CONNECTED) {
    delay(500);
    Serial.print(".");
  }

  Serial.println("");
  Serial.println("Wi-Fi Connected!");
  Serial.print("IP Address: ");
  Serial.println(WiFi.localIP());
}

void loop() {
  // Nothing to do here
}
```

Steps to Upload:

1. Open the **Arduino IDE** and connect your ESP32 to your computer via USB.
2. Copy and paste the code into a new sketch.
3. Replace `your_SSID` and `your_PASSWORD` with your Wi-Fi credentials.
4. In **Tools > Board**, select **ESP32** and the correct COM port.
5. Click **Upload** to transfer the code to the ESP32.

Check Output:
Open the Serial Monitor after uploading the code. You should see the ESP32 attempting to connect to your Wi-Fi. Once connected, the IP address of the ESP32 will be displayed.

MicroPython Programming Section

MicroPython Syntax:

- *network.WLAN()*: Initializes the Wi-Fi interface.
- *wlan.connect(ssid, password)*: Connects to the specified Wi-Fi network.
- *wlan.ifconfig()*: Retrieves the network information, including the IP address.
- *print()*: Displays output in the terminal.

MicroPython Code:

```python
import network
import time

# Replace with your network credentials
ssid = 'your_SSID'
password = 'your_PASSWORD'

def connect_to_wifi():
    wlan = network.WLAN(network.STA_IF)
    wlan.active(True)
    wlan.connect(ssid, password)

    print("Connecting to Wi-Fi...")
    while not wlan.isconnected():
        print("Attempting connection...")
        time.sleep(1)

    print("Wi-Fi Connected!")
    print("IP Address:", wlan.ifconfig()[0])

connect_to_wifi()
```

Steps to Upload:

1. Open your **MicroPython IDE** (such as Thonny) and connect the ESP32 via USB.
2. Copy and paste the code into the editor.
3. Replace `your_SSID` and `your_PASSWORD` with your Wi-Fi credentials.
4. Click **Run** to execute the program.

Check Output:
The terminal will display the connection status. Once connected, it will show the IP address of the ESP32.

Troubleshooting Tips

- **Wrong SSID or password**: Double-check that the SSID and password match your Wi-Fi network.
- **No connection**: Ensure that the ESP32 is within the range of your Wi-Fi network.
- **Incorrect baud rate**: In the Arduino Serial Monitor, ensure that the baud rate is set to 115200.
- **Wi-Fi module not initialized**: Make sure Wi-Fi is enabled using `WiFi.begin()` or `network.WLAN()`.

Further Exploration

- **Reconnect Logic**: Add logic to automatically reconnect if the ESP32 loses connection to Wi-Fi.
- **Web Server**: Expand the project by creating a simple web server that can be accessed via the ESP32's IP address.
- **Wi-Fi Signal Strength**: Display the signal strength of the connected network using the `WiFi.RSSI()` function (Arduino) or `wlan.status()` (MicroPython).

Note

This project introduces the basic concepts of connecting the ESP32 to a Wi-Fi network and retrieving the IP address. It's an essential step for building IoT projects that rely on network communication.

2. Connection Status & IP Information

Checking WiFi Connection Status

WiFi.status() is a function that lets you check if your Arduino or ESP-based device is connected to a WiFi network. It tells you if the device is connected, disconnected, or still trying to connect.

Use Purpose

This function is used to find out if the device has a WiFi connection or not. You can use it to make sure your device is connected before you send or receive data over the internet.

Arduino Syntax Use

```
WiFi.status();
```

Arduino Syntax Explanation

- *status()*: Returns a number that tells you the connection status:
    - *WL_CONNECTED*: The device is connected to WiFi.
    - *WL_DISCONNECTED*: The device is not connected to any network.
    - *WL_IDLE_STATUS*: The device is doing nothing and not trying to connect.
    - *WL_CONNECT_FAILED*: The attempt to connect failed.
    - *WL_NO_SSID_AVAIL*: The network name (SSID) is not available.
    - *WL_CONNECTION_LOST*: The connection was lost after being established.

Arduino Simple Code Example

```
if (WiFi.status() == WL_CONNECTED) {
Serial.println("Connected to WiFi");
} else {
Serial.println("Not connected to WiFi");
}
```

Notes

- It's a good idea to check the connection status before trying to send data over the network.
- You can check this status repeatedly to monitor whether your device is still connected.

Warnings

- The status can change while the device is running, so check it regularly to avoid connection issues during operation.

MicroPython Syntax Use

```
sta_if.status()
```

MicroPython Syntax Explanation

- *status()*: In MicroPython, this function also returns a number that tells you the connection status:
    - *0*: Not connected.
    - *1*: Trying to connect.
    - *2*: Connected.
    - *3*: Connection failed.

MicroPython Simple Code Example

```
if sta_if.status() == 2:
print("Connected to WiFi")
else:
print("Not connected to WiFi")
```

Notes

- Useful for checking if your device is connected to WiFi before trying to communicate over the network.

Warnings

- Always keep an eye on the connection status, especially if your device depends on constant network communication.

Getting the Local IP Address

WiFi.localIP() is a function that retrieves the local IP address of your Arduino or ESP-based device after it has successfully connected to a WiFi network. The local IP is the address your device uses to communicate on the network.

Use Purpose

You can use this function to get the device's IP address assigned by the router or a manually configured static IP. It's useful for identifying the device on your network, for tasks such as accessing a web server running on the device.

Arduino Syntax Use

```
WiFi.localIP();
```

Arduino Syntax Explanation

- *localIP()*: This function returns the IP address assigned to your device by the router or the static IP you set.

Arduino Simple Code Example

```
IPAddress ip = WiFi.localIP();
Serial.println(ip);
```

Notes

- The IP address will be displayed in the serial monitor. It can be used in other parts of your code to display or work with the device's IP.
- You must be connected to a WiFi network for this function to return a valid IP.

Warnings

- If the device is not connected to WiFi, the returned IP address may be 0.0.0.0.
- Ensure that the connection to the network is established before calling this function.

MicroPython Syntax Use

```
sta_if.ifconfig()[0]
```

MicroPython Syntax Explanation

- *ifconfig()*: This function returns a tuple with the device's network settings, including the local IP as the first item.

MicroPython Simple Code Example

```
ip = sta_if.ifconfig()[0]
print(ip)
```

Notes

- This will print the device's local IP address to the console.
- Like in Arduino, you need to be connected to WiFi to get a valid IP address.

Warnings

- Without a network connection, the returned IP will be invalid, such as 0.0.0.0 or an error.

Getting the Access Point IP Address

WiFi.softAPIP() is a function that retrieves the IP address of your Arduino or ESP-based device when it is acting as a WiFi access point. When you use your device to create its own WiFi network (access point), this function provides the IP address that other devices will use to connect to it.

Use Purpose

This function is useful when your device is set up as an access point, and you want to know its IP address so other devices can communicate with it. The IP address allows other devices to connect to the access point and interact with your device (for example, accessing a web server hosted on the device).

Arduino Syntax Use

```
WiFi.softAPIP();
```

Arduino Syntax Explanation

- *softAPIP()*: This function returns the IP address of your device when it is in access point (AP) mode.

Arduino Simple Code Example

```
IPAddress apIP = WiFi.softAPIP();
Serial.println(apIP);
```

Notes

- After calling *WiFi.softAP("YourSSID", "YourPassword");* to create an access point, you can use this function to get the IP address of the access point.
- The default IP address is usually *192.168.4.1*, but this can be changed with *WiFi.softAPConfig()*.

Warnings

- This function only works if your device is in AP mode. If it's not, the IP address may return as 0.0.0.0 or an invalid value.

MicroPython Syntax Use

```
ap_if.ifconfig()[0]
```

MicroPython Syntax Explanation

- *ifconfig()*: This function returns a tuple with network settings, including the IP address of the access point. The IP address is the first value in the tuple.

MicroPython Simple Code Example

```
ap_ip = ap_if.ifconfig()[0]
print(ap_ip)
```

Notes

- Make sure your device is in AP mode before using this function.
- The default IP in access point mode for MicroPython devices is also typically *192.168.4.1*, unless otherwise configured.

Warnings

- If the device is not in access point mode, the returned IP may not be valid. Ensure the access point is active before calling this function.

Project: Display ESP32 IP Address

Objective
Connect the ESP32 to a Wi-Fi network and display its IP address on the Serial Monitor.

Programming Fundamentals
This project demonstrates how to connect the ESP32 to a Wi-Fi network and retrieve its IP address, which is then displayed on the Serial Monitor.

Requirement Components

- **ESP32 microcontroller**
- **USB cable**
- **Computer with Arduino IDE or MicroPython IDE installed**

Circuit Diagram
This is a software-only project, so no additional circuits are required.

Circuit Connection

1. Connect the **ESP32** to your computer using the USB cable.
2. Ensure that your ESP32 drivers are properly installed to allow communication with the IDE.

Arduino Programming Section

Arduino Syntax:

- *WiFi.begin(ssid, password)*: Initializes the Wi-Fi connection with the specified SSID and password.
- *WiFi.status()*: Checks the connection status.
- *WiFi.localIP()*: Retrieves the ESP32's local IP address after connecting.
- *Serial.print() / Serial.println()*: Displays output on the Serial Monitor.

Arduino Code:

```
#include <WiFi.h>

// Replace with your network credentials
const char* ssid = "your_SSID";
const char* password = "your_PASSWORD";

void setup() {
  Serial.begin(115200);  // Start the serial monitor
  delay(1000);

  Serial.println("Connecting to Wi-Fi...");

  WiFi.begin(ssid, password);  // Connect to Wi-Fi

  // Wait until connected
  while (WiFi.status() != WL_CONNECTED) {
    delay(500);
    Serial.print(".");
  }

  Serial.println("");
  Serial.println("Wi-Fi Connected!");
  Serial.print("IP Address: ");
  Serial.println(WiFi.localIP());
}

void loop() {
  // Nothing to do here
}
```

Steps to Upload:

1. Open the **Arduino IDE** and connect your ESP32 to your computer via USB.
2. Copy and paste the code into a new sketch.
3. Replace `your_SSID` and `your_PASSWORD` with your Wi-Fi credentials.
4. In **Tools > Board**, select **ESP32** and the correct COM port.
5. Click **Upload** to transfer the code to the ESP32.

Check Output:

Open the Serial Monitor after uploading the code. You should see the ESP32 attempting to connect to your Wi-Fi. Once connected, the IP address of the ESP32 will be displayed.

MicroPython Programming Section

MicroPython Syntax:

- *network.WLAN()*: Initializes the Wi-Fi interface.
- *wlan.connect(ssid, password)*: Connects to the specified Wi-Fi network.
- *wlan.ifconfig()*: Retrieves the network information, including the IP address.
- *print()*: Displays output in the terminal.

MicroPython Code:

```python
import network
import time

# Replace with your network credentials
ssid = 'your_SSID'
password = 'your_PASSWORD'

def connect_to_wifi():
    wlan = network.WLAN(network.STA_IF)
    wlan.active(True)
    wlan.connect(ssid, password)

    print("Connecting to Wi-Fi...")
    while not wlan.isconnected():
        print("Attempting connection...")
        time.sleep(1)

    print("Wi-Fi Connected!")
    print("IP Address:", wlan.ifconfig()[0])

connect_to_wifi()
```

Steps to Upload:

1. Open your **MicroPython IDE** (such as Thonny) and connect the ESP32 via USB.
2. Copy and paste the code into the editor.
3. Replace your_SSID and your_PASSWORD with your Wi-Fi credentials.
4. Click **Run** to execute the program.

Check Output:
The terminal will display the connection status. Once connected, it will show the IP address of the ESP32.

Troubleshooting Tips

- **Wrong SSID or password**: Double-check that the SSID and password match your Wi-Fi network.
- **No connection**: Ensure that the ESP32 is within the range of your Wi-Fi network.
- **Incorrect baud rate**: In the Arduino Serial Monitor, ensure that the baud rate is set to 115200.
- **Wi-Fi module not initialized**: Make sure Wi-Fi is enabled using `WiFi.begin()` or `network.WLAN()`.

Further Exploration

- **Reconnect Logic**: Add logic to automatically reconnect if the ESP32 loses connection to Wi-Fi.
- **Web Server**: Expand the project by creating a simple web server that can be accessed via the ESP32's IP address.
- **Wi-Fi Signal Strength**: Display the signal strength of the connected network using the `WiFi.RSSI()` function (Arduino) or `wlan.status()` (MicroPython).

Note
This project introduces the basic concepts of connecting the ESP32 to a Wi-Fi network and retrieving the IP address. It's an essential step for building IoT projects that rely on network communication.

3. Wi-Fi Mode Selection

Setting the WiFi Mode to Station

WiFi.mode(WIFI_STA) is a function that configures your Arduino or ESP-based device to operate in **station mode** (STA). In this mode, the device acts like a client (station) that connects to an existing WiFi network, just like how your phone or computer connects to a router.

Use Purpose

This function is used when you want your device to connect to a WiFi network instead of creating its own. In station mode, the device can access the internet and communicate with other devices on the same network, such as sending data to a server or receiving commands from a mobile app.

Arduino Syntax Use

```
WiFi.mode(WIFI_STA);
```

Arduino Syntax Explanation
- *WIFI_STA*: This tells the device to operate in **station mode**, allowing it to connect to a router or any other access point.

Arduino Simple Code Example

```
WiFi.mode(WIFI_STA);
WiFi.begin("YourSSID", "YourPassword");
```

Notes

- Station mode is the most common mode for IoT projects where the device needs internet access or needs to communicate with devices over a local network.
- After setting the mode, you must use *WiFi.begin(ssid, password)* to connect to a specific WiFi network.

Warnings

- Make sure that the SSID and password are correct when using *WiFi.begin()* to connect; otherwise, the device will not be able to connect to the network.

MicroPython Syntax Use

```
sta_if = network.WLAN(network.STA_IF)
sta_if.active(True)
```

MicroPython Syntax Explanation

- *network.STA_IF*: This sets the device in station mode.
- *active(True)*: This activates the WiFi interface in station mode, allowing the device to connect to a network.

MicroPython Simple Code Example

```
sta_if = network.WLAN(network.STA_IF)
sta_if.active(True)
sta_if.connect('YourSSID', 'YourPassword')
```

Notes

- After setting the device to station mode, you can use *sta_if.connect()* to connect to a WiFi network.
- In station mode, the device will behave like a client, joining an existing network.

Warnings

- Ensure the WiFi credentials are correct; if not, the device will fail to connect.

Setting the WiFi Mode to Access Point

WiFi.mode(WIFI_AP) is a function that configures your Arduino or ESP-based device to operate in **access point mode** (AP). In this mode, the device creates its own WiFi network, allowing other devices (such as smartphones or computers) to connect directly to it, just like connecting to a router.

Use Purpose

This function is useful when you want your device to act as a WiFi hotspot or network hub. Other devices can connect to the network created by your device, making it ideal for projects where you want local control or communication without an external WiFi router.

Arduino Syntax Use

```
WiFi.mode(WIFI_AP);
```

Arduino Syntax Explanation

- *WIFI_AP*: This sets the device to **access point mode**, which creates a WiFi network for other devices to join.

Arduino Simple Code Example

```
WiFi.mode(WIFI_AP);
WiFi.softAP("MyAccessPoint", "MyPassword");
```

Notes

- After setting the mode, you must use *WiFi.softAP(ssid, password)* to create a WiFi network with the specified name (SSID) and password.
- The default IP address for the access point is usually *192.168.4.1*.

Warnings

- An open network (no password) can be insecure, so always use a strong password when setting up an access point.
- Devices connecting to the access point can only communicate locally unless you set up internet sharing.

MicroPython Syntax Use

```
ap_if = network.WLAN(network.AP_IF)
ap_if.active(True)
```

MicroPython Syntax Explanation

- *network.AP_IF*: This sets the device to access point mode.
- *active(True)*: This activates the access point, allowing other devices to connect.

MicroPython Simple Code Example

```
ap_if = network.WLAN(network.AP_IF)
ap_if.active(True)
ap_if.config(essid='MyAccessPoint', password='MyPassword')
```

Notes

- Once the access point is active, other devices can connect to it using the provided SSID and password.
- You can also configure the access point's IP address using *ap_if.ifconfig()* if needed.

Warnings

- Without a password, your access point will be open, allowing any device nearby to connect. Be cautious of this for security reasons.
- Devices connected to this network won't have internet access unless additional network routing is configured.

Setting the WiFi Mode to Both Access Point and Station

WiFi.mode(WIFI_AP_STA) is a function that configures your Arduino or ESP-based device to operate in both **access point (AP) mode** and **station (STA) mode** simultaneously. In this mode, the device can connect to an existing WiFi network (as a station) while also creating its own WiFi network (as an access point) for other devices to connect to.

Use Purpose

This mode is useful when you want the device to act as a bridge between a network and other devices. It allows your device to be connected to the internet (via station mode) while also allowing local devices to connect directly to it through access point mode. This is commonly used in IoT applications where devices need to be controlled locally, but still send data to a cloud server or another network.

Arduino Syntax Use

```
WiFi.mode(WIFI_AP_STA);
```

Arduino Syntax Explanation

- *WIFI_AP_STA*: This sets the device to work as both a station (STA) that connects to a router and an access point (AP) that creates its own WiFi network.

Arduino Simple Code Example

```
WiFi.mode(WIFI_AP_STA);
WiFi.begin("YourSSID", "YourPassword");
WiFi.softAP("MyAccessPoint", "MyPassword");
```

Notes

- In station mode, the device connects to an existing network using *WiFi.begin(ssid, password)*.
- In access point mode, the device creates a network using *WiFi.softAP(ssid, password)*, allowing other devices to connect.
- The device will have two IP addresses: one for the local network (as a station) and one for the access point (usually *192.168.4.1*).

Warnings

- Devices connected to the access point will not automatically have internet access through the device unless additional networking (like routing) is configured.
- Be mindful of network security and always set a strong password for your access point.

MicroPython Syntax Use

```
ap_sta_if = network.WLAN(network.AP_IF)
sta_if = network.WLAN(network.STA_IF)
ap_sta_if.active(True)
sta_if.active(True)
```

MicroPython Syntax Explanation

- *network.AP_IF*: Sets the device in access point mode.
- *network.STA_IF*: Sets the device in station mode.
- *active(True)*: Enables both station and access point modes.

MicroPython Simple Code Example

```
ap_sta_if = network.WLAN(network.AP_IF)
sta_if = network.WLAN(network.STA_IF)
ap_sta_if.active(True)
sta_if.active(True)
sta_if.connect('YourSSID', 'YourPassword')
ap_sta_if.config(essid='MyAccessPoint', password='MyPassword')
```

Notes

- In this mode, the device can connect to a WiFi network and create its own WiFi network simultaneously.
- You can check the connection status and IP addresses using *sta_if.ifconfig()* and *ap_sta_if.ifconfig()*.

Warnings

- Devices connected to the access point cannot access the internet unless routing is manually configured.
- Ensure proper security settings (passwords) for both networks to avoid unauthorized access.

Project: Dual Mode ESP32: Wi-Fi Client (Station) and Hotspot (AP)

Objective
Create a project where the ESP32 simultaneously connects to a Wi-Fi network as a client (Station mode) and acts as a Wi-Fi hotspot (Access Point mode) for other devices.

Programming Fundamentals
This project demonstrates how the ESP32 can operate in **dual mode**, both as a Wi-Fi client (station mode) to connect to a home network and as an access point (AP mode) to provide a hotspot for other devices to connect.

Requirement Components

- **ESP32 microcontroller**
- **USB cable**
- **Computer with Arduino IDE or MicroPython IDE installed**

Circuit Diagram
This is a software-only project, so no additional circuits are required.

Circuit Connection

1. Connect the **ESP32** to your computer using the USB cable.
2. Ensure that your ESP32 drivers are properly installed to allow communication with the IDE.

Arduino Programming Section
Arduino Syntax:
- *WiFi.begin(ssid, password)*: Initializes the Wi-Fi client connection with the specified SSID and password.
- *WiFi.softAP(ap_ssid, ap_password)*: Initializes the ESP32 in AP mode with the given SSID and password.
- *WiFi.status()*: Checks the connection status for the station (client) mode.
- *WiFi.softAPIP()*: Retrieves the IP address of the access point (AP mode).
- *Serial.print() / Serial.println()*: Displays output on the Serial Monitor.

Arduino Code:

```
#include <WiFi.h>
// Station (Client) Mode credentials
const char* ssid = "your_SSID";
const char* password = "your_PASSWORD";
// Access Point (Hotspot) Mode credentials
const char* ap_ssid = "ESP32_Hotspot";
const char* ap_password = "12345678";
void setup() {
  Serial.begin(115200);
  delay(1000);

  // Connect to Wi-Fi as a client (Station mode)
  Serial.println("Connecting to Wi-Fi...");
  WiFi.begin(ssid, password);

  while (WiFi.status() != WL_CONNECTED) {
    delay(500);
    Serial.print(".");
  }
  Serial.println("\nWi-Fi Connected!");
  Serial.print("Station IP Address: ");
  Serial.println(WiFi.localIP());
  // Set up the ESP32 as a Hotspot (AP mode)
  WiFi.softAP(ap_ssid, ap_password);
  Serial.println("Hotspot started!");
  Serial.print("AP IP Address: ");
  Serial.println(WiFi.softAPIP());
}

void loop() {
  // Nothing to do in the loop
}
```

Steps to Upload:

1. Open the **Arduino IDE** and connect your ESP32 to your computer via USB.
2. Copy and paste the code into a new sketch.
3. Replace your_SSID and your_PASSWORD with your Wi-Fi credentials for Station mode.
4. In **Tools > Board**, select **ESP32** and the correct COM port.
5. Click **Upload** to transfer the code to the ESP32.

Check Output:

Open the Serial Monitor after uploading the code. You should see the ESP32 connecting to your home Wi-Fi (Station mode) and simultaneously starting a Wi-Fi hotspot (Access Point mode). The IP addresses for both modes will be displayed.

MicroPython Programming Section

MicroPython Syntax:

- *network.WLAN()*: Initializes the Wi-Fi interface for both station and AP modes.
- *wlan.connect(ssid, password)*: Connects to the specified Wi-Fi network (Station mode).
- *ap.active(True)*: Activates the AP mode.
- *ap.config()*: Configures the AP mode SSID and password.
- *print()*: Displays output in the terminal.

MicroPython Code:

```python
import network
import time

# Station (Client) Mode credentials
ssid = 'your_SSID'
password = 'your_PASSWORD'

# Access Point (Hotspot) Mode credentials
ap_ssid = 'ESP32_Hotspot'
ap_password = '12345678'

def dual_mode_esp32():
    # Connect to Wi-Fi as a client (Station mode)
    wlan = network.WLAN(network.STA_IF)
    wlan.active(True)
    wlan.connect(ssid, password)

    print("Connecting to Wi-Fi (Station mode)...")
    while not wlan.isconnected():
        print("Attempting connection...")
        time.sleep(1)

    print("Wi-Fi Connected!")
    print("Station IP Address:", wlan.ifconfig()[0])

    # Set up the ESP32 as a Hotspot (AP mode)
    ap = network.WLAN(network.AP_IF)
    ap.active(True)
    ap.config(essid=ap_ssid, password=ap_password)

    print("Hotspot started!")
    print("AP IP Address:", ap.ifconfig()[0])

# Run the dual mode setup
dual_mode_esp32()
```

Steps to Upload:
1. Open your **MicroPython IDE** (such as Thonny) and connect the ESP32 via USB.
2. Copy and paste the code into the editor.
3. Replace `your_SSID` and `your_PASSWORD` with your Wi-Fi credentials.
4. Click **Run** to execute the program.

Check Output:
The terminal will display the IP address for both the station (client) mode and the access point (AP mode). Other devices can connect to the hotspot with the credentials set in `ap_ssid` and `ap_password`.

Troubleshooting Tips

- **Wrong SSID or password**: Double-check that the SSID and password match your Wi-Fi network for station mode.
- **No connection in Station mode**: Ensure that the ESP32 is within the range of your Wi-Fi network.
- **Devices not connecting to AP**: Make sure the devices are entering the correct SSID and password for the ESP32 hotspot.

Further Exploration

- **Web Server on AP Mode**: Create a simple web server on the ESP32 hotspot that allows devices connected to the AP to interact with the ESP32.
- **Monitor Traffic**: Capture and display the number of devices connected to the ESP32's AP.
- **Dual Network Communication**: Add functionality that allows the ESP32 to forward information from devices connected to the AP to the network it's connected to as a client.

Note

This project demonstrates the ESP32's ability to operate in **dual mode**, where it can act as both a Wi-Fi client (station mode) and a Wi-Fi hotspot (access point mode) simultaneously. It's a powerful feature for IoT applications where the ESP32 needs to communicate with other devices while maintaining a connection to a broader network.

4. Network Scanning

Scanning for Available WiFi Networks

WiFi.scanNetworks() is a function that scans for all available WiFi networks within the range of your Arduino or ESP-based device. It returns the number of networks found and allows you to retrieve information such as the SSID, signal strength, and encryption type for each network.

Use Purpose

This function is useful when you want to list all nearby WiFi networks. It helps in selecting which network to connect to or simply for monitoring available networks.

Arduino Syntax Use

```
WiFi.scanNetworks();
```

Arduino Syntax Explanation

- *scanNetworks()*: This function initiates a scan of all WiFi networks in range and returns the number of networks detected.

Arduino Simple Code Example

```
int numNetworks = WiFi.scanNetworks();
for (int i = 0; i < numNetworks; i++) {
Serial.print("Network Name (SSID): ");
Serial.println(WiFi.SSID(i));
Serial.print("Signal Strength (RSSI): ");
Serial.println(WiFi.RSSI(i));
Serial.print("Encryption Type: ");
Serial.println(WiFi.encryptionType(i));
Serial.println("----------------------");
}
```

Notes

- *WiFi.SSID(i)* returns the name of the network (SSID).
- *WiFi.RSSI(i)* returns the signal strength of the network in dBm (negative values; the closer to 0, the better the signal).
- *WiFi.encryptionType(i)* returns the encryption type (WEP, WPA, etc.) used by the network.

Warnings

- Scanning for networks can take a few seconds, so it may block code execution until the scan is complete.
- Repeatedly scanning for networks can reduce performance or slow down the program.

MicroPython Syntax Use

```
sta_if.scan()
```

MicroPython Syntax Explanation

- *scan()*: In MicroPython, this function scans for available WiFi networks and returns a list of tuples containing network information such as SSID, BSSID, channel, RSSI, security, and hidden status.

MicroPython Simple Code Example

```
networks = sta_if.scan()
for network in networks:
print("SSID:", network[0])
print("Signal Strength (RSSI):", network[3])
print("Security:", network[4])
print("----------------------")
```

Notes

- Each tuple in the list contains details about a network: *network[0]* is the SSID, *network[3]* is the signal strength (RSSI), and *network[4]* indicates the security type.

Warnings

- Scanning takes a little time, and frequent scans can affect performance.

Getting the SSID of a WiFi Network

WiFi.SSID(i) is a function that retrieves the name (SSID) of a WiFi network found during a network scan. It is used after calling *WiFi.scanNetworks()* to access the SSID (Service Set Identifier) of the network at index *i*.

Use Purpose

This function is useful when you want to get the names of all available WiFi networks after scanning for networks. You can display these SSIDs to let the user select which network to connect to or just monitor available networks.

Arduino Syntax Use

```
WiFi.SSID(i);
```

Arduino Syntax Explanation

- *SSID(i)*: Retrieves the SSID (network name) of the WiFi network at index *i* after a network scan.

Arduino Simple Code Example

```
int numNetworks = WiFi.scanNetworks();
for (int i = 0; i < numNetworks; i++) {
Serial.print("Network Name (SSID): ");
Serial.println(WiFi.SSID(i));
}
```

Notes

- You must first scan for networks using *WiFi.scanNetworks()* before you can use *WiFi.SSID(i)*.
- *i* is the index number of the network in the list of scanned networks, starting at 0.

Warnings

- If the index *i* is out of range (greater than the number of networks found), the function will not return a valid SSID.
- Scanning for networks can take time, so ensure the scan is completed before accessing the SSID.

MicroPython Syntax Use

```
networks[i][0]
```

MicroPython Syntax Explanation

- After using *sta_if.scan()* in MicroPython, the SSID of the network at index *i* can be accessed by calling *networks[i][0]*, where *networks* is the list of scanned networks.

MicroPython Simple Code Example

```
networks = sta_if.scan()
for i, network in enumerate(networks):
    print("Network Name (SSID):", network[0])
```

Notes

- The SSID is the first item in the tuple returned for each network in the list.
- Ensure that the scan is complete before trying to access the SSID.

Warnings

- Make sure the index *i* is within the range of the number of networks found, or you may get an error or invalid SSID.

Getting the Signal Strength of a WiFi Network

WiFi.RSSI(i) is a function that retrieves the signal strength (RSSI - Received Signal Strength Indicator) of a WiFi network found during a network scan. The RSSI is measured in dBm, and it indicates how strong the signal is. The closer the value is to 0 (less negative), the stronger the signal.

Use Purpose

This function is useful when you want to evaluate the strength of nearby WiFi networks. It helps in determining the quality of a network connection before deciding which one to connect to.

Arduino Syntax Use

```
WiFi.RSSI(i);
```

Arduino Syntax Explanation

- *RSSI(i)*: Retrieves the signal strength (RSSI) in dBm of the network at index *i* from the list of scanned networks.

Arduino Simple Code Example

```
int numNetworks = WiFi.scanNetworks();
for (int i = 0; i < numNetworks; i++) {
Serial.print("Network Name (SSID): ");
Serial.println(WiFi.SSID(i));
Serial.print("Signal Strength (RSSI): ");
Serial.println(WiFi.RSSI(i));
}
```

Notes

- The RSSI value will be a negative number. The closer to zero, the better the signal. For example, -30 dBm is a very strong signal, while -90 dBm is quite weak.
- This function can only be used after scanning for networks with *WiFi.scanNetworks()*.

Warnings

- If the index *i* is out of range (greater than the number of networks found), the function may return an invalid value.
- RSSI is a dynamic value and may fluctuate depending on environmental factors.

MicroPython Syntax Use

```
networks[i][3]
```

MicroPython Syntax Explanation

- After using *sta_if.scan()* in MicroPython, the RSSI (signal strength) of the network at index *i* can be accessed by *networks[i][3]*, where *networks* is the list of scanned networks.

MicroPython Simple Code Example

```
networks = sta_if.scan()
for i, network in enumerate(networks):
print("Network Name (SSID):", network[0])
print("Signal Strength (RSSI):", network[3])
```

Notes

- The RSSI value in MicroPython works similarly to Arduino and provides a measure of signal strength in dBm.

Warnings

- Make sure the index *i* is within range of the scanned networks to avoid errors.

Project: Wi-Fi Network Scanner Using ESP32

Objective
Program the ESP32 to scan for available Wi-Fi networks and display the SSIDs and signal strengths (RSSI) on the Serial Monitor.

Programming Fundamentals
This project demonstrates how to use the ESP32 to scan for Wi-Fi networks, retrieve network details like SSIDs and signal strength (RSSI), and display them in the Serial Monitor.

Requirement Components

- **ESP32 microcontroller**
- **USB cable**
- **Computer with Arduino IDE or MicroPython IDE installed**

Circuit Diagram
This is a software-only project, so no additional circuits are required.

Circuit Connection

1. Connect the **ESP32** to your computer using the USB cable.
2. Ensure that your ESP32 drivers are properly installed to allow communication with the IDE.

Arduino Programming Section

Arduino Syntax:

- *WiFi.scanNetworks()*: Scans for available Wi-Fi networks and returns the number of networks found.
- *WiFi.SSID(i)*: Retrieves the SSID of the i-th network.
- *WiFi.RSSI(i)*: Retrieves the signal strength (RSSI) of the i-th network.
- *Serial.print() / Serial.println()*: Displays output on the Serial Monitor.

Arduino Code:

```
#include <WiFi.h>

void setup() {
  Serial.begin(115200);  // Start serial communication
  delay(1000);

  Serial.println("Scanning for Wi-Fi networks...");

  int networkCount = WiFi.scanNetworks();  // Scan for networks

  if (networkCount == 0) {
    Serial.println("No networks found.");
  } else {
    Serial.print(networkCount);
    Serial.println(" networks found:");

    for (int i = 0; i < networkCount; i++) {
      // Display SSID and RSSI for each network found
      Serial.print(i + 1);
      Serial.print(": ");
      Serial.print(WiFi.SSID(i));
      Serial.print(" (");
      Serial.print(WiFi.RSSI(i));  // Signal strength
      Serial.println(" dBm)");
    }
  }
}

void loop() {
  // Do nothing in the loop
}
```

Steps to Upload:

1. Open the **Arduino IDE** and connect your ESP32 to your computer via USB.
2. Copy and paste the code into a new sketch.
3. In **Tools > Board**, select **ESP32** and the correct COM port.
4. Click **Upload** to transfer the code to the ESP32.

Check Output:
Open the Serial Monitor after uploading the code. You will see a list of available Wi-Fi networks with their SSIDs and signal strengths (RSSI) in dBm.

MicroPython Programming Section

MicroPython Syntax:

- *network.WLAN()*: Initializes the Wi-Fi interface.
- *wlan.scan()*: Scans for available networks and returns a list of networks with SSID and RSSI.
- *print()*: Displays output in the terminal.

MicroPython Code:

```python
import network

def wifi_scan():
    wlan = network.WLAN(network.STA_IF)
    wlan.active(True)

    print("Scanning for Wi-Fi networks...")
    networks = wlan.scan()  # Scan for networks

    if not networks:
        print("No networks found.")
    else:
        print(f"{len(networks)} networks found:")
        for i, network in enumerate(networks):
            ssid = network[0].decode('utf-8')
            rssi = network[3]  # Signal strength (RSSI)
            print(f"{i + 1}: {ssid} ({rssi} dBm)")

# Run the Wi-Fi scan function
wifi_scan()
```

Steps to Upload:

1. Open your **MicroPython IDE** (such as Thonny) and connect the ESP32 via USB.
2. Copy and paste the code into the editor.
3. Click **Run** to execute the program.

Check Output:
The terminal will display a list of available Wi-Fi networks with their SSIDs and RSSI (signal strength in dBm).

Troubleshooting Tips

- **No networks found**: Ensure that your ESP32 is within the range of Wi-Fi networks.
- **Incorrect baud rate**: Ensure that the baud rate in the Serial Monitor (Arduino) is set to 115200 for proper display.
- **Network list not appearing**: Check if the Wi-Fi module is properly initialized using `WiFi.scanNetworks()` (Arduino) or `wlan.scan()` (MicroPython).

Further Exploration

- **Network Filtering**: Modify the program to filter and display only networks with certain signal strength thresholds (e.g., networks with RSSI greater than -70 dBm).
- **Network Type**: Display whether each network is open or secured (encryption type).
- **Multiple Scans**: Set up the program to scan for Wi-Fi networks periodically, e.g., every 30 seconds, and update the results.

Note

This project provides a practical introduction to using the Wi-Fi capabilities of the ESP32 to scan for available networks. It's a useful tool for network diagnostics and learning about the surrounding Wi-Fi environment.

5. Advanced Network Management

Manually Configuring Network Settings

WiFi.config(ip, gateway, subnet) is a function used to manually configure the IP address, gateway, and subnet mask for your Arduino or ESP-based device when connecting to a WiFi network.

Instead of using DHCP to automatically assign network settings, this function allows you to specify a static IP configuration.

Use Purpose

This function is useful when you need your device to have a static IP address. A static IP ensures that your device always has the same IP address on the network, making it easier to communicate with other devices or set up local servers without worrying about changing IP addresses.

Arduino Syntax Use

```
WiFi.config(ip, gateway, subnet);
```

Arduino Syntax Explanation

- *ip*: The static IP address you want to assign to the device (e.g., *IPAddress(192, 168, 1, 100)*).
- *gateway*: The IP address of the router or gateway (e.g., *IPAddress(192, 168, 1, 1)*).
- *subnet*: The subnet mask that defines the network range (e.g., *IPAddress(255, 255, 255, 0)*).

Arduino Simple Code Example

```
IPAddress local_IP(192, 168, 1, 184);
IPAddress gateway(192, 168, 1, 1);
IPAddress subnet(255, 255, 255, 0);
WiFi.config(local_IP, gateway, subnet);
WiFi.begin("YourSSID", "YourPassword");
```

Notes

- A static IP can be useful in controlled environments where you need the device to be consistently reachable.
- Make sure the static IP address is outside the DHCP range of your router to avoid IP conflicts with other devices.

Warnings

- Incorrect IP settings can prevent the device from connecting to the network.
- You need to know your network's configuration (gateway and subnet) to set these values manually.
- If you don't set the DNS server manually, it will use the default one assigned by the router.

MicroPython Syntax Use

```
sta_if.ifconfig((ip, gateway, subnet, dns))
```

MicroPython Syntax Explanation

- *ifconfig()*: This function manually sets the network configuration for the device, including the IP, gateway, subnet mask, and DNS server.
    - Example: *sta_if.ifconfig(('192.168.1.184', '192.168.1.1', '255.255.255.0', '8.8.8.8'))*

MicroPython Simple Code Example

```
sta_if = network.WLAN(network.STA_IF)
sta_if.active(True)
sta_if.ifconfig(('192.168.1.184', '192.168.1.1', '255.255.255.0', '8.8.8.8'))
```

Notes

- This will assign the static IP and other network details to your device.
- The last parameter, DNS, can be set to a public DNS like Google's (8.8.8.8) or your router's IP.

Warnings

- Ensure the IP address is not in conflict with another device on the network.
- Incorrect settings can prevent the device from connecting or communicating with other devices.

Setting the Hostname for Your Device

WiFi.setHostname(name) is a function that sets a custom hostname for your Arduino or ESP-based device on the network. The hostname is a human-readable name that identifies your device on the local network, similar to how computers and smartphones have recognizable names when they are connected to WiFi.

Use Purpose

Setting a hostname makes it easier to identify your device on a local network, especially when multiple devices are connected. Instead of using an IP address, you can access or identify the device using its hostname, which is useful in large networks or when managing multiple devices.

Arduino Syntax Use

```
WiFi.setHostname(name);
```

Arduino Syntax Explanation

- *name*: The desired hostname you want to assign to your device. This should be provided as a string (e.g., *"MyDeviceName"*).

Arduino Simple Code Example

```
WiFi.setHostname("MyESPDevice");
WiFi.begin("YourSSID", "YourPassword");
```

Notes

- This function should be called before connecting to the WiFi network using *WiFi.begin()*.
- The hostname can make it easier to access the device on your local network, for example, through `http://MyESPDevice.local` (if your router supports mDNS).

Warnings

- Not all routers support resolving hostnames to IP addresses, especially without mDNS.
- Ensure the hostname is unique within your network to avoid conflicts.

MicroPython Syntax Use

```
sta_if.config(dhcp_hostname=name)
```

MicroPython Syntax Explanation

- *config(dhcp_hostname=name)*: This sets the DHCP hostname for the device, which is similar to assigning a network name. For example, *sta_if.config(dhcp_hostname="MyMicroPythonDevice")*.

MicroPython Simple Code Example

```
sta_if = network.WLAN(network.STA_IF)
sta_if.active(True)
sta_if.config(dhcp_hostname="MyMicroPythonDevice")
sta_if.connect('YourSSID', 'YourPassword')
```

Notes

- This will set the hostname for the device on the network and make it easier to identify when checking connected devices on the router.

Warnings

- Some routers might not support DHCP hostname, so the device might still show up with its IP address only.
- The hostname should not contain spaces or special characters.

Adjusting WiFi Transmission Power

WiFi.setTxPower(power) is a function that adjusts the transmission power of your Arduino or ESP-based device's WiFi module. This setting determines how strong the WiFi signal will be when your device transmits data. Adjusting the transmission power can help you control the range and power consumption of your device.

Use Purpose

This function is useful when you need to optimize the balance between signal range and power consumption. For example, you may want to reduce the power if your device is close to the WiFi router to save energy, or increase the power to extend the range when the signal is weak.

Arduino Syntax Use

```
WiFi.setTxPower(power);
```

Arduino Syntax Explanation

- *power*: The transmission power level. It should be one of the predefined power levels:
    - *WIFI_POWER_MINUS_1dBm*: Lowest transmission power.
    - *WIFI_POWER_MINUS_10dBm*: Low power.
    - *WIFI_POWER_MINUS_20dBm*: Medium power.
    - *WIFI_POWER_MINUS_30dBm*: Highest transmission power (default).

Arduino Simple Code Example

```
WiFi.setTxPower(WIFI_POWER_MINUS_10dBm);
WiFi.begin("YourSSID", "YourPassword");
```

Notes

- Lowering the transmission power can save energy, which is helpful in battery-powered projects.
- Higher transmission power can help extend the range but may consume more energy.

Warnings

- Setting a very low transmission power might cause connection instability if the signal strength is too weak to maintain a stable connection.
- Always test the connection after adjusting the power to ensure it works in your environment.

MicroPython Syntax Use

```
sta_if.config(txpower=power)
```

MicroPython Syntax Explanation

- *config(txpower=power)*: This sets the transmission power for the device. The power value is usually in dBm (decibel milliwatts), with typical values like *78* (for maximum power) or *20* (for lower power).

MicroPython Simple Code Example

```
sta_if = network.WLAN(network.STA_IF)
sta_if.active(True)
sta_if.config(txpower=20)
sta_if.connect('YourSSID', 'YourPassword')
```

Notes

- In MicroPython, transmission power is typically adjusted by providing a value directly in dBm.
- Adjusting the power can help fine-tune the device's connection strength in different environments.

Warnings

- Reducing power too much may cause the device to lose connectivity if it's too far from the router.
- Always ensure the device remains stable after changing the power settings.

Disabling WiFi Sleep Mode

WiFi.setSleep(false) is a function that disables the WiFi sleep mode on your Arduino or ESP-based device. By default, many WiFi modules enter sleep mode to save power when they are not actively transmitting data. Disabling sleep mode ensures that the WiFi connection remains always active, which can improve responsiveness and connection stability but may increase power consumption.

Use Purpose

This function is useful in scenarios where constant WiFi connectivity is essential, such as when the device needs to maintain a stable connection for real-time data transfer or when the device is hosting a server. Disabling sleep mode can prevent connection interruptions caused by the device entering power-saving states.

Arduino Syntax Use

```
WiFi.setSleep(false);
```

Arduino Syntax Explanation

- *false*: Disables WiFi sleep mode, keeping the connection always active.
- *true*: (Optional) Enables sleep mode, allowing the WiFi to save power when not in use.

Arduino Simple Code Example

```
WiFi.setSleep(false);
WiFi.begin("YourSSID", "YourPassword");
```

Notes

- Disabling sleep mode ensures the WiFi remains active and responsive, which is useful in server-hosting applications or real-time monitoring systems.
- Enabling sleep mode (*WiFi.setSleep(true);*) helps save power, especially in battery-powered projects, but might cause temporary disconnections during data transmission.

Warnings

- Disabling sleep mode will increase power consumption, which may reduce battery life in portable projects.
- If your device doesn't need constant WiFi activity, consider keeping sleep mode enabled to save energy.

MicroPython Syntax Use

```
sta_if.config(ps_mode=network.WIFI_PS_NONE)
```

MicroPython Syntax Explanation

- *ps_mode=network.WIFI_PS_NONE*: This disables the power-saving mode (sleep mode) for the WiFi connection, ensuring it stays awake and active.
- *ps_mode=network.WIFI_PS_MAX*: Enables power-saving mode (default).

MicroPython Simple Code Example

```
sta_if = network.WLAN(network.STA_IF)
sta_if.active(True)
sta_if.config(ps_mode=network.WIFI_PS_NONE)
sta_if.connect('YourSSID', 'YourPassword')
```

Notes

- By disabling sleep mode, the WiFi module stays active at all times, which is beneficial for continuous data streams or web servers.
- If energy efficiency is a priority, consider leaving the default power-saving mode on.

Warnings

- Disabling sleep mode may lead to increased power consumption, so it's important to balance performance needs with power efficiency.

Made in United States
Orlando, FL
19 November 2024